Eighteenth Century Painting

Title page illustration:
Jean-Honoré Fragonard
Grasse 1732-Paris 1806
Fantasy Figure, called *Inspiration*
Oil on canvas 2′7″ × 2′2″
Paris, Louvre

Cover illustration:
Antoine Watteau
Late 1720
L'Enseigne de Gersaint
(Signboard for Gersaint)
Oil on canvas 5′5″ × 10′0″
Berlin, Charlottenburg Palace

Eighteenth Century Painting

Claire Gay

Funk & Wagnalls, New York

Series edited by Claude Schaeffner
Artistic Adviser:
Jean-Clarence Lambert
Illustrations chosen by Claude Schaeffner
Assistant: Martine Caputo
Translated from the French by Paul Eve

Library of Congress Catalog Number: 75-100538

Published by Funk & Wagnalls,
A Division of Reader's Digest Books, Inc.
by arrangement with Editions Rencontre
Printed in Italy

The colour illustrations in the first part and on the
cover were provided by André Held, Lausanne,
except:
Scala, Florence: pages 45, 46 and 50;
Courtauld Institute, London: pages 65, 74 (right), 75,
79 and 80;
R. B. Fleming, London: pages 73 and 88;
Brompton Studio, London: page 66;
Giraudon, Paris: page 70 (lower);
Rijksmuseum, Amsterdam: page 91.

The black-and-white illustrations in the dictionary
were provided by:
Giraudon, Paris: pages 146, 147, 148, 149, 152, 153,
156, 157, 159, 160, 161, 163, 165, 169, 177, 180,
181, 183, 186, 191, 192 (right), 194, 195, 197, 198
and 200;
André Held, Lausanne: pages 150, 151, 154, 168,
176, 179, 184, 185, 190, 192 (left) and 202;
Bruckman-Giraudon, Paris: page 166;
Hanfstaengl-Giraudon, Paris: page 171.

Table of Contents

Pietro Longhi
Venice 1702-85
The Dentist
Oil on canvas 2′0″ × 1′7″
Venice, Academy

Introduction

A character of great unity may rightly be attributed to the culture of the 18th century, but in that case it must also be recognised as having a strong element of complexity.

The 18th century lends itself well to the title of " Elegant Century", or " Century of Enlightenment", one of epicurean behaviour and rationalist philosophy. It is also known as the " French Century", although it should be emphasised that this title is not of French invention but comes from across the mountains and the Rhine.

Historically, the century begins and ends with two events which, although emanating from France, are of European importance: the hegemony of Louis XIV and the imperialism of Napoleon. In the years between, although they are studded with political or economic defeats and setbacks, France maintains her place at the head of a Europe which spontaneously accepts the pre-eminence of her language, her literature and her art and adopts the etiquette of her court for its social usages.

It is taken for granted that foreign sovereigns go to the studios of French artists for their portraits, or to buy paintings to adorn the walls of distant palaces. In the same way French artists, or those trained in France, make triumphant journeys throughout Europe, staying to carry out highly-paid commissions or to found academies and art factories modelled on those of Paris. Thus is to become established the type of royal portrait painted by Rigaud, the mythological portrait perfected by Nattier, the worldly type of Van Loo, Tocqué and Perronneau; the same applies to genre paintings such as Watteau's Fêtes galantes which his successors, in more or less worthy manner, triumphantly paint on overmantels, illustrating sentimental or licentious scenes from mythology ... or the Bible.

" But was that the whole of European art? Did the powerful wave of French art submerge all national specialties and traditions?" We pose the question as did Louis Réau, principal architect of the " defence and illustration" of a French Europe, and we accept his answer: " Art as elaborated at Versailles and in Paris had an all-powerful influence on court and society art, which is international, but had no effect on religious and popular art." It must also be remembered that reservations about French expansion are manifest across the Channel and the Alps: in England because of a fierce Franco-British national rivalry and in Italy from " the proud consciousness of 18th-century Italians of a national school whose glory stems not only from its past but from the living and is made illustrious with great names".

In fact it is a Venetian, Tiepolo, who dominates the important sector of decorative painting, a derivation from and organic complement to the Baroque architecture of palaces and sanctuaries, while fresco, after the death of Louis XIV, is hardly used in France. The superb ceiling of the Hercules Salon at Versailles and some of the other works of François Lemoine and those who emulated him are only exceptions to the general rule represented by Boucher. Boucher's genre painting is better suited to the new style of interior architecture which favours blank ceilings and leaves to the decorative painter only overmantels above doors or panels. As for churches, France builds hardly any.

The situation is different in Germany and Austria, recovering after the Thirty Years

War and the Turkish invasion. Churches and monasteries are rebuilt in thanksgiving. Vast abbeys, libraries, refectories, bishops' palaces and "imperial apartments" offer a rich field to the Italian fresco painters who before long are joined by native artists trained in the academies of Augsburg or Vienna.

The art of displaying the virtuosity of the brush over large but capriciously-divided surfaces calls for a real science in which the basic ideas of ceiling perspective, laid down in books by Andrea Pozzo and Paulus Decker, are combined with theological concepts or the commonplace ideas of Cesare Ripa's Iconology (that "Artists' Bible" which drew the condemnation of Winckelmann and which combines pagan mythology with Christian allegory).

Here, indeed, is an important aspect of 18th-century painting which deliberately stands aloof from a French Europe and the "Century of Enlightenment"!

In the same way, the Italians must be acknowledged as leaders in another form of painting: the urban panorama. The travels of the two Venetian "Vedutisti", Canaletto and Bellotto, throughout Europe produce a series of particularly vivid pictures of London, Vienna, Dresden and Warsaw.

If today we are to discover the "masters of reality of the 16th century", predecessors of those of the 17th century who held sway for thirty years, tomorrow we may do as much for the 18th century and find, near or far from the great Chardin and in France or elsewhere, a whole crop of lesser masters devoted to naturalism. The portrait abandons all pomp and becomes intimate. The landscape swings away from the Roman countryside and the precepts of Claude Lorrain towards opposite ideas which have no pretensions to a monopoly of beauty; like Ruisdael and other Dutch painters of the 17th century, the artist seeks to delve directly into nature. Finally, genre painting, not only that of Chardin, shows scenes of daily life far from the sophistication of the boudoir or the prowesses of the bedchamber.

Nor must the "Caravaggists" of the 18th century be forgotten, those isolated "tenebrists" who dot the "Century of Enlightenment" and with whom is joined, albeit incidentally, the great David with his Marat Assassiné (Murder of Marat). By the same token international Mannerism, which the historians say disappeared about 1620, shows some curious resurgence in the 18th century as with Magnasco or Fuseli.

Another example of the complexity of the 18th century is found in the second half in the sudden and total change in aesthetic conception which puts an end to the reign of the Baroque, by now 200 years old or very nearly, and installs neo-classicism, which develops in imitation of an antiquity brought to life by archaeological discoveries. This revolution in taste has its origin in Rome, cosmopolitan melting-pot of intellectuals and artists from all over Europe.

However, the classical inclinations of the French spirit, which consist of a feeling of keeping within bounds, exist outside of imitation of the ancients. They are to be found as much in the 13th century, golden age of Gothic art (was not Amiens Cathedral called the "French Parthenon"?), as in the works of Delacroix, head of the Romantic school. As for *the 18th century, it is to be noted in the Régence and Louis XV styles, called " rocaille" (rococo), creations that are free but in which capriciousness is kept in check, and which contrast with the frenzied exuberances of the Rococo of Italo-German Baroque, in their last phases.*

It is these contrasts, this variety and these metamorphoses which make for the charm and show the richness of painting of the European 18th century.

Boris Lossky
Curator of the Museums of Tours,
Amboise and Richelieu

Thomas Gainsborough
Sudbury 1727-London 1788
Conversation in a Park
Paris, Louvre

The European 18th Century

From Paris to St Petersburg, by way of London, Venice or Potsdam, the 18th century develops a European unity above national divisions. The essential mutations, those of thought and taste, operate collectively. In spite of her military defeats, France holds Europe fascinated. Venice, already prey to the decadence that is to push it under the Austrian yoke, beckons Europe to its feasting. England, welcoming all intellectual "delinquents", presents the seductive model of her constitutional monarchy. The idea of "divine right" gives way to the "enlightened despotism" which Frederick II now practises in Prussia. His *Anti-Machiavel*, rejecting the theory of unscrupulous statecraft, paves the way, with Montesquieu's *Esprit des Lois* and Rousseau's *Social Contract*, for the downfall of absolutism.

However, enough intolerance remains at the dawn of the "Century of Enlightenment" to hold respect for traditions. The repeal of the Edict of Nantes, hunting the French Huguenots from their country, is followed by the ebb of the triumphant Anglicanism which has dethroned the Stuarts and driven English Catholics on to the Continent. But from now on the prestige of the exiles puts a premium on freedom of thought and, against obscurantism, gives added influence to ideas which soon will rule a new world. An intuitive feeling that great changes are imminent enlivens international thought. From the English empiricism of Locke* and Hume* come the principal philosophical movements. Scepticism and sensualism spread wide on the atheistic materialism of Diderot* and Helvetius* before Kant* brilliantly crowns the accumulated philosophical wealth of the last decades of the century.

This century, which lends itself to structural changes, constitutes *par excellence* a transitory era in which the opposing forces feign co-operation. It is the tumultuous period where a civilisation enters into the precarious balance of the apogee, the stage of splendour before the fall. A decisive factor for art, the state of society explains all the contrasts of this epoch which embraces equally happily the serious and the frivolous, the real and the imaginary, in a vast liberation of senses and spirit. The most disparate elements join together in a coherent whole. The aristocracy, although its decline is beginning, none the less maintains its traditions. It adds elegance to grandeur and pours out its riches in bidding for the ostentatious. Proud of their economic prosperity, the middle classes gradually move into the category conceived by and for the nobility, bringing with them the lusty strength of their rationalism and faith in progress and spreading profusely their religious scepticism, their curiosity and their culture. This change takes place with the reassuring courtesy of the period. "They had manners, even in the street", Paul Valéry remarks. What do they say in the Salons*, the daily battlefields of this lace-bound revolution? There one is deafened by passionate discussions on the theatre, on music. There talents are measured. There creative ardour is revived. There culture is never restricted but is distributed like pleasure and matches it in charm. Madame Geoffrin has given the lead to Europe, for the salon, at the beginning of the century, is feminine. From La Camargo to Julie de Lespinasse or to Lady Hamilton

11

An asterisk placed after a word indicates that it is the subject of an article or explanation in the dictionary at the end of this volume.

and whatever her beauty, culture or talent, woman reigns. "Everywhere," say the Goncourts, "spreads a refinement of elegance, a delicacy in voluptuousness."

To meet the insatiable curiosity of the times an *Encyclopaedia** is needed, learned in all matters of science, politics, literature, arts and philosophy.... The progress of science and techniques is followed enthusiastically by the public, hence the astonishing success of works like Voltaire's *Elements of Newton's Philosophy within Reach of Everyone* or Algarotti's *Newtonianism for Women*, or the Abbot Nollet's *Essay on the Electricity of Bodies*. The passion for travel which grips Europe stems from the same thirst for knowledge. No longer do people hesitate before journeying from Naples to Madrid or London, from Venice to Paris or St Petersburg. Literature and painting open up to the exotic. Frontiers are abolished, often scorning military alliances. Helped by Diderot and Grimm*, Catherine II amasses a gigantic collection of works of art, often buying *en bloc* whole private collections from the best-known collectors. Her reign crowns the golden age of patronage of the arts. European princes vie in munificence with

Nicolas de Largillière
Paris 1656-1746
Portrait of Voltaire
Versailles Museum

such famous collectors as Walpole, Crozat, Algarotti*, Bruhl and the extravagant William Beckford, who had the neo-Gothic Fonthill Abbey built to house his treasures. This cosmopolitanism gives rise to a sort of collective cultural patrimony in which figure such names as Hume, Voltaire*, Diderot, Daniel Defoe*, Swift*, Fielding*, Jean-Jacques Rousseau*, Metastasis, Goethe*. . . .

At first, licentious in France and satirical in England, the course of the novel flows towards the pool of sentimental naturalism, revealed by Richardson* and Rousseau. The aristocratic taste for show and gaiety seizes on the theatre. Propagated by the Commedia dell'Arte, the theatre gradually brings itself up to date. Traditional with Gozzi, it assumes an elegant frivolity with Marivaux*, becomes realistic with Goldoni* and mocking with Beaumarchais*. It transforms the Opera which, like it, came from that Italy whose singers are eagerly sought by the European capitals. From elegant music to pre-romantic drama it is the same progression that throws up the names of Campra, Vivaldi, Couperin, Rameau, Handel, Bach, Haydn, Cimarosa, Mozart and Gluck in an unprecedented creative rivalry. Again it is the theatre which marks the great Italian and German decorative religious painting. The French painting of Watteau* and Greuze* is full of it. The century is rich and innovationist and thus is busy building. All the

Jean-Marc Nattier
Paris 1685-1766
Penitent in the Desert
Oil on canvas 2′4″ × 2′6″
Paris, Louvre

sensualism of the epoch is reflected in the new conception of the plan for living.

Prosperity no longer is characterised by trappings for collective use but in a profusion of luxurious or charming detail conceived for individual pleasure. Great reception halls give way to the favoured small, light and warm rooms adorned with mirrors, gilts or scrolled stucco.

The quarrel between the "Ancients", admirers of Poussin, and the "Moderns", followers of Rubens, is settled in favour of the latter by the Baroque. Henceforth the gods are Flemish and Venetian: Rubens, Tintoretto, Veronese, Titian. Rome, which has ruled over the arts since the Renaissance, bows down to Venice and Paris. The line snakes round, twirls, winds itself up and springs back again. Under a transparent glaze, colours become lighter. Fashionable and unfettered, the Baroque goes to the limit of Rococo possibility. It finds disciples all over Europe but is produced essentially in three main centres: France, Italy and England. The other countries, although receptive to this art form, remain aloof. European courts compete for Italian and French artists capable of bringing out local talent.

Rome, however, becomes the cosmopolitan haven where people gather round the erudite such as Mengs*, Winckelmann* and the Count de Caylus*. Reformers, assured of their "good taste" and moral sense, mount an attack on the deplorable "French taste". About 1760 they are helped by historical and social evolution. The literary works of Voltaire and Montesquieu* already have foreseen this turn of events. The *Salons* of Diderot are devoted to it. Neo-classicism, style of the militant middle class, comes only a short time before the French Revolution. It has the same significance.

The French School

Between two periods of militant classicism, French art has a breathing spell. It is a pleasant, easy-going period. But a reversion to the old moderation, opposed to violent change, brings a caution born of previous transitions. France slides slowly from the age of Louis XIV into that of Louis XV. To understand the painting of this period we must plant its leading exponents into the heart of the new society which follows equally the cults of serious thought and pleasure. Court art, noble and emphatic, is as tiring as that old Sun King whose twilight lingers on. The Régence institutes drastic changes. Philip of Orleans abandons Versailles for Paris—the court for the city—a simple move, but a determining factor in the evolution of ideas and art. Emerging from a long-numb state, society bursts into joy in revenge for so much accumulated austerity. The Régence initiates licentiousness; Louis XV becomes the incarnation of the epoch. He has its tastes, its nonchalance and its culture. His reign sees the prestige of Paris grow even greater. Political vicissitudes do not customarily lessen the artistic vitality of France, but never yet has the strategic superiority of thought over arms been so evident! From now on art is aimed at a cultivated class which must be reckoned with. Renown is built up in the "salons" of Madame de Tencin, the Marchioness Deffand, Baron d'Holbach* or Mademoiselle de Lespinasse. Here mingle the encyclopaedists, writers, actors and high

15

noblemen. Madame Geoffrin, whose prestige is international, reserves her Mondays for artists. The privilege of being invited there bestows the cachet of celebrity. Selective domains where the critical or erudite mind shines, the salons assume the importance which the court has lost.

With sociability as a common denominator, all the arts dovetail harmoniously. Music is the rage. The century opens on Campra's *Europe Galante* and *Fêtes Vénitiennes*, whose titles alone show the joint admiration with painting. At the home of the Prince de Conti at the Temple there are crowds to hear an infant prodigy, the little Mozart. Alexandre la Riche de la Pouplinière entertains the musical élite of his time centred around the composer Jean-Philippe Rameau. In the opera-ballet the dance breaks away from court traditions and in its new-found freedom brings unprecedented success to talented dancers like Mesdemoiselles Prevost and Salle. The theatre, which creeps in everywhere, has a quick evolution. Marivaux brings a certain rakishness to it. Beaumarchais tinges it with a satirical philosophy, Voltaire gives it the novel and Diderot dramatises it. Romantic, philosophical or political, French literature spreads its clear language throughout Europe.

Contributing to this stimulating atmosphere, the artist is governed by a series of official institutions peculiar to his calling. Outside the old St Luke Academy, which adhered to its medieval origin and corporate traditions, there has existed since the middle of the 17th century a Royal Academy of Painting and Sculpture whose more modern outlook bears down so hard on that of its rival that it is to secure suppression of the latter before the end of the century. All great painters of the time submit to its teachings and its discipline, which requires them to exhibit at the Salon*.

These institutions come under the authority of the King's Superintendent of Buildings, whose influence can be considerable. Thus the Duke d'Antin revives the Beauvais Factory and gives his protection to the *avant-garde* of his day: Charles de Lafosse*, Restout*, Lemoine*. After him in 1737 Philibert Orry de Vignory, a friend of La Tour, restores the biennial salon, named after the square salon of the Louvre. Two superintendents who follow are protégés of Madame de Pompadour: her uncle Lenormant de Tournehem, then her brother Abel Poisson de Vandieres, Marquis de Marigny. The latter sets off a return to classicism without too much of a blow to individual conceptions. Only the Count d'Angivillers, authoritarian partisan of painting morals, exercises a debatable dictatorship over art under Louis XVI. In this epoch appear the first signs of a sobriety which owes less to the indeterminate tastes of Louis XVI than to the evolution of ideas and the underlying permanence of a basis of classicism. Lafont de Saint-Yenne long has railed against the Rococo. The position of a Rigaud * or Restout, whose death barely precedes the advent of Greuze and Vien*, shows the complexity of aesthetic tendencies in the middle of the century. The pictorial upsurge which began in the Régence period becomes married in its different styles to the graph of ideas and tastes and assumes four successive aspects. After a transitory period during which it sheds the frilly trappings of the Grand Siècle, art becomes intoxicated with elegance and uninhibited worldliness. Contrasting with the frivolity which made a

16

Antoine Watteau
Valenciennes 1684-Nogent-sur-Marne 1721
Gilles (Pierrot in The Commedia dell'Arte)
Oil on canvas 6′0″ × 5′0″
Paris, Louvre

Antoine Watteau
The Faux Pas (sketch)
Oil on canvas 1′8″ × 1′4″
Paris, Louvre

travesty of princely subjects, and inspired the pastorales of Watteau or the decorative allegories of Boucher*, bourgeois realism brings forth the tender integrity of Chardin* and the formidable psychology of La Tour*. A reaction sets in and the landscapes of Hubert Robert* and Vernet* reveal a naturalism that, by now, is Romantic. Deemed purged by the elevating influence of Greuze, it merges finally into the neo-classicism which triumphs only shortly before the Revolution of 1789.

The end of the reign of Louis XIV and the Régence see the complete evolution of the grandiose style inherited from Le Brun. Austerity becomes less severe. The " grand genre " which still co-exists with lighter subjects gives fresh life to its myths and opens up to a smiling world of Venus-saints and Eros-angels. Everything prepares the way for the advent of Boucher. If a Jean Jouvenet*, in whom religious convictions are instilled and who has been brought up on the principles of his master Le Brun, sees too little in the century for it to support sacred painting for long, his nephew Jean Restout is to advance very late, such a wayward apostle in a heterodox century. Departing from the traditional subjects sought by the Carthusians and the Benedictines he gives himself over voluntarily to a new style. A precise science of perspective is added to a Flemish influence typical of the 18th century. While he feels the need to get away from pious subjects, Restout delves into mythology for a mundane repertory. Because his respect for sacred things is too great, he would not have dared to draw his creations from the Bible, as did his predecessor J.-B. Santerre*, who succeeded at the end of the reign of Louis XIV in making an immense success for himself by shocking the public. For him *Lot and His Daughters*, *Suzanna at the Bath*, etc., pass into current mythology. His Eve, quite logically deprived of a navel, has already caused some murmuring. But his Saint Theresa in the Chapel of Versailles, it appears, horrifies virtuous priests and makes them avert their chaste eyes because, as L. Reau remarks, " Santerre does not distinguish very well between the ecstasies of divine love and the spasms of human love ". Quite obviously austerity was no longer current in religious decoration ! It is Charles de Lafosse who, drawing on his double Venetian and Flemish training, first paints in the new style, decorating the cupola of the Invalides Church. Moreover, historical and mythological subjects provide the inspiration for his work, which Watteau is to see and admire at the home of their common patron Pierre Crozat. Sensing that he is to be asked to decorate the vault of the Chapel of Versailles, he uses a subterfuge to have the commission passed on to Antoine Coypel*, who enjoys the double patronage of the Duke of Orleans and the Grand Dauphin. With Coypel, religious sentiment makes way for quite profane qualities of colour and movement. He also uses his talents better in extracting diverting subjects from mythology, such as that nymph daubing the face of Silene with mulberries, or a frolicsome Bacchus beckoning the spectator to his love-feast. Antiquity offers its great legends as material for his theatrical passion. His son Charles Coypel* is to inherit both his father's princely protection and his taste for the spectacular. Quite freed from the transitional period, he and François Lemoine inaugurate the decorative allegories of the glittering Boucher school.

Another type, the ceremonial portrait, retains at the beginning of the 18th century a strong attachment to the " grand style ", but with a Rubensian touch. The ability to achieve the plasticity of expression of majesty with which his contemporaries adorned their king wins for Hyacinthe Rigaud a record of celebrity which may be astonishing today.

Soon every European prince is begging the master to give him a little of the splendour of the Sun King. All the same, apart from an undeniable aptitude for capturing the essentials of a face—as evidenced by the remarkable portrait of his mother—Rigaud scarcely bothered to individualise characters. Hardly varying under their leonine masks, they are worthy effigies surrounded by cohorts of velvet, columns, all the pomp that is supposed to go with princes. The whole is painted by a team of " pupils ", some specialising in tapestry hangings, others in robes, still others in wigs. . . . Out of the same austere mould come Louis XIV and all his offspring, Peter the Great and the European monarchs, a crowd of artists of every school and the full list of French cardinal-politicians and marshals of the salons. Rigaud's art furnishes the best possible expression of an epoch in which all individual aspiration already is snuffed out. But he has made the portrait into a noble type, thus opening the way for the liberating movement which is to heap laurels on Maurice Quentin de La Tour.

Rigaud's success is such that it eclipses the not inconsiderable talents of others. Joseph Vivien*, forerunner of the Italian Rosalba Carriera* and La Tour in the delicate art of the pastel, reveals remarkable qualities in his portrait of Samuel Bernard. But he has to go to German princes to seek the success his own country denies him.

Nicolas de Largillière*, whose qualities of plasticity and sensitiveness are reckoned with some justification to be superior to those of his rival, has lived for some time in London. Under his master Peter Lely, the English Rigaud, he becomes imbued with the spirit of Van Dyck before being introduced into the entourage of the last Stuarts. But the Stuarts are dethroned and Largillière returns to France where, outside Rigaud's princely circle, he has no great difficulty in being recognised as gifted. His light and true tonalities, allied to scrupulous technique, stand him in good stead with the élite of an upper middle class whose importance at the beginning of the century grows incessantly. His superiority rests perhaps in his eclecticism. Largillière knows the value of variety, he can compose a detailed landscape behind two children at play, or break the monotony of the individual portrait by grouping members of a family or a corporate body. Most often the pomp remains, movement is still fixed, as if cramped by the sumptuousness of the robes. But the delicacy of his colours, their clarity, and an atmosphere of distinction already hint at Watteau. Largillière also starts, with François de Troy*, the vogue of the mythological portrait which later is to make the name of Nattier illustrious. The innovation consists less in the use of fancy dress than in the choice of the hero. To meet the new criteria of grace and beauty the hierarchy of Olympia are jostled a little. The terrestrial hierarchy, too; for deification no longer belongs only to blood princes. Venus takes the lead from Mars with her retinues of Diana, Flora, Ariadne and Ceres. The court is peopled with goddesses of blue and pink, scantily dressed.

But if F. de Troy and Largillière confine themselves to putting several original patricians into fancy dress, Jean-Marc Nattier* sets himself up as a specialist in this type and builds his renown on the shifting sands of a fashion. Maria Leczinska has him brought to the court. The Ladies of France pass through all the metamorphoses judged worthy of their rank. Nattier has satiated the court *ad nauseam* with his dolls' heads with faces of pink porcelain and staring eyes. Moreover, his success has obliged him to carry them out in series and their qualities of plasticity have suffered accordingly. The versatile clientèle that brought him glory takes it away from him, for the very reasons they had bestowed it on him. Then he tries to drop the allegory. But psychology does not come suddenly and Nattier is not able to match La Tour. The aristocracy turn their backs on him and, temporarily, become interested in more sincerity. Nattier is to find himself emulated belatedly by François-Hubert Drouais, who is to disguise Madame du Barry as Flora. All the futility of the century seems to have found a place in his light portraits of little princes beribboned or in fancy dress. The contribution of Jean Raoux* has aspects that are more complex. Preceding Nattier at the court which he peoples with divinities, Raoux also monopolises mundane success with actresses and dancers whom he disguises in their turn. Mesdemoiselles Duclos, Prevost, Camargo or Deschamp, often painted in the character of their roles, thus "democratise" mythological costume! His work is a delightful testimony to the conjugate importance of the theatre and mythology, which he alone has demonstrated so clearly in a type different from but contemporary with that of Watteau.

22

Nicolas Lancret
Paris 1690-1743
The Game of Pied-de-bœuf, c. 1738
Oil on canvas 1′5″ × 1′6″
Berlin, New Palace

In the same way that any revolution comes only after long underground maturing, the appearance of Antoine Watteau, decisive figure in the French school, at the uncertain dawn of the century, is a sunburst of what is to come. The scope of his audacity is all the more striking when it is recalled that thirty of the thirty-seven years of his short life are passed under the reign of Louis XIV. Watteau has not lived through the ostentation of a frivolous and refined epoch. But he has wanted it. Arriving too early in the century to meet with the success of a Boucher, a Fragonard* or a La Tour, he passes as such a bewitching meteor that his contemporaries are left with no time to realise the importance of what he has done.

Watteau is an innovator in all the aspects of his very abundant work, and primarily in form. So soon after the domination of Le Brun, the subtlety of his idle little personages and the clarity of his silvery half-tones bring out a boldness that has only a slight classic flavour. Watteau, however, has not been to Venice, nor to Antwerp. For him the Crozat Collection and the Luxemburg Gallery, of which Audran is now the curator, take the place of Flanders and Italy. The working method of the master of the *fêtes galantes* is known. His notebooks of drawings in three colours taken from life provide a bottomless reservoir of heads, attitudes, personages always ready to play the role of extras or actors in the great pictorial dramas of their creator. It even happens that the producer sometimes has recourse several times to the same interpreter. He has a genius for arranging his compositions with an original balance. He is fond of seated groups whose mass gives a breadth to the landscape-décor in which he often places one

23

Jean-Honoré Fragonard
Bacchant Asleep
Oil on canvas 1′6″ × 1′10″
Paris, Louvre

person alone and standing up. But all creative activity implies a choice. The aesthetic paradise of Watteau ignores poverty, old age, grossness and the other ugly sides of life. His various types are based on a poetic homogeneity for which others long envy him without, however, discovering its secret. Audran has taught him, for the decoration of arabesque panels, the elegance which wells up in his *fêtes galantes*. Claude Gillot *, his first teacher, has given him this theatrical taste which, with music, penetrates not only his scenes from Italian drama or the *Embarkation for Cythera*, but his entire work, even to his portraits. Harlequin, Pierrot, Colombine and Mezzetin are introduced everywhere; they bring the colours of their costumes, their joy or their melancholy. They are present in the rustic fairylands alongside even more imaginary, silky images. No learned subject taken from an ancient odyssey—reality also is a spectacle, even camp life, above all the sparkling elegance of those who come and go in the shop of friend Gersaint*, for whom he paints the famous "Enseigne". At the height of his mastery, with the assurance that comes from having well assimilated the sparse elements that comprise his language, he invents the *fête galante*. This contemporary of Marivaux finally brings to life the sumptuous domain of his confused desires. In it life becomes diluted in ostentatious spectacle, in an atmosphere of Paradise Regained. The accuracy of his attitudes, the mobility of his faces and the softness of his landscapes bring a selective realism into this oasis of purity. That a *Rural Entertainment* may dissolve into a *Hunting Rendezvous* or a *Venetian Festival* is not important. His themes are generally interchangeable but have no philosophic pretensions. Less affected by classical culture than his predecessors, Watteau thus is only the more human. "A libertine in spirit but morally prudent", he sticks to games, to the poetic preludes to love. His love affairs are always linked with courtliness. They never violate that purity with which he surrounds even his nudes. The *fête galante* is to become gradually degraded throughout the century until it becomes erotic in the hands of decadent petty painters. Watteau disappears at a time when the Régence is abandoning austerity. The sudden eruption of festivals and pleasure gives an air of truth to his work. But Watteau gives it the elegant air that too often is missing in the carousals of the Regent and his mistress Madame Parabère. Watteau has not known this ideally-refined society but he has dreamed of it and sensed its coming. Fifteen years later the insatiability of Frederick II and the posthumous fame of Watteau open the way for a host of more or less slavish imitators.

In the immediate aura of Watteau, however, Jean-Baptiste Pater* and Nicolas Lancret* deserve special mention. If they lack something of the poetry of their master, they retain faithfully the delicacy of those *fêtes galantes*, which gains them entry to the Royal Academy. At the end of his life Watteau, in a fit of remorse over the son of his sculptor friend Antoine Pater, calls Jean-Baptiste to him. Pater admits later to Gersaint that he "owes all I know to that brief time which I have turned to good account". Excessively faithful in military scenes as well as in pastorals, he revives almost unchanged Watteau's sparkling atmosphere, the attitudes of his characters and his composition. . . . He might almost be accused of plagiarism except that at this time frequent borrowing by

artists is not considered reprehensible. To the themes of the *Concert, Conversation Galante* and *Blind-man's Buff* are added that of *Les Baigneuses*, which has been repeated many times. Also attributed personally to Pater are the illustrations for La Fontaine's *Fables* and the *Roman comique* of Scarron, where the artist shows he can be as truculent as required.

Although never a pupil of Watteau, Nicolas Lancret benefits from advice he received from the master to work particularly from nature. After Lancret is admitted to the Academy at a very young age, a princely clientèle ranging from the Duke d'Antin to Frederick II bid for his paintings. It is, in fact, following the fashion, for his elegant pastorals assume something of the form of imitations of Watteau although shorn of his poetry. On the other hand his series of "games" are coloured with all the freshness of childhood. His genre paintings of modest interiors couple the grace of his people with a sense of reality quite new at this time. A predilection for "cycles" makes him devote series of paintings to the "hours of the day" or "seasons of the year", which come only from his own personal imagination, while the theatre, life-blood of the century, is insinuated everywhere into works which are a wonderful testimony to the atmosphere in which they have been created.

Among more distant disciples Jean-François de Troy*, son of the portraitist, contributes an unexpected eclecticism. Decorative painting sometimes claims him, mythology and the Bible provide elegance; contemporary high society furnishes his best subjects. Spirit and verve are free in the rapid brushwork of his genre paintings such as *Déjeuner de Jambon, Déjeuner de Chasse* or *Death of a Stag*. He is also "mundane

25

chronicler", which suits him delightfully. More original than many others he has a high standing in the prolific line of artists who have been able to exploit the dainty, flowery French spirit and spread it throughout the whole of Europe; for each of the types practised by Watteau has found one or more artists who emulate it. François Octavien* and Bonaventure de Bar* take up elegant subjects again. Charles Parrocel* perpetuates the small military scenes. Christopher Huet* decorates the Chateau of Chantilly and the Hotel Rohan with arabesques and "singeries". The "three-colour drawing" finds fervent admirers throughout the whole of the century before it reaches the spiritual heights of Gabriel de Saint-Aubin*. However, the range of Watteau's influence is not limited to this handful of imitators. His elegance underlines the plasticity of expression throughout the whole of the century, but in perpetuating itself thus it is submitted to a process of accentuation which transforms it completely in the uproarious decades that are to follow. The *fin de siècle* version is provided by Jean-Honoré Fragonard.

The joyous Mediterranean seems to have picked the most fragrant flowers from its garden of elegance to offer a back-handed bouquet to the virtuous preachers of a return to antiquity (and to good morals). From the rural festival to landscape, from scenes of courtliness to the allegorical portrait or the touching family scene, not only is the type foreign to him but his style remains resolutely anti-classical. *Coresus Sacrificing Himself to Save Callirhoe* opens the doors of the Academy to him, but he discards a career as historical painter as too dull, and it is such paintings as *Hasards Heureux de l'Escarpolette* that give him access to the boudoirs of bankers and dancing girls, that is, to fame and fortune.

The bedchamber scene is to Fragonard what the *fête galante* is to Watteau. It suits him well. As an historical painter he would have been nothing but a Deshays*, whose succession had been reserved for him. The "man of matchless mythology and undressed rogues" makes a mockery of the high-minded watchwords of the neo-classicists. His preferred field is *Début du Modèle*, *La Gimblette*, *Les Baisers*, *La Chemise Enlevée*, *Le Verrou*. . . . The most daring scene is always tempered with exquisite delicacy. Fragonard never insists, he touches lightly on the subject and moves on. His is the poetry of voluptuousness, the essence of the Latin temperament. It takes a rare talent to handle ticklish subjects in this way. Nobody ever had the facility this "sketching genius" possesses for capturing and turning to his own use the successive contributions of his predecessors. From his master Boucher he takes the voluptuous curve, which he corrects with the elegance of Watteau and the virtuosity of Tiepolo*. "I was mad about Tiepolo in Venice; I should like to have been that man," he admits. Fragonard has taken rakishness to the ultimate beyond which it no longer is a part of art. But beside him, or in his wake, collect a host of licentious little painters bent on the business of satisfying the lewd leanings of this golden age of pleasure. Apart from Boucher, whose name remains linked with greater productions, the only one worth recalling is his son-in-law and pupil, Pierre-Antoine Baudouin. His field is gouache. His reduced format allows of all subjects. His *Bride Going to Bed*, *Confessional*, *Carquois épuisé* and *Fille conduite* raise the admiration of thousands of fervent art lovers, and the ire of the Archbishop of Paris who, in 1765, demands their withdrawal from the Salon on the grounds of immorality.

In the luminous wake of Watteau, decorative painting also is transformed. It shows a marked preference for light subjects, allegories without particular emphasis or pretensions to edification. It gets in everywhere, uses up the smallest overmantel, vies for the smallest space with stuccos, mirrors and brocade. The Hôtel de Soubise, in whose decoration most of the great names of this school participated, furnishes the most shining example. In several European countries at the same time decorative painting maintains a strength inherited from the Baroque and is the dominant type. The Solimenas*, Sebastiano Ricci*, Tiepolo and Maulbertsch* have confidence in it. In France it is represented by Boucher, whose affectations draw the fire of international critics against "French taste", and a series of lesser painters suffering from a confusion of influences.

Of Dutch origins, the cosmopolitan dynasty of the Van Loos demonstrates throughout Europe and the century talents that are tinged by a variety of reminiscences. France has the greatest, Carle Van Loo*, who was principal painter to Louis XV before Boucher and realised, in the middle of the century, a success that went far beyond French boundaries. A similar unselfconscious wealth, very appealing, characterises his portraits and his sacred or mythological themes. His elder brother, Jean-Baptiste*, has spread his work haphazardly in his many travels as painter-courtier on which he spent some time at the court of Savoy in Turin. The two sons of Jean-Baptiste Van Loo are to follow in their father's footsteps. Charles-Amédée* becomes painter to the King of Prussia; the court of Spain is host for several years to Louis-Michel Van Loo, painter of that "pretty" portrait of Diderot which the stern scribe of the salons says makes him look like "an old coquette still trying to charm". In fact the eclectic production of the Van Loos is always to keep a relative reserve inherited from their Dutch origins which makes them a class apart in the school of Boucher.

Typical as it may be of the school of Watteau, the art of François Boucher draws its style from a Baroque tradition of which Rococo is only one of a number of possible manifestations. His master, François Lemoine, still borrows his favourite themes from traditional mythology. But his manner already betrays a lively admiration for the

27

François Boucher
Paris 1703-70
La Petite Jardinière
Oil on canvas 2′0″ × 1′6″
Rome, National Gallery of Ancient Art
Barberini Palace

contemporary Italians, Solimena and Sebastiano Ricci. After several religious compositions the fine ceiling of the Hercules Salon in the Chateau de Versailles wins him the title
of Principal Painter to the King. If his mind, impaired by overwork, had not led him to
suicide a year later, Lemoine might perhaps have brought great vigour to French
decorative painting. Boucher's temperament leads to more lewdness. His blue and pink
pastorales, full of sensuality, seem to have lost the initial purity of the *fêtes galantes*.
Doubtless they are equally imaginary. High society, however, was bound to find in his
" daintiness, his romantic gallantry, his fantasy, his facility, his variety, his brilliance, his
made-up flesh tints and his debauchery "[1] the scarcely inaccurate picture of their
customary atmosphere and thus raise him to a pinnacle and put him in the front rank of
the French school. Qualities which Diderot sometimes attributed to him are easily
recognised in the delicate decoration of the Hôtel de Soubise and the portrait of Madame
de Pompadour. He also leaves some admirable drawings. The generous protection of
the royal mistress has given him access to the tapestry works at Beauvais and Gobelins.
But the arduous nature of this particular art, combined with ailing eyesight, distorts his
sense of colour, and his tonalities, particularly after 1750, become very insipid. Although
acceptable as an adjunct to ornate architecture, Boucher's art does not stand up well by
itself. His voluptuous nymphs do not bear comparison with the elegant ladies of
Watteau, or the likeable libertines of Fragonard, whose spirit they lack. Diderot, having
dared to become involved in aesthetics, is reproached for having been too severe with
Boucher. The philosopher's criticism is occasionally prophetic.

Another pupil of Lemoine, Charles Natoire*, a former director of the French
Academy in Rome, wins a measure of fame alongside Boucher in the decoration of the
Hôtel de Soubise and the Medal Room of the King's Library, where he paints the story
of Psyche and that of the nine Muses. Even more so than Boucher he has contributed to
the decline of the Baroque with his sugary, superficial painting. Rococo ornamentation,
it is true, leaves little room for great themes. The reduction of space available for
decorative painting in the new style of architecture sends the painters back to tapestry.

The phenomenon of Chardin throws light on a less pretentious but primordial
aspect of this same epoch, whose diversity is surprising. Modest and home-loving, this
son of a cabinet-maker in Paris is to reveal a form of poetry that imitators of Watteau
have passed by, but which is full of significance. Nearer to Vermeer or the Le Nains,
Chardin is classified by the Academy as a " painter of animals and fruit ". He takes this
little regarded style to the highest level and keeps it there until 1733. " This is the painter,
this is the colourist, " cries Diderot, filled with enthusiasm at the fidelity of his " mute
compositions ". Alone in a dimensional way where only Jeaurat* and Lépicié*, or more
rarely Desportes* and Oudry*, ever came near him, Chardin subconsciously discovers
the aesthetic equivalent of the most advanced philosophical reasoning. The trueness of
his colour harmonies, the bloom of his fruits, the softness of his materials, the quality of
his silence catch simultaneously the eye, the feeling and the ear. . . .

[1] Diderot, *Salon 1761.*

Related to the "sensualism" of Condillac*, his art also reflects the rationalist thought of the period with his persistence in searching right into the substance of an object to root out its secret, which is not the "soul" attributed to it by the Romanticists but its profound truth beneath the visible skin. It is undoubtedly this "magic" which makes him revered by Diderot, who feels the deep naturalism of his work. "One might say of M.Chardin and M.de Buffon* that nature has taken them into her confidence." At the derisive suggestion of his friend, Aved*, he ventures into other pictorial types in 1733 with *Lady Sealing a Letter*. A series of domestic scenes, bathed in a padded silence, makes poetry of the daily tasks of his class. No question of rowdy ostentation. No question, either, of gross misery. But a tenderness, a sensitivity, an accent on truth, which, added to his divided touch and his handling of reflection, go beyond realism to show the universality and continued existence of the human race. The liking of Catherine II, Frederick the Great and rich art lovers for these peaceful little scenes explains why the artist is asked to make frequent replicas which spread his work all over Europe without ever bringing him more than very relative material wealth.

Not very imaginative, he takes his characters from his immediate friends. The children of his friend Godefroy the jeweller are seen drawing, playing with tops, building houses of cards—marvellous portraits, each the essence of an anecdote. At the end of his life the results are equally happy when he moves into the specialised field of the pastel, leaving us that moving self-portrait which shows a Chardin grown old, sheltering his poor eyes behind round spectacles which even accentuate his legendary bonhomie. Appreciated as it may be by artists and amateurs, Chardin's art at the time has less appeal than that of Watteau. But the importance of Chardin is not measured by its immediate influence. A *fête galante* by Watteau, a composition by Chardin, they are the very essence of the French 18th century.

The rising tide of popularity of the portrait throughout the century is evidence of the multiple aspects of this moving period. Regal pomp had its Rigaud, elegant mythology its Nattier. Realism pushes the type to its peak with the psychological portrait, bringing out once more the characteristic of Chardin at his peak of going beyond outward appearances.

Nattier's son-in-law, Louis Tocqué*, has already shown himself to be too realistic for a clientèle accustomed to flattery. His sense of realism soon closes the doors of French nobility to him and he has to turn to the middle classes. However, his portrait of Queen Maria Leczinska brings him invitations to the courts of Russia and Denmark.

The qualities of Maurice Quentin de La Tour come to light at a moment when contemporary society has reached its greatest intensity of culture and refinement. Admitted to the Academy with his portrait of his master Restout, he assiduously frequents the salons of Madame Geoffrin, Grimod de La Reynière and Le Riche de La Pouplinière, the theatre, the Opera, every place where new ideas are affecting literature, philosophy, politics and music. La Tour, apt as all portraitists in capturing a physical resemblance, excels in animating a face. The grain of the skin, the gleam of an eye suggest in a quick stroke that intensity which seems to be concentrated in the depth of a gaze.

The multiple smile of the century is there. The softness of the pastel is flattering and seductive. Everyone who matters in the kingdom is at the feet of La Tour who, lavish with superfluous advice, demands exorbitant prices. They find him charming. But are they always aware of the psychology of this mischievous pastellist? "They think I have only taken the features of their face; but unbeknown to them I go right down to the depths and show the whole of them."

The self-importance of a banker is drawn into his attitude and the expression of his mouth; the habitual charm of his "celestial friend" Mademoiselle Fel, the intelligence of d'Alembert*, the sensuality of Maurice de Saxe can be seen particularly in the impressive "preparatory sketches" gathered together at the Saint Quentin Museum in his native town. But the artist becomes obsessed with Diderot's idea that his pastels will not last long. He becomes absorbed in long research on different methods for possible fixing of the colours. A sudden outburst from Tocqué prompts him to retouch a great number of his works. Thus he brings back the freshness which made their charm before sinking into a mental twilight which brought him a lamentable death. "This perfection I seek is out of human reach," he cried, revealing the total distressing despondency that was to topple his reason. Adulated by an aristocracy that saw in his insolence only the caprices of a gifted child, he captivated no less the *avant-garde* of bourgeois intellectuals and the fiercest detractors of the gallant style, Diderot and Lafont de Saint-Yenne.

While La Tour held out for four years before agreeing to paint the portrait of the Marquise de Pompadour, his rival Perronneau* scoured the provinces and the whole of Europe in search of clients. He was to be found in Holland, Italy, England and Russia. The virtuosity of the one easily eclipsed the more sober talent of the other. However, Perronneau's gifts of colouring, the subtlety of his blue and grey colour harmonies, win out over those of La Tour. He also succeeds in finding a choice clientèle of whom he has left some admirable portraits such as those of Madame de Sorquainville, J.-B. Oudry, J. Cazotte and numerous local officials whom he met in his provincial travels. He dies in Amsterdam, in this Holland which welcomes French painters and where Aved, called the Batavian, has made his second home. The latter, in the middle of the century, paints the Stadhouder William IV in his armour. The official portrait barely befits him more than the "Turkishness" to which he gives himself for some time. But Holland has put her stamp on him and to her he owes his greatest work, a portrait of Madame Crozat which is admirable in its simplicity and faithfulness. He goes on to confine himself at last to the humble world of his friend Chardin, where he has the ability to be great. In the same time nostalgia for lost simplicity brings a new wave of portraitists even into the court.

Joseph Duplessis* excels as the anti-Nattier of the reign of Louis XVI. Approved by the Academy in 1769, this modest man, more concerned like Chardin with portraying human resemblance than deifying his subjects, gives pre-Revolutionary society the style which responds to its feeling of expectation. The middle class, harbouring some mistrust regarding virtuosity, appreciates the conscientiousness and precision of his drawing, which is shorn of any concessions to facility. It offers him, outside female subjects, an abundance of clients from men of letters, artists and politicians, such as Caffieri, Vien,

Glück, Necker, Benjamin Franklin. . . . As official portrait painter to Louis XVI he tries out the formal portrait. But the grandiose style does not suit him so well; he is not made of the same stuff as Rigaud, but his access to the court at such a time gives him a certain prestige. Meanwhile the vogue for the pastel, consolidated since Rosalba Carriera's success in Paris and hallowed by La Tour, has brought about an unprecedented surge of feminine talent, which feeds the most abundant market of the century. But the pastel is not the only reason for it, and two women achieve fame through a less specialised contribution. The masterpiece of Adelaide Labille-Guiard*, pupil of La Tour and her husband Vincent, a vigorous portrait of the sculptor Pajou, undoubtedly wins her entry to the Academy. The more feminine talent of Elisabeth Vigée-Lebrun* derives successive styles from Greuze, Nattier or Drouais. Her light and pleasing summation of the century's portrait art soon wins over to her the city and the court. Her charm and her spirit make Madame Vigée-Lebrun the official portraitist and friend of Marie-Antoinette. Her name is made. It seems that in this effervescent period beauty, unconscious of what was happening around it, is concerned only with superficial modes easily satisfied by a versatile brush. Shortly before 1789 the style of David brings a taste for antique poses and she adopts the Greek head-band and tunic which refine the figure. As the Revolution approached, the illustrator of " The Austrian " was inspired to leave France. It is said that during ten years of her exile a certain painting of Marie-Antoinette, draped in black, was her Sesame to the doors of the princely élite of Europe.

To be accurate, the reign of Louis XVI does not produce a genius in the field of specialisation. The best portraits of the period are those by Greuze and Fragonard. The former reveals himself as a much better portraitist than moralist. Here there is no longer any melodrama. In the portraits of his father-in-law, the bookseller Babuti, of his friend the engraver Wille or of the musician Glück, Greuze displays unsuspected gifts as a colourist; realism is tempered with all the delicacy of the refined century, but its simplicity avoids all mannered style. In his enthusiasm Diderot compares it to a Rembrandt or a Van Dyck! He appreciates less, on the other hand, the dazzling virtuosity of Fragonard, perhaps too audacious for the period. His brush envelops a face in a fine swirl of vivid colours until no resemblance is retained, but only the symbol: reading, inspiration, music. . . . How could this " busybody genius " have failed to top off the most representative type of the century with an original contribution?

But the long vogue of the portrait, which made some artists rich, brings about such competition that a number of artists must either vegetate where they are, go abroad or specialise in a style that is less practised. Thus Louis XV's passion for hunting restores this sport to a place of honour and brings about the rise of the animal painter. In the first part of the century Desportes and Oudry occupy a quite exceptional place. François Desportes has been portraitist to the King of Poland before becoming hunting painter to Louis XIV and making an international success for himself as painter of animals. His great tapestry, *Nouvelles Indes*, a series of eight pieces, remains celebrated. Also leaving portraiture, J.-B. Oudry devotes himself to the hunt just at the time when his contemporary Watteau dies. As hunting historiographer to Louis XV he makes an immense

Jean-Baptiste-Siméon Chardin
Paris 1699-1779
Lady Sealing a Letter, 1733
Oil on canvas 4′9″ × 4′10″
Berlin, Charlottenburg Palace

contribution to the royal tapestry factories, in particular the great *Hunts of Louis XV in the Compiègne Forest.*

These open-air compositions introduce realistic landscape to painting and carry the seeds for a renewal of the classic. Aristocratic by the nature of its clientèle and its themes, animal painting satisfies a latent need for the natural and prepares the way for that cult of nature of which Jean-Jacques Rousseau is soon to become one of the high priests. Desportes and Oudry also have had merit enough to show that the beribboned sheep and the foolish virgin have no monopoly in decorative painting. After them painters of battles such as Charles Parrocel, still quite dazzled by Watteau's military scenes, François Casanova*, brother of the Venetian adventurer, and his eclectic pupil Loutherbourg*, contribute to reviving the taste for landscapes in France. Nature still figures as an accessory, but it is felt to be closer and ready to overrun the animal or human story. Fantastic Loutherbourg, whose escapades are to have him exiled to England, sees the rhythm of the sun and the seasons in the countryside or borrows seascapes from Vernet, sometimes shrouding them in storms. But sea or mountain, it is their dramatic intensity which brings profuse praise from Diderot. He likes this "man of

33

pathos who speaks to the soul". Finally, content with the art of his time, the philosopher-critic rejoices while he deals with Joseph Vernet.

This elder of a diffuse dynasty has passed nearly twenty years in Italy before coming to conquer a France that is the better prepared to receive him. The quite classical serenity of his Italian landscapes is to lend colour for several years to his seascapes and his "Ports of France", ordered by the King, which the skilful topographer animates with a handful of people. But soon a darkness pervades his seascapes, setting off to advantage only the light of the moon or the flashes of the storm. Vernet dramatises nature, seeking more and more striking contrasts. His international fame is owed to clients who are more concerned with the effect than with delicacy. His workshop becomes a sort of factory producing nocturnal storms and stereotyped moonlight.

It is a very different interpretation that his contemporary Hubert Robert puts on the landscape. The Marquis of Stainville, later Duke de Choiseul, takes him to Rome in 1754 just as Vernet returns from the Italian capital. He passes ten years there during which he makes many friends and acquaintances. Panini*, then very well known in his own country, passes on to him his passion for ruins. A little later Fragonard arrives and they become friends. Both pass bewitching months at the Villa d'Este, drawing to their hearts' content, with the Abbé St Non* "about whom there was nothing ecclesiastical except his little collar". Fragonard fills nature with poetry, Hubert Robert decks it out with melancholy ruins into which he puts picturesque lower-class people. Back in France he never departs from these romantic ruins, which become the rage. "It was very much in the fashion and very magnificent to have one's salon painted by Robert," Madame Vigée-Lebrun relates. The ancient monuments of Nîmes and Orange take the place of the Coliseum of Rome for Robert. His imagination supposes the great gallery of the Louvre to be in ruins and he assembles there, at will, monuments from many sources.

This curious frame of mind makes him an attentive chronicler of demolitions in Paris. Precise and rapid strokes tell of the burning of the Opera, or the destruction of the bridge at Neuilly, encroaching on the domain of the charming Gabriel de Saint-Aubin, who multiplies the picturesque scenes of Parisian life. In his personal version of restitution of conjugality to nature and the antique, "Robert of the Ruins" links two aspects of the preoccupations of his time, in a technique that is a forerunner to Impressionism.

In the century of Watteau and Fragonard, Jean-Baptiste Greuze would hardly have been important had he not made concrete the evolution accomplished in the ideas of the eve of the Revolution. The social phenomenon has assumed more and more importance. Throughout its philosophers and its writers the middle class imposes its conceptions. Marmontel's *Moral Fables* and Rousseau's *Social Contract* appear in 1761.

The outbidding in eroticism which has made fortunes for small masters begins to provoke a disgust which is echoed by Diderot. The Count of Angivillers makes use of his powers to ban not only licentious subjects but all showing of nudity in paintings. At the same time it becomes good taste to be tender. The "tearful play" of Nivelle de La Chaussée comes shortly before the "bourgeois drama" of Diderot and Sedaine*.

Chardin
La Pourvoyeuse
Oil on canvas 1′6″ × 1′3″
Paris, Louvre

Maurice Quentin de La Tour
Saint-Quentin 1704-88
Portrait of Jean-Jacques Rousseau
Pastel 1′6″ × 1′3″
Geneva, Museum of Art and History

Maurice Quentin de La Tour
The Negro, 1741
Pastel 2′2″ × 1′8″
Geneva, Museum of Art and History

From this mixture comes the painting in Greuze's style, " the first ", according to Diderot, " to be advised to give morals to art and to put together events from which it should be easy to make a novel ". Unfortunately, morals and literature do not constitute the criteria of a quality of plasticity. Greuze never accepted the title of " genre painter " which the Academy bestowed on him at his reception. To realise his dream of a " grand style " he draws on comedy and the novel for this literary painting which preaches " good upbringing " in a series of paintings whose tonalities are grey and faded. The actors in his *Paternal Curse* and *Bad Son Punished* play out the bitter melodrama.

In fact the whole of Greuze's production seems to rest on a misunderstanding. This man was not born to eulogise virtue. Hence the equivocal aspect of his symbolic paintings in which a non-genuine simple young girl with her bodice half-open has always lost or broken something: *Broken Mirror*, *Bird Flown Away*, *Broken Pitcher*, so many poor implications which, by comparison, are so rewarding as they stand without the deviations of a Fragonard. Despite their dullness and greyness, these compositions are a great success in France and abroad, particularly in Russia. One wonders if Diderot and his contemporaries did not like Greuze for the wrong reasons. Like an old rake repenting late, this declining century proclaims a doubtful Puritanism.

But the new style expresses an aspect of the era important enough to be the decisive factor in a pictorial movement of which Nicolas-Bernard Lépicié remains the best exponent, a movement half-way between Chardin and Greuze. Fragonard himself, around 1775, comes under the joint influence of Greuze and Jean-Jacques Rousseau. Family bliss is made the object of a series of paintings whose titles, from Fragonard, are somewhat surprising: *Happy Family*, *Visit to the Nurse*, *Education Does Everything*. Fragonard shows all the symptoms of an edifying conversion.

The return to virtue is to be accompanied by a return to the antique. As the elegant style slowly deteriorates, this is countered by the ever-insistent neo-classical pressure. There, during the last few decades, art records the approach of the Revolution.

Elisabeth-Louise Vigée-Lebrun
Paris 1755-1842
*Portrait of Madame Vigée-Lebrun
and her Daughter. c.* 1789
Oil on wood 4′0″ × 2′11″, Paris, Louvre

Jean-Baptiste Perronneau
Paris 1715-Amsterdam 1783
Portrait of Jean-Baptiste Oudry
Oil on canvas 4′3″ × 3′3″
Paris, Louvre

The ideals of the Tiers-Etat movement gradually sap the tastes of the decadent class, while the far-off reputation of Roman republics makes scintillating mirages of their uprightness. The Roman cult to which Voltaire and Montesquieu have been devoted since 1730 has recruited followers among cultured minds such as the Count de Caylus and Lafont de Saint-Yenne. The craze for archaeological expeditions first at Hercula- neum in 1738 and then at Pompeii, the anti-French theories of Mengs and Winckelmann, have given such an interest to Roman aesthetics that a veritable fashion is established, even down to costume. Madame de Pompadour's own brother, who has become the Marquis de Marigny and is superintendent of the King's Buildings, takes this reaction in hand, aided by a sworn enemy of Rococo, the engraver Cochin. Against the "little style" the immutable perfection of the antique is established. Imitation of sculpture in painting is advocated. It is the age of *trompe-l'œil*, monochrome and judicious. The major part of the great decorative painting comes from the pupils of Boucher. It retains all its Baroque dynamism with Doyen*, Deshays, Durameau* and J.-B. Pierre*. But the Marquis de Marigny had maintained a taste and critical sense that were to be lacking in his successor, the Count d'Angiviller. From 1774 to 1791 the latter seeks to impose the artistic ideas of Louis XVI by recommending artists to seek inspiration from the great examples of antiquity, and not to neglect French history. The artists are patriotic. A horde of lesser painters benefit simultaneously from the infatuation of the rich with Pompeian simplicity, from artistic privileges and official commissions. Hence the vast compositions of Menageot*, the insipid *Marchande d'Amours* by Vien and illustrations of French history by J.-B. Suvée* and F.-A. Vincent*. Louis-J. Le Lorrain* reverts to Homeric themes and decorates a room for Lalive de Jully in the Greek manner. Lines are strained, movement fixed. Vincent may perhaps acquire a lasting name for his acclimatised "Spartan" style but his small talent is eclipsed by the triumph of Louis David*, whose *Oath of the Horatii* in the Salon of 1785 marks the advent of a new era, long anticipated in the process which culminates in the Revolution of 1789.

39

Jean-Baptiste Oudry
Paris 1686-Beauvais 1755
Still-life with Violin
Paris, Louvre

Jean-Baptiste Greuze
Tournais 1725-Paris 1805
Portrait of a Little Girl
Oil on canvas 1'7" × 1'3"
Rome, National Gallery of Ancient Art,
Barberini Palace

The Italian School

It is very difficult to discern an Italian entity in the 18th century. Italy appears as a juxtaposition of independent principalities between natural common frontiers. This division, together with the overthrow of successive dominations, means that each city retains its own local peculiarities, sometimes even a local language that is more widely spoken than Italian. Austria, Spain, Savoy and the Church share out the territory; Naples passes from Austrian domination to that of the Spanish Bourbons who are also installed in Parma, succeeding the Farnese in 1731.

Since the Infante Don Philip, son of Philip V and his second wife Elisabeth Farnese, is the son-in-law of Louis XV, the court of Parma becomes a place of Franco-Spanish influence. Beyond these divisions the names of Servandoni* or Galli Bibiena*, whose genius has organised the most brilliant festivities in European capitals, become international. Throughout this avidly ostentatious century the great scenography is Italian. But in an area more worthy of the artist's brush, the rare common characteristics linking the regions of the peninsula belong in the social field. As everywhere in Europe the middle class has acquired importance in a social structure that is still aristocratic. Painting records this phenomenon in finding a new realism. On the other hand, the penetration of rationalist ideas has not done much harm to religion which, with the language, remains the most important linking factor. Quite cleared of its inquisitorial aspects, the Church insinuates itself into all levels of society from one end of the territory to the other. Aristocratic in Rome with Popes, who are patrons of art, and the ecclesiastical élite, it assumes a middle-class complexion in Bologna, where its priests frequent the salons. In Venice it plays its part in the craze for luxury which seizes the whole of society. Right throughout the century hardly a painter is to be found who has not made his contribution to it. But if religious subjects are excluded, the Italian school of this century presents the greatest variation in themes and styles.

From Neapolitan Baroque to Lombardian realism, from Venetian gracefulness to Roman austerity, each city reveals its own particular style. It is true that in most cases the great outburst of art hardly extends beyond the first one-third of the century. After that the situation clarifies itself, to boil down to a Rococo movement which triumphs first in Venice and is countered at the end of the century by the neo-classic movement which Rome is to impose on Europe. Chronologically, distant Naples, still vibrant from the memory of Luca Giordano, inaugurates the period.

Far from the great centres of living art and prey to political upheavals, Naples has Francesco Solimena to thank for maintaining its artistic position in the 18th century. In 1709 Austria takes possession of it and gives it a Viceroy, Charles III. Solimena profits without difficulty from successive protections. But as against the vicissitudes of temporal power the Church offers a permanence that is beneficial or formidable as the case may be. It constitutes an economic and moral power that is better cultivated than alienated. From the beginning Solimena has been careful to ensure the favour of the Jesuits by decorating the chapel of the Gesu Nuovo. Soon overwhelmed with orders, he covers the churches of his city in spirited frescoes. Recollections of Luca Giordano, brought out with a tumult of colour in the manner of Pietro da Cortona, they also contain traces of the influence of the Carracci. From the Baroque the ensemble retains volumes, rhythm and inventive power but a clarity and new lyricism is already heralding Tiepolo. For these reasons Solimena, at the beginning of the 18th century, occupies a key position. However, he does not hold a complete monopoly on local decorative painting. Francisco de Mura represents a calmer trend, in which solemnity vies with refinement of form. But de Mura allows himself to be coaxed to Turin, leaving only the prolific radiance of Solimena to justify the maintenance of the Neapolitan painting movement.

The likeable Corrado Giaquinto* already displays a joyous and Rococo-tinted lightness of touch. To Rome, Turin and Madrid he takes an affected refinement of art in which mythology and religion are adorned with elegance. Giuseppe Bonito* turns gradually from sacred subjects to the more temporal universe. Painter to the King of Naples in the middle of the century, he transforms the casual anecdote or the rustic genre picture by means of coloured light and shade. But without realising how he excels in this sort of refined genre painting he gives it up for collective portraits in the cold, neo-classic style. Bonito also loses much of his importance when some of his best works, from *Neapolitan Masks* to *Wounded*, are attributed to his junior, Gaspare Traversi*. Abandoning the popular scene, Traversi opens up a veritable comedy of morals, full of irony and psychological finesse. As far as he is concerned the Baroque style in great decorative painting has gone for ever from Naples to be supplanted by the realism which from now on appears even in sacred painting itself.

This new current, which is to have so great a place in Italian painting, flows first through Bologna where, from the early decades of the century, it is fuel for the audacity of several modernists such as Giuseppe Maria Crespi*. Dubbed "The Spaniard", Crespi blends the teachings of the Carracci and Guerchino in his own fashion and is able to draw his own personal style, essentially human, from the mixture. His independence of art patrons and of tradition wins him renown that sometimes is tinged with censure. It is true that this product of the austere 17th century has little concern for metaphysical qualms. Sacred or profane subjects become one in an anecdotal style in which all grandiloquence disappears in favour of discreet humour. *St John Nepomuk Hearing the Confession of the Queen of Bohemia* is bathed in the same luminous serenity as *The Flea* or *The Massacre of the Holy Innocents*, which wins him the favour of Ferdinand of Tuscany. Little inclined to pathos, Crespi's brush blithely colours the *Seven Sacraments* and brings to life the humblest scenes such as his *Woman Washing Dishes*, a forerunner of Chardin. Central figure of the Bologna school of the 18th century, the man who instructs Piazzetta* and Pietro Longhi* is partly responsible by his teaching for the dazzling Venetian sunburst. But Bologna has reigned too long over European art not to put up some resistance to a realism born of the most advanced philosophical ideas. Against Crespi, Donato Creti* puts forward his aristocratic mythologies and rural paintings which have a more candid link with local tradition. In other respects his arcadian idylls with their subtle elegance are nearer to the works of the French *fêtes galantes* painters than those of his own daring compatriot.

The first half of the century sees an intensification of the flow of exchanges between the cities of the north. Artists move about easily and Verona, Piacenza, Parma, Milan, Turin and Modena are dependent even on nomad painters attracted to those prosperous cities on the roads to Europe. The most original Florentine has just that sort of vagabond nature. Francesco Zuccarelli*, painter of idyllic pastorals and beribboned mythologies, abandons his native city for London, where most of his works are to be found, and for Venice, whose "Accademia" welcomes him to membership and even makes him its president.

While Florence lies dormant, the extravagances of the House of Savoy and the geographical and political position of Piedmont give Turin a special aura. The genius of one of the greatest artist-decorators of the century, Juvarra, gives it simultaneously a

Rococo framework and luxurious festival productions that remain celebrated. At the Royal Palace and Stupinigi Castle a profusion of stuccos, of Chinese lacquers, of overmantels raise great pictorial themes up towards the ceilings. A local painter, Claude de Beaumont*, and the Nice-born Savoy national Carle Van Loo cover the ceilings and the apartments of the Queen with decorative allegories. The famous Stupinigi hunting lodge, attributed to Juvarra, and the Royal Palace, are decorated by numerous painters from France, like the Van Loos, or more often from other regions of Italy. On the road to Madrid, to London, to St Petersburg, artists in perpetual transit like Giaquinto, Bellotto*, F.de Mura, Guglielmi* and Bigari* make more or less protracted halts at the court of Savoy and leave their works in its palaces and churches.

Challenged by this brilliance Lombardy seems to take up the gauntlet with Giacomo Ceruti. Ceruti belongs to that realist movement that already has nurtured the art of Crespi or Ghislandi*. But as his nickname suggests, " Il Pitochetto " (The Beggar) confines his world to the most poverty-stricken classes. Not for him the shelter of a powdered wig, but humanity in rags, the needy with their burning stares, those grave faces of premature adulthood which daily misery fixes on children. Little information is available on the painter of *Portarolo* and *Meeting in the Wood*. Traces of him are found in Brescia, Bergamo and Padua in the first part of the century. Despite the strength of realist trends in Italy, his style must isolate him and limit his success.

Genoa, particularly in the 18th century, has given birth to an exceptional genius, a forerunner of the daring Romanticists, Alessandro Magnasco*, known as Lissandrino. In his tragi-comic universe the weird invades daily life. A nervous stroke gives a disturbing mobility to his objects. A fantastic imagination transfigures the anguish of the century of his birth and Magnasco preserves its dark obscurity as part of his magic. But his obsession with light, his theatrical taste, his spaces limited or terrestrial, his broken line, make up the originality of his contribution to the new era. Half-demoniac, half-playful, an hallucinating atmosphere of macabre animation surrounds these groups of poor wretches and half-starved mountebanks. To what fantastic Witches' Sabbath are they going, these bewitched punchinellos whose clothing catches up little pieces of fire? What strange rites are those Capuchin monks practising as they dance at the funeral of one of their order, or bustle about in a weird library? Magnasco's universe encompasses, in its relentlessly close spaces, sarabands of frenetical skeletons, strange funerals, carousals that are less elegant, more romantic but also more imaginative than those of Watteau. He uses darkness as a pretext for bursts of light which put a hem of gold around the poorest objects, accentuate each break of line, and gets into the heart of a cameo browns with sumptuous troughs of incandescent reds or muted blues. The tragic disappears before his unrepentant taste for the picturesque, noticeable in his monastic scenes as well as in his chronicling of everyday life, in which Magnasco abandons the field of dreams. An attentive observer, he captures a gesture or an attitude almost to the point of caricature in one rapid stroke. He brings to mind Goya* and Daumier. Revival of interest in Magnasco at the turn of the century after a long oblivion brought on by his

44

Alessandro Magnasco
Genoa 1667-1749
Landscape
Naples, Capodimonte

own unorthodox miracles and daring art forms is not just accidental. When he finally paints the patrician *Meeting in a Garden*, in which all terror has been eliminated, it has the elegant pleasures of a sister society to that of Watteau. In the movement to secure freedom of style that leads to Guardi, Magnasco's contribution is considerable. But his genius stems from his own imagination alone and has no link with anyone around him. It does not inspire any local painter to carry on his tradition. When Magnasco dies before the middle of the century, Genoa in its turn drops out of the art world.

Among this number of dormant cities Venice reasserts herself again with the final bouquet of a society that wants to die as it has lived, with elegance. After this the 18th century resumes its way with an almost schematic opposition between a brilliant Venice, which has the rare essence of the new aesthetics, and a nervous Rome which works furiously to destroy this style. Their struggle winds up in two successive reigns of international importance. In the first part of the century Venice spreads the influence of her young and successful school and the glory of her past throughout the whole of Europe. From 1750 onwards Rome begins to reap the fruits of its sombre demolition work before definitely reducing different European aspects of the Rococo to ruins. Venice, international city of luxury and pleasure, crossroads for adventurers and the élite of the whole world, races through its last century of grandeur as if seeking by a wave of the wand to bring on its own inevitable decadence. Venice blends life and the theatre, the reality and the game, in an intense confusion symbolic of all that 18th-century Europe has loved. From the celebrated " Ridotto " (Casino), where crowds gather to play, to the cafés where everything is discussed with passion, and to the watery thoroughfares which for six months of the year carry a carnival masquerade, Venice is at the same time Europe's bawdy-house and its permanent theatre. And like all theatres Venice, indulging in its own pleasures, occasionally reveals a glimpse of the other side of the curtain. The painter or writer must find there a profusion of material, dazzling or ironical. Moreover, as in the rival city of Paris, an innate sense of knowing how to live produces a co-existence of mind and pleasure. More than any other form of expression the theatre raises a tumult of passions. Everyone takes sides for or against the satirical comedy of manners of Carlo Goldoni or the more traditional *Fiabe* of Carlo Gozzi. In a way they are also taking part in a decisive struggle. Goldoni's realistic common sense represents the middle class against the aristocracy as defended by Gozzi. When both sides fail to gain a victory, the Most Serene Republic declines into a combination of patrician frivolity, grandeur and ostentation and middle-class realism, simplicity and scepticism. Hence, undoubtedly, the extraordinary range of Venetian genius which in less than one hundred years breeds such theatrical, mythological and sacred successes as those of Sebastiano Ricci, Piazzetta and Tiepolo, the meticulous precision of Canaletto and Bellotto, the calm irony of Longhi and the poetry of Francesco Guardi*. At the end of the 17th century, which has only been a long fallow period between two flourishing harvests, Venice shakes off the paralysing complexes which have made it a slave to its great ancestors, the Tintorettos, Veronese, Titian. . . . The aristocrats need decorators for their palaces, the Church for its churches. This revival at first touches on the painting

47

of religious history and mythology. From the end of the 17th century the academic principles of the Baroque begin to lose their severity and allow of more colourful elements.

Jacopo Amigoni*, who borrows something of the vast mythological composition of his master Solimena, spreads his work haphazardly throughout his many travels. Traces of it are found in London, Bavaria and Madrid, where he becomes court painter before ending his errant life there. But the first great luminary of the Venetian revival is another vagabond artist, Sebastiano Ricci. At the instigation of his nephew Marco, already in London, Ricci leaves Venice for England—not, however, before visiting Paris where he is received into the Academy with a flattering *Allegory to the Glory of France*. Queen Anne's England, still poorly endowed with great painters, gives him a warm welcome which is to last for ten years. His itinerant life, which takes him through Germany and Flanders, explains why his abundant works, of which the best examples are found in Schönbrunn and Hampton Court, are so widely disseminated. Ricci is the first to change the Baroque into Rococo. Receptive to all that is new, he represents the spearhead of a coloured religious painting movement which is to be propagated by his pupils Marco Ricci* and Gasparo Diziani*. But it is Antonio Pellegrini* who benefits most from his lessons, which have consolidated the example of Luca Giordano. Travelling tirelessly through England, Flanders, Germany, Austria and France, Pellegrini leaves throughout Europe works that are particularly remarkable for the coloured sensitivity of his features. A particular work of his is a series of fourteen paintings glorifying the Elector Palatine. His contemporary Antonio Balestra* is only a Venetian by adoption. But he is assured of a position and soon receives commissions from several European courts. Teacher of Rosalba Carriera, Pietro Longhi and Pietro Rotari*, he exercises his influence on several other Italian artists. Among those emulating him, Giovanni Battista Pittoni*, during time spent with Sebastiano Ricci and Tiepolo, draws on the graces of his most brilliant period before drifting into the zone of indefinity that

48

Alessandro Magnasco
Composition, Landscape
Lugano, Vanotti Collection

Giambattista Piazzetta
Venice 1682-1754
The Fortune Teller
Oil on canvas 5'1" × 3'9"
Venice, Academy

Giambattista Tiepolo
Venice 1696-Madrid 1770
The Embarkation
Sketch for fresco in the Labia Palace, Venice
Strasbourg Museum

separates the Rococo from neo-classicism. This ineptitude of choice, while giving his prolific work an impression of improvised stylistics, causes him to be considered, about 1760, as the great master of historical painting. He constitutes an interesting exception in the Venetian school. But his predecessors, transitional painters, have paved the way for the prodigious outburst of the last great decorative painting.

A pupil of Crespi, G. B. Piazzetta remembers the lessons of Guerchino and Caravaggio. But a new spirit soon bursts out everywhere, with sculptural dimensions and sharply-defined contours. The "Venetian Caravaggio" turns tradition to his own use, using only coloured shading. This skill in contrast, which fills the *Beheading of St John* with a dramatic intensity, more easily brings fame to his "Assumptions", which already begin to resemble the work of Tiepolo. The emotional vigour of the Baroque lights up with softness when he touches on the Bible with Rebecca or Suzanne. But it is particularly in the fantasy of his non-religious compositions, his genre scenes and pastorals, that Piazzetta is the precursor of Tiepolo. In his sumptuous ochres and blues, in his masterful range of light tonality he traces the regal progress of the Venetian school. This liberation of his style dates from about 1725. The end of his career is also capped by the official ratification of his position at the head of the Venetian school. He occupies the highest post as Director of the Venice Academy in 1750. Apart from the influence he exercises on Tiepolo, Piazzetta has many admirers and pupils. Giuseppe Angeli* has assimilated his master's art so well that after Piazzetta's death he is given the job of completing some of his paintings. As for the Dalmatian Federico Bencovitch*, he takes to Vienna the new Venetian colours to which he adds a sort of personal romanticism which is not without influence on the Austrian school.

It is Giambattista Tiepolo who brings the new Baroque to full autonomy. Early in the century the precocious fame of this great admirer of Veronese causes jealousy. Most flattering orders for religious or non-religious decoration start off his intense activity.

50

Vittore Ghislandi
San Leonardo 1655-Venice 1743
Signboard for the Barber Oletta
Bergamo, Carrara Academy

Venice, Germany and Spain are to be the main beneficiaries of painting which owes its sources and its atmosphere to the theatre. In this era, in fact, wasn't aristocratic life just one vast parade? Tiepolo brings together, with the same elegance, allegory, religion, history and mythology in a gigantic ballet spectacle, courtly or impious at will. Great tumults of bodies are grouped together and dispersed into the infinite space of his light-coloured ceilings. A crowd of curious people, painted in illusionist fashion, lean on the balustrades which run along the cornices. The Baroque lights up with a smile. In his ardour for aerial ballet, bare legs move about under the yellow or red brilliance of costumes which gives added value to the adjacent cold tones. Trumpets spread across clouds that also let through the light. Bodies appear in the giddy foreshortening of upward movements. It is impossible to go into the detail of works which, from the Rezzonico, Clerici or Canossa Palaces to the Villas Contarini, Soderini or Cordellina, cover the walls of aristocratic residence with delirious allegories. Rarely has decorative painting assumed such diverse aspects. A motley carnival crowd bursts into the Papadopoli Palace with their masks, their mountebanks and their musicians. The frescoes of the Labia Palace narrate the tragic love of Antony and Cleopatra, and the palace becomes a theatre. But it is probably the Villa Valmarana which, from the Baroque to the Rococo, has the widest range of endlessly recurring fantasy. There tribute is paid to the theatre with the *Sacrifice of Iphigenia* in the Grand Saloon. The epic poetry of Virgil, Homer, Ariosto and Tasso provides the themes for the elegant décor of four consecutive rooms; and a dazzling animation of mythology and carnival is let loose in the seven rooms of the guest-house where also are to be found some surprisingly natural rustic festivals and chinoiseries. The reason for this diversity lies partly in the fact that Tiepolo's sons, Gian Domenico and Lorenzo, collaborated with him, following their father on his frequent travels. The former seems to have played a far more important role than was once thought. It is this "Tiepoletto", responsive to the daily spectacle of the city, who paints most of those little Venetian chronicles, from masquerades to minuets,

51

Gian Domenico Tiepolo
Venice 1727-1804
Pierrots at Rest
Mural, painting on canvas 6'6" × 4'11"
Venice, Ca'Rezzonico

Pietro Longhi
Venice 1702-85
The Perfume Seller
Oil on canvas 2'0" × 1'7"
Venice, Ca'Rezzonico

Pietro Longhi
The Concert, 1741
Oil on canvas 2′0″ × 1′7″
Venice, Academy

with their poetic realism. In the Villa Valmarana may be found themes identical with those he is to paint later in his villa at Zianigo. Declining an invitation from the King of Sweden, Giambattista Tiepolo accepts, in the middle of the century, another invitation from the Prince-Bishop of East Franconia to decorate his residence at Wurzburg. In three years of intense work he covers the great reception room and the monumental staircase with frescoes. There he tells the story of Frederick Barbarossa, the Holy Roman Emperor, amid the stuccos, the gilding, the leafwork and mouldings which make up the Rococo ornamentation of Neumann's construction. The virtuosity in the flight of Apollo's Chariot in the ceiling of the great reception room, or in the deification of the Prince-Bishop on the arch of the staircase, marks the peak of an art still using the powerful themes of the High Baroque while surpassing them in the boldness of its multiple colouring and its planning. At sixty-five, indefatigable, Giambattista Tiepolo goes off to glorify the Spanish monarchy on the walls of the royal palace in Madrid, from where he never returns. An incessant lightness increasingly demonstrates his incomparable mastery. Terse, rapid drawing underlines the extemporaneous look of his compositions painted after his return from Wurzburg. Diametrically opposed to the realism which preoccupies a whole concept of Italian painting of the period, Tiepolo does not bother either with the human content or religious considerations in his relentless quest for spectacular quality. The imaginary suffices to arouse his enthusiasm. Thus before it disappears the Baroque finds a dimension which its splendour has lacked.

It was inevitable that Venice, having applied the great part of its genius to the decoration of its palaces and churches, would also feel the need to perpetuate the likenesses of its most illustrious citizens. As everywhere else in Europe the taste for portraiture runs parallel with prosperity. However, compared with their French or English opposite numbers, Italian portraitists occupy only a minor place in the world of painting. The first half of the century has already provided its best in this field with Vittore Ghislandi, known as Fra Galgario, whose education rather than his life as a wondering monk links him with Venice. Honorary member of the Clementine Academy in Bologna, he has a curious way of linking a taste for the ostentatious with that of truth. In his case an indispensable richness of costume balances rather than overshadows the sincerity of a face. His extravagances in attitude or in surroundings contrast with this style of realism and make him the psychologist of the formal portrait. Ghislandi has not placed his brush at the service of any one class, but his masculine portraits always show an admiring predilection for the lustrous robes of local officials. A master of colour harmony, he remains the best of a school of portraitists distinguished particularly by a sense of elegance wedded to the sumptuousness of period and place. Among other exponents of this style which remains secondary, the high-society pastellist Rosalba Carriera suddenly wins Europe-wide fame in 1720 after a triumphant stay in Paris. Today a comparison with the pastels of La Tour makes Rosalba's look chalky and lacking in vigour. The absence of strictly disciplined construction gives the impression of inconsistency. However, the delicateness of her materials and the softness of her light are seductive enough to bring quickly to the Venetian artist some of the most brilliant

Antonio Canal, called Canaletto
Venice 1697-1768
The Piazzetta in Venice
Ascona, von der Hoyt Collection

commissions. Thus is the modest pupil of Balestra honoured with a clientèle that includes the Elector Palatine, the King of Denmark, Crozat and Law, and particularly the amazing Augustus III, who had nearly one hundred of her works! But the best Venetian portraits, after Ghislandi, are found in the occasional contributions of masters of other styles. Tiepolo excels in posing a high dignitary in his special surroundings. Pietro Longhi, Amigoni and Francesco Guardi paint admirable portraits, but it is particularly Alessandro Longhi* who, profiting from his father's fame, paints the portraits of all Venetian society. From the aristocratic Giulio Contarini da Mula to Cimarosa and Carlo Goldoni he leaves detailed pictures in which he combines accuracy of expression with the delicate harmony of his colours.

The relative reserve of Venetian artists towards the portrait is no doubt explained by the thousands of other attractions which their extraordinary city and its spectacles offered them the whole year round.

In striking contrast to the great flights of Tiepolo, the modest art of Pietro Longhi, with its realism tinged with slightly waggish foppishness, shows a completely different aspect of Venetian art. Longhi takes from his masters, Balestra and Crespi, a liking for the picturesque, as shown by the *Visit to the Rhinoceros* or the crowd gathered in the "Ridotto". Like his friend Carlo Goldoni, the writer, Longhi is above all a representative of the middle class of his time, a middle class still quite awestruck by its new-found importance. He captures with finesse the first steps of the Venetian *nouveau*

54

riche into the fashionable world. He shows them receiving dancing lessons or having their hair dressed in their own homes. He shows them singing to the accompaniment of the clavichord played by a companionable priest. Pastel tones of equal strength are subtly placed alongside one another without the least worry about contrast. Hence an air of sobriety, of quasi-indifference in which powdered figurines put up with a life to which they do not seem to become accustomed. The slightly naïve indecision of his characters also helps to give them that look of puppets in their Sunday best which sometimes borders on dryness. The well-behaved little world of Longhi has neither the caricatural faults of Hogarth nor the tenderness of Chardin. However, both are brought to mind and the worth of his work may be judged by the enthusiastic way in which his contemporaries acclaim his little accounts of daily life.

While Longhi sticks to observing his contemporaries, numerous artists yield to the lure of travel. Since the beginning of the century, a Marco Ricci with his romantic characters, a Zuccarelli with his dream pastorals, have gone to satisfy the innate taste of the English for landscapes. Those with an inquiring turn of mind move about, eager to see and learn. This ambulatory phenomenon assumes fantastic proportions throughout the century. In the summer of 1785 alone, 40,000 Englishmen make the classic tour of Italy which is an indispensable part of their education as gentlemen. They take a passion for Roman archaeology, go into ecstasy over the marvels of Venice. Everyone wants to take something back as a souvenir of their travels. Well before the end of the

Gianantonio Guardi
Venice 1698-1760
Il Ridotto (The Casino)
Oil on canvas 3'7" × 6'8"
Venice, Ca'Rezzonico

17th century artists painted the urban landscape and there is no doubt that many a smart painter lived well on this trade, particularly in Venice. But with the dawn of the 18th century the "vedutists" assume an artistic character which they never had before except as a background to the religious compositions of Carpaccio or Pintoricchio. Now Luca Carlevaris*, who has done his first work in Rome, introduces the urban panorama into art by means of engravings. From 1703 onwards his compilation of 120 *Fabbriche e vedute di Venezia* assures him of a considerable English clientèle, and starts a school. But it is his great pupil Antonio Canal*, called Canaletto, who concentrates on raising up this style. After a childhood passed among the great city decorations that his father painted, Canaletto goes to Rome, where his contemporary Panini enjoys youthful renown from his paintings of ruins and opulent receptions. Little is known of his life, but the atmosphere of his youth in the first twenty years of the century predestined him for the art of the Venetian landscape.

Tirelessly, lovingly he is to paint and repaint the coloured variations of his city with perspectives of strict accuracy down to the smallest detail. In an atmosphere as luminous as it is humid, serene architectures set up delicate contrasts between sky and sea. Honoured with the influential friendship of Count Algarotti and the less disinterested admiration of the British consul, Joseph Smith, Antonio Canal acquires at the same time mastery and renown. A perfect business man, Smith had the ingenious idea of combining his diplomatic functions with the business of acting as intermediary between the artist and the English gentry, thus setting up a sort of brokerage in art. The master of Venetian architectural scenes gets out of this arrangement, under which he was being

exploited, and goes to London to enjoy his fame personally. His success is so great as to eclipse even that of his fellow-countryman Marco Ricci, whose landscapes, however, are greatly appreciated. It is a decisive voyage by reason of the impetus it gives to English architectural painting, of which Samuel Scott* is to become the leading exponent.

Canaletto takes advantage of two successive stays in England to paint views of the Thames and the English countryside before returning by way of Germany, where the name of his nephew Bellotto is becoming known. There he paints views of Munich. But the works of this voluntary expatriate often appear rigid. By comparison, they provide an understanding of the marvellous balance represented in his Venetian " vedute ", which are bathed in the special light of the lagoon. In fact, to compensate for the rectangular immobility of his palaces, and add more interest to them, he needs all the picturesque animation of the gondolas and the little world of colour interposed between stretches of sky and water. It is in Venice that Canaletto is great. On the other hand the landscapes of the second Canaletto, Bernardo Bellotto, often suffer from an excess of precision, even more noticeable when he exercises his talents outside Venice. He has benefited and suffered from his uncle's fame. Too ambitious to be satisfied with second place, this impenitent traveller goes off to seek fame with European princes, particularly in Dresden, which becomes his second home, and in Warsaw, where he dies.

The two Canalettos, meticulous artisans of the great city perspective with the aid of the *camera obscura*, centred all their art round their concern for topographical accuracy. They enjoyed the success that technical prowess, providing it is tangible, never fails to bring. The inspired fantasy of Francesco Guardi is less appreciated—even to the point where he is forced to yield to his elder brother Gianantonio*, who directs the family *bottega* (shop). But he has since been recognised as the painter of the *Life of Tobias*, the previously disputed frescoes which so lyrically adorn the church of San Raffaello in Venice. Thus history does him justice. With his " vedute " and his " fantasies " Guardi is already opening the way for Impressionism. In subordinating the insensitive objectivity of the landscape to his own personal feeling he shows a very daring individualism. Too much, probably, for an era which did not appreciate, either, the dazzling virtuosity of his little figures in whom he captures in pale bright colour the changing attitude or the gesture which is made. His way is quite different from that of Canaletto, who is tied to the lasting idea of a petrified and serene Venice.

Little concerned with the permanent, Guardi wants to show the succession of fleeting moments which animate a city. His *capriccios* quiver with a continual coming and going. His poetic vision makes too rigid perspectives more supple and gives a silvery sheen to the dirty waters of the canal. It transforms the ordinary with a sparkle of gold which is emphasised by changes in his line. At the turning of a street the carmine of a robe makes a hole in the ochre of a wall. Guardi is the Venetian depository of that part of pre-Romanticism which otherwise is demonstrated by Magnasco or Loutherburg. He is the enthusiastic onlooker whose brush captures with the same sprightly zest a strolling vendor at the corner of a thronged *calle*, the historical event of the visit of Pope Pius VI, the flight of a balloon above the Giudecca, or that traditional Ascension Day when the

Doge embarked on the *Bucentaur* decked out in crimson and gold for ritual nuptials with the sea. Guardi dots the gala atmosphere of the lagoon with black gondolas, a fabulous scene of an immense theatrical fairyland. In the final years of its splendour, in which Venice comes under the rule of the sinister " Council of Ten ", the appetite for luxury and pleasure which portend its collapse turns into a mad race. Guardi's work perpetuates a resplendent picture of that Venice and confirms, if confirmation were necessary, that periods of political or economic decadence often bring extreme refinement to art. Guardi, with his brother-in-law Tiepolo, represents the finest of the Venetian 18th century. His death in 1793 comes as a symbol of the disappearance of a republic, the decline of a class and the end of an aesthetic period.

In the era of the death of Venetian art, Rome frees opposing forces that have been building up for a long time. She intends to govern European art from now on. In the first part of the century her pretensions, expressed locally, hardly cause any worry. The prestige and richness of her past make her a mecca for tourists rather than a city involved in living art movements. Wealthy tourists come to admire the vestiges of past grandeur, pupils of the French Academy come to complete their classical education. Some even prolong those much-appreciated visits, but it is rare to see them settle in Rome. Impervious to outside influences, Rome is the ideal setting for a new attitude to antiquity.

The first typically Roman expression naturally comes in landscapes. Andrea Locatelli blends traces of Claude Lorrain and Albani into his pastorals, in which Arcadian mythology takes the place of grandiloquent artifice in the manner of Salvator Rosa. His best pupil, Giovanni Paolo Panini, frequently recalls this rural atmosphere. But in his case the monumental balances out the bucolic. In addition to an incontestable knowledge of the antique which gives his compositions great documentary value, Panini possesses the art of being able to " tame " a ruin, always setting against the solemnity of a

Roman arch the colourful spectacle of ordinary people going about their daily affairs. Yet his transitional realism is tempered by a jauntiness which may be responsible for the pleasant fantasy of his *Imaginary Views*. His perspective shortcomings make his compositions both mobile and seductive. At a time when his contemporary Canaletto, as yet unknown, was arriving in Rome, the city already knew the name of Panini. Prestigious commissions for the Alberoni Palace, the Villa Patrizi and the Quirinal have made the young painter known. An opportune marriage with the sister of Vleughels, director of the Academy of France, adds the favour of French society.

Panini, in whom it would be wrong to recognise only a clever painter of ruins, has an acute sense of the fête and the crowd. His *Visit of Charles III to Benedict XIV* is a veritable social ballet in the most brilliant tradition. He pictures, with the same obvious pleasure, the Piazza Navona artificially inundated to the very great joy of an elegant crowd of onlookers. These diverse qualities make him one of the great figures of the *Settocento*.

Too much in the same period as the Rococo to be quite free of it, these artists, despite their local renown, have not reached a height of fame equal to that of Pompeo Batoni*, pupil of Sebastiano Conca* of Naples. Combining the study of Raphael with that of the ancients, he first composes great frescoes for palaces and churches. His subjects and styles come directly from classical antiquity. One seems to be present at the *Education of Achilles by Chiron* and the *Farewells of Hector and Andromache* in an atmosphere of cold solemnity. The Romans, proud of this apparent communion with their prestigious ancestors, proclaim their Batoni as " the restorer of art " and equate him with the celebrated Mengs. At this time neo-classicism has broadened its field. Batoni, who has already painted frescoes in numerous provincial churches of the north, in Milan, Brescia, Lucca and Parma, exports his remodelled mythology throughout the whole of Europe. From the courts of Russia, Poland, Prussia or Portugal, commissions flow in. Portraitist of the princes of the locality—Benedict XIV, Clement XIII and Pius VI—and of titled travellers, he freely places his lofty subjects in front of antique stones and statues. His clients, particularly Englishmen such as the Hon. John Staples or Joseph Leason, Earl of Milltown, greatly appreciate his sense of the grandiose. Batoni, however, allows something to penetrate through his work that indicates regret for the not-distant Baroque and shows the transitory aspect of his art.

But this triumph has gone far beyond his personality. It is the abolition of a complete style that is credited to him. His friendship with the German archaeologist Winckelmann puts him in the centre of Roman cosmopolitanism. After 1755 Winckelmann publishes his *Reflections on the Imitation of Classic Works in Painting and Sculpture*, followed in 1764 by a monumental work of erudition, *History of Art Among the Ancients*. From this springs the theory that beauty is not contingent, but one and universal and that, the Ancients having discovered it and brought it to perfection, the only way to revert to it is in imitating them.

Two years earlier another German, Anton Raphael Mengs, published *Reflections on Beauty and Taste in Painting*, which constitutes an authoritative declaration of the proposed new line. Mengs exercises an influence that is wider because of the fact that he moves about freely and thus joins practice with theory. After his début in Rome as a pupil of Benefial*, he makes frequent visits there. From the court of Dresden to that of Madrid the wandering theoretician spreads his theory throughout a Europe which by now is ready to be converted. His opposition to the great Tiepolo at the court of Madrid is a good illustration of the struggle between the two tendencies. At this time the Rococo is conquered. The immense glory which Europe accords to Mengs makes him the master of the new era. This reputation seems more justified by his theoretical works than by the manner in which he applies them. He shows himself to be in effect a transitional painter. His style, certainly simplified, is still nurtured by the golden fairness of Titian and traces of Correggio. Relegated today to a more equitable rank, Mengs in any case deserves to be recognised for his quality as a portraitist.

And likewise with Angelica Kauffmann*, whose portraits retain a pleasant likeness and a finesse in colour compatible with the new simplicity as is proved by, among others, the very fine portrait of Winckelmann. Of Swiss origin, Angelica Kauffmann divides her time between London, where she becomes a founder-member of the Royal Academy, and a Rome triumphant in the final years of the century. Her studio becomes a centre for intellectuals and artists won over to the new ideas which they are to propagate in their respective countries.

The English School

The 18th century is England's Golden Age of painting. Arrogant and fertile after a long lethargy, it suddenly makes a striking contribution to European artistic patrimony. It has needed a mixture of political, economic and cultural circumstances to cultivate such a bloom of artists and to preserve the originality of the English school in the bosom of Gallic Europe. After the Treaty of Utrecht a rich and victorious royalty is ready, after so much else, for great mental feasting. Still poor in indigenous talent, the England of William III, Queen Anne, George I and George II is content to spread its benevolence among foreign artists. She entrusts commissions to the Italians Ricci, Amigoni and Pellegrini; she makes the journey to London a veritable triumph for the two Canalettos. Philippe Mercier* follows his patron, the Prince of Wales, across the Channel and sets in England the *fêtes galantes* inspired by Watteau, who also made the voyage. The English go to Italy to study, and pass through France, with whom there are fertile exchanges.

Painting in the English 18th century, which is to extend to nearly 1820 with Raeburn and Lawrence*, gets off to a slow start. Its birth coincides with the era of prosperity opened in 1760 by the accession of the popular and cultured George III. The comfort of material riches and peace releases the pent-up desire for luxury and pleasure. The whole of English high society travels, dances, has a portrait painted. Painting becomes the mirror of this society, fiercely and passionately decried by some and glorified with elegance by others.

The cultural context is brilliant. Music profits from the pro-English propensities of Handel, two of whose works are interpreted to celebrate that capital event for England, the Treaty of Utrecht. With Berkeley*, philosophy discovers in sensationalism the very principle of existence, although it remains very steeped in the materialism of Locke and Newton, which the French are to "civilise".

As for literature, it experiences some of its most intense moments with the poet Young, the writers Swift, Pope, Daniel Defoe, Fielding, Goldsmith* and Richardson, grand masters of the novel and often companions of painters in intellectual meeting-places. The exceptional fecundity of this period could not fail to stimulate the whole of artistic creation; England no longer is to be dependent on foreign contributions for she raises her own painters who come up to the expectations of her society. A century earlier she had had to call in the prestigious Flemish painter Van Dyck, whose spirit played a capital role in the orientation of the English school. It was Van Dyck who brought a breath of Venice across the Channel and it is Van Dyck who is responsible for the long vogue for the portrait, lasting up to the beginning of the 19th century. Finally, it is Van Dyck who holds the admiration of all the young painters who become masters of English painting. But the birth of an important school is not without its troubles. England has also experienced the quarrel between ancient and modern. Tired of fruitless dogmas, the poet Young and the painter Hogarth* assume leadership of an anti-classical revolt about 1740. At a time when continental Europe is beginning the inverse movement of a return to classicism, England alone builds her own form of expression which is able to retain its originality without ever clashing with the general concerted harmony of Europe.

This originality is manifest at first in style. Impervious to the tumult of decorative painting, the movement is also alone in standing up to academic pressures, which come too early to shake it. The English movement proceeds from the Baroque, but it finds an excess of Rococo too repugnant. The styles it practises are few. Apart from the very insular satirical tendency with its caricatured realism, the portrait occupies the majority of talents and is perpetuated throughout the reign of George IV in almost identical form.

The landscape, on the other hand, gradually assumes importance, but attempts at " grand painting " are too tied to neo-classic movements to make themselves felt.

One trait in the English character is a critical sense which is expressed through a typically national process, humour. While the morals of a society or the attitude of its public figures are not irreproachable and while, in addition, there is sufficient freedom of speech, painters and writers set themselves up as censors of an era whose failings they paint from life, either as purely descriptive observers or as pitiless critics. At the beginning of the century, all the favourable conditions for this existed. The suppression of censorship in 1695 prompts numerous artists and painters to become caricaturists. The print facilitates denunciation of turpitude of all kinds. The novel of manners becomes biting. Everyone is able, through his art, to attack with impunity a government which is the butt of opposing factions or a frivolous, opulent society that is oblivious to mass misery. The year 1722 sees the appearance of Daniel Defoe's *Moll Flanders*, the story of a courtesan. The way is open for painting of morals, of which Hogarth is to become the leading exponent ten years later.

Born of a modest family, William Hogarth lives at first on portrait painting, a lucrative type which permits him to devote a considerable part of his time to forms of expression more suited to his temperament. He frequents the studio of Sir James Thornhill*—and elopes with his daughter. This starts a quarrel that ends only with the genuine celebrity accorded to Hogarth in 1732 for his first satirical suite, *The Harlot's Progress*. As an engraver he is able to make mass reproductions of his work in the form of prints. He suddenly becomes so popular that reproductions of his work are used for

Giovanni Paolo Panini
Piacenza 1691-Rome 1765
Benedict XIV Lambertini and Cardinal Silvio
Valenti Gonzaga
Oil on canvas 4′0″ × 5′10″
Rome, Rome Museum, Braschi Palace

decorative purposes, and his prints are even counterfeited. Honour is bestowed on him with the title of Sergeant-Painter to the King, while his work raises polemics of all sorts. Apart from his portraits, of which more later. Hogarth, the indefatigable reformer, has devoted his art to satirising his period.

On the moral level debauchery and adultery, intemperance and gambling, vanity and prodigality are vilified in *The Harlot's Progress*, *The Rake's Progress*, *Marriage à la Mode*, and others—so many scathing satires on his contemporaries. No class of society escapes his censure.

If he tolerates religion, he is ruthless with bigotry and the clergy and, in his own words, fights " the monstrous effects of a base and literal conception of holy things as well as the idolatry tendency of church paintings and images of piety ".

In the political field he devotes the *Election* series to the corruption of Parliament and electoral venality. His nationalism wanders slightly towards xenophobia. Thus he is dead set against the Italians, whose success in the London Opera annoys him, and particularly against the French, whom he has never forgiven for expelling him from Calais on suspicion of spying when they caught him making sketches of the city gate. That adventure brings down on France a venomous print entitled *Calais Gate or O the Roast Beef of Old England*.

On the artistic level, however, Hogarth, arriving early in the century, has to fight to defend his convictions. With the poet Young he first demands an art stripped of antiquated formulas and a return to creative freedom. In 1745 he intrigues the art world by drawing beneath a very fine self-portrait a sinuous line with the enigmatic inscription:

William Hogarth ►
London 1697-1764
Calais Gate
London, National Gallery

William Hogarth
The Graham Children
London, Tate Gallery
▼

" The Line of Beauty and Grace ". But he goes beyond the concrete expression of his ideas and in 1753 publishes the *Analysis of Beauty*, a text illustrated with plates, containing his views on aesthetics and some violent criticisms which, in return, earn him insults and caricatures. The work is of the greatest importance to the development of art. It exhorts artists to return to the school of nature and, finding the prime cause of beauty in the idea of variety, formulates his famous definition of the " serpentine line ", the keystone of the whole of his theory. An admirer of Rubens and Correggio, he advocates live, light and brilliant colours and a clear-cut touch. Much can be written about his style, emphasising his realism or the detail of his art, the dramatic effects of his work or his imagination, and in showing certain weaknesses in his composition. In fact, Hogarth's importance lies in the fact that he was an originator. This great destroyer of prejudice struggled all his life to leave a new horizon for posterity in painting. The young English school is indebted to him for written formulations on art form and for a number of successful " genres " such as the suites of six or eight paintings showing the unfolding of a drama with the power of moral improvement, his collective portraits and his conversation pieces. The type is exploited by a swarm of artists who leave a variegated picture of their contemporaries.

Logically painters of moral subjects deriving from Hogarth are confined to this descriptive attitude. Among them several pamphleteers are constrained to paint a far from pleasant picture of a society wallowing in political struggles, promiscuous immorality and indifference to mass poverty. Thus Thomas Rowlandson* takes up in turn painting, caricature and illustration. Particularly concerned with poverty, he devotes to the lower classes an immense production of series with such eloquent titles as *Miseries of Human Life* and *The Microcosm of London*. He illustrates several literary works including *The Vicar of Wakefield* and *The Sentimental Journey*.

The political climate of the period lends itself to caricature, and the press, freed from censorship for more than half a century, urges artists to follow their natural bent for the satirical. Some devote themselves passionately to it, such as James Gillray*, known to have drawn more than 1,000 biting caricatures, and John Collet*, Dighton*, Nixon*, Boyne*, and others. While pursuing its solitary way in this field, British painting tackles wholeheartedly the most highly-valued theme of the century.

If we are to believe Hogarth, " England combines egoism with vanity; so portrait painting in this country has always had and will always have a greater vogue than in any other ". And in fact the portrait in England is a style dating back much farther than the 18th century in which Kneller*, in a number of works, retains the grandiose traditions of the 17th century. But the real forerunner is still Van Dyck, whose radiance has affected the style of a whole century of portraitists. The English school is to succeed in evolving a new form for the portrait, so compatible with the taste of the day that it soon eclipses all other styles. What painter, in an era where the only thing that matters is glamour, would damage his career by not taking it up? All the great painters of the English school were exponents of a type that in other times was considered secondary; each painting is like the magnified and finely-analysed detail of a vast picture of contemporary society.

By reason of its subjects, its revival and the fact that it fills a need, English portraiture blends well into the European 18th century. However, it retains an originality which ensures immediate recognition of its national character. Hogarth's advice, recommending a return to nature, probably has been taken. After Kneller, in effect, wigs, drapery and other formal trappings disappear; light and lively colours replace browns and blacks; the natural triumphs. Childhood acquires considerable importance; its spontaneity, its freshness are characteristics sufficiently representative of the taste of the period to provide the subject for several masterpieces.

Before the reign of George III the type has not yet acquired the seductive qualities which are to give it an unprecedented vogue. The formal portrait is a good illustration of the pompous mediocrity of several court painters little qualified to hold their posts, such as Sir James Thornhill, whose main claim to fame seems to lie in the fact that he taught Hogarth and was his father-in-law. Here again Hogarth figures as innovator.

Actually, Hogarth was not to continue for long in the field which he despised and referred to as "manufacturing likenesses". But a series of portraits remarkable for their intensity and sense of the natural show how much he contributed to this type. He excels

66

Allan Ramsay
Edinburgh 1713-Dover 1784
Portrait of a Man
London, Tate Gallery

in the use of light and shade in a way that puts the subject in relief and pushes back into the shadows the multiple explanatory details which he likes to put with the subject. After setting them in their daily surroundings, he invests his subjects with far more than semblances and brilliantly inaugurates the sort of psychological work that leaves the dull, formal portrait far behind. He could have had a brilliant career as a portraitist if, like others, he had been willing to flatter the vanity of a client, but he could never do so. It is because of this intransigent streak in his nature that he paints such strikingly truthful portraits as those of Lord Lovat, the celebrated *Shrimp Girl*, his self-portraits and particularly the admirable composition in which he gathers his domestic staff together.

With such a precursor, British portraiture is set on a very fertile track. In fact the quintessence of English genius, from Ramsay* to Romney*, is concentrated in the reign of George III. The indispensable journey to Italy soon takes Allan Ramsay to Rome, where he has Imperiali for a master and Pompeo Batoni as co-follower, and to Naples where he works under Solimena. On his return to London the young Scotsman is assured of rapid celebrity in high society. As official painter to George III, of whom he painted more than sixty portraits, he brings the formal portrait up to date with a little French

67

William Hogarth
Portrait of Viscountess de la Valette
Oil on canvas 2'6" × 2'1"
Geneva, Museum of Art and History

rakishness. Essentially a portraitist, he is helped by his psychological qualities. His sense of aristocratic style and elegant detail is well suited to captivate a frivolous clientele which he sets freely against the verdant backgrounds of parks and gardens. He paints with spirit but, soon overloaded with orders, sometimes in a hasty fashion. This leads to the risky business of setting up workshops in which numerous " pupils " collaborate in the completion of works which, in losing their originality, lower the prestige of the artist. However, Ramsay remains an excellent portraitist, as shown by his studies of Dr. Mead, Lord Drummore and numerous women subjects. But if he is enchanting in his refinement, he never attains the authoritative mastery of posture which Sir Joshua Reynolds* brings to painting.

Reynolds, with Hogarth and Gainsborough*, form the most representative trio of the English school of the 18th century. The great opportunity in his life is undoubtedly a cruise offered him in 1749 by Captain Keppel, of whom he painted some admirable portraits. After Portugal, Gibraltar, and the Balearics, Reynolds discovers Rome and stays there for two years. From his return voyage through Florence, Arezzo and Parma he brings back the coloured memory of Veronese, of Titian and particularly a lasting admiration for Correggio. Then, imperturbably, he passes through the middle of the contemporary French art bloom. Soon after his return to London he goes from success to success. His customary charm and culture win him, in addition to a fashionable clientele, the friendship of artists of all types. He is a member of the same literary club as Goldsmith; his studio becomes a veritable salon. To have been received and appreciated there is to become the key to success for more than one young artist. The year 1768 sees the foundation of the Royal Academy in England and Reynolds is named its president. On the death of Ramsay in 1784 the vacant post of Principal Painter to the King is handed to Reynolds as a legitimate tribute to his work. This double official position provides the occasion for him to pronounce his famous fifteen Discourses, which constitute one of the most important summations of English aesthetics. A necessary counterbalance to the over-disparaging Hogarth, Reynolds is able to provide Georgian society with the exact picture, discreetly tinged with complaisance, that they expect of him. Also it is not surprising that, up to his death, he exerted an artistic domination that was far more effective than it was pleasant. In some 2,000 portraits which constitute his work, Reynolds contributes a natural freedom and an austereness to the High Baroque tradition. His tireless variety, his sense of light and shade and his finesse in making an atmosphere decisive are to be appreciated. Masculine portraits, like those of Colonel Tarleton or John Stuart, come out in their daily surroundings, always with some judicious detail. Feminine portraits are presented, according to the various parts the woman plays in society, in various aspects. The grace of Lady Bamfylde, who appears before the splendour of a moving landscape, is achieved without stressing distinction. The marvellous portrait of Nelly O'Brien has the subtle harmony of luminous half-tints hidden in its simplicity. The dignity with which he is able to invest all his models does not stop him from becoming tender at the so-often-repeated sight of affectionate young mothers. For Reynolds adores children, of whom he leaves

Sir Joshua Reynolds
Plympton 1723-London 1792
Portrait of Master Hare, 1788
Oil on canvas 2′6″ × 2′0″
Paris, Louvre

many portraits. With his children he puts a spontaneity into English painting. Reynolds also has tried several incursions into genre painting which suits him less well, such as decorative painting borrowed from mythology or legend (*Ugolino and his Sons*) or religious painting. But his quality as a portraitist is sufficient to make him a master of English painting.

The genius of Thomas Gainsborough is quite different. More than the venerated example of Rubens or the lessons of Gravelot* and Francis Hayman*, it is intuition and feeling which teach him the refinements which are to captivate England. Circumstances combine to provide him with an existence that hardly conforms to his character. Here is a peaceful man leading a provincial life at Ipswich, where he carries on his work and indulges his passion for music, when there arrives on the scene a military man named Thicknesse who prides himself on being a patron of the arts. His authoritative manner soon persuades the gentle Gainsborough to make his home in Bath, the centre of luxury, debauchery and culture which the aristocracy makes its winter quarters. His triumph there is as sudden as it is unanimous. He passes the fourteen most fertile years of his life there, painting the portraits of anyone who matters in England at that time, from the Duke of Argyll to General Honywood and Georgina Spencer, Duchess of Devonshire. The finesse with which he was able to profit from a frivolous society, which he despised, without ever stooping to the ever-present lure of artificiality, forces admiration for him. In 1774 he leaves Bath for London where, as court painter, he paints the portrait of every member of the royal family before his death, in his beautiful house in Pall Mall, ends a life heaped with honour and money which could never shake his authenticity.

Gainsborough seems to have gained in psychology and feeling what he never acquired in culture. Unlike his fellow-students, there is in effect nothing of the erudite about him. He is not well-read and never decides to venture out of his own country. There are enough works of Van Dyck in England for him to admire and take some lessons from, but the audacity of his style is very personal. It is all emotion. "I am quickly lost from the moment I try to reason," he says. His rapid and light touch makes laces flow, evaporates muslins in an apparent confusion that seems to point to later Impressionism. He suggests more than he says, acts more on feeling than on understanding, as is demonstrated in the delicious *Musidora*. The charming detail (plumes, velvety materials), the quality of his air and his light, create an atmosphere. From his unrequited love of the landscape undoubtedly comes the affection he has for leafy backgrounds which, as they do with Watteau, procure for him a harmonious balance between landscape and person. He excels at painting women and children. The sad and far-away look of *Perdita*, the noble pride of *Mrs Siddons* and particularly the grace of the celebrated *Blue Boy* bring the most daring of English painters close to continental painters.

Sophistication is better suited to George Romney, who illustrates the very type of cultivated and brilliant portraitist who is an instant success in a society whose image he is able to portray in a sufficiently flattering way. Otherwise, Romney shows himself to be extremely scrupulous about the technical problems of his art. He uses eight basic colours by means of which he obtains all his warm and luminous tonality, those transparencies which made him famous in his day and which have lasted up to now without changing. The precision of his drawing and his sense of harmony make him one of the best portraitists of the reign of George III. Nelson's mistress, Lady Hamilton, became his beloved pretext for a long series of portraits in which she reappeared in the guise, always exquisite, of Cassandra, Miranda, Circe, Hebe—or simply Emma.

The reign of George IV ensures the continuity of a taste which in England suffers no rupture similar to that caused in France by the Revolution and the Empire. However, evolution is slow. The appearance of subjects becomes modified; it becomes the rage to dress subjects in ancient robes. But the fundamental moral basis of continental neo-classicism is disparaged by the growing immorality of English society after George III. More than ever before, everything there is luxury, pleasure, feasting, the desire to show off.

The portrait experiences an even greater vogue; there is not a portraitist of any talent who does not amass a fortune and live at a fast pace, often owning a castle or manor-house and staff. Frivolity also overtakes the painter. He entrusts his too-numerous orders to obscure pupils who provide immature and flattering work in the taste of the day. There are abundant portraitists who make illustrious names without always deserving such immortality. However, we should mention John Hoppner*, for whom George III gains entrance to the Royal Academy and who later becomes official painter to George IV. His work, sometimes a little conventional but still boldly drawn, owes its importance to the picture it paints of that *fin de siècle* society, torn between the thirst for pleasure, romanticism and the solicitations of a neo-classicism too soon arrived from the Continent.

But the last great luminary of the century is an original and scrupulous Scotsman, Henry Raeburn. Noticed by Reynolds in London, he passes two years in Italy, then returns to his native city, Edinburgh, where he distinguishes himself by his independent will and his dedication to his work. Such an attitude often makes Lawrence preferred to him, but his mastery of the portrait and his irreproachable drawing work for his reputation. Given a title by George IV and with honours heaped on him, he never deviated from his stubborn quest for perfection. His great personalities, full length on a background of verdure, seem more natural. In this Raeburn is an innovator, as in his broad, clear touch, the very balanced construction and the general harmony of his compositions. He represents that trend which seeks to steep the portrait again in reality. But the horror of plainness inherent in the period tones down his realist inclinations and more tangible evolution is shown by a greater simplicity which heralds the 19th century.

In another direction painting continues the way traced by the preceding generation with Sir Thomas Lawrence. This *enfant terrible* of painting at the end of the century takes the plastic movement to the ultimate limits of elegance and futility. From his immense production emerge some masterpieces such as the fine portrait of Sir John Angerstein and his wife, or that of Master Lambton, better known under the title of *Red Boy*. Despite the great vogue for the portrait throughout the century, no artist had yet

received the adulation given to Lawrence. After Hoppner, he becomes official painter to King George IV and then, his fame having spread far across the Channel, he hastens to reply to requests from the Continent. He goes to paint portraits of Pius VII, Metternich, Wilhelm of Prussia and Tsar Alexander I. His successes go to his head. Burdened with orders, he carries out a series of hastily-painted portraits. His art of covering up spreads and precipitates the ruin of this genre. With his off-hand manner and his show-off propensities Lawrence becomes a part of the artificial and amoral society which he serves. He has so well assimilated all its faults that his work, little inspired as it might be, is the best possible reflection of that society.

If the portrait, predominant type of the English school, shows evidence of strong originality, its arrival is too late to have an influence on continental taste. On the other hand, the primacy of the English in the modern conception of landscape must be recognised. Certainly, at the beginning of the century, the Venetians have contributed pretty pastorals which have had a great success. But there nature is still subjugated to mythology or history. Only the urban landscape has been able to stand out as an independent type. Around 1740 verdant nature makes its appearance as the principal subject in English painting, well before the ideas of Richardson and Rousseau are circulated. It is as if the intensity of a favourable movement has suddenly crystallised an ancestral liking for the countryside. The landscape insinuates itself behind the portrait to vie for space which it appropriates little by little. Then the vogue for archaeology, coming in a period of prosperity, incites travel. Rich aristocrats take topographers with them to make views whose austere precision calls for basic greenery to make them more pleasant. Thus topography has its share of responsibility for the advent of the English landscape. It has its little masters who all excel in the art of water-colouring, with which they bring up their topographical drawings. From these it is only one step to the great florescence of the English landscape.

74

Sir Thomas Lawrence
Bristol 1769-London 1830
John Julius Angerstein and his Wife
Oil on canvas 8'4" × 5'2"
Paris, Louvre

Richard Wilson* crosses this step and is the first to dare regard the landscape as a genre noble enough to justify its use in great oil compositions. Brought up first under Dutch influence, he takes a long trip through Italy, allowing him to see the works of Tiepolo, Guardi and Canaletto. He makes the acquaintance of Reynolds in Rome, where he opens an academy. It is a portrait, that of Admiral Smith, which brings him fame. But the best of his work is found among his Italian and English landscapes bathed in beautiful luminosity which is dotted with the silhouettes of minuscule characters. The landscape moves towards complete autonomy, but the corners of ruins, the vestiges of architecture are still there in more or less modest form as if the artist wants to ensure a minimum of decency. This permanent contrast between the fragility of human endeavour and the perennial triumphant nature bears witness to a new will.

Gainsborough goes further and, to an apathetic society which expects from him only seductive portraits, delivers landscapes in which nature, devoid of humans, is glorified for itself alone. Their spontaneity, their conjuring up in almost anecdotal manner of country life, make them very representative works of the 18th century and would have been sufficient to make the master famous. Warm colours, browns and golds settle at canvas level, vaguely on the surface, to determine at a distance the harmonious balances of shade and light.

In the following generation, John Crome*, without denying the influence of Gainsborough, claims particularly that of Wilson. "Old Crome", from a poor family, began as a sign painter before meeting Sir W.Beechey, a portraitist of the "gentry", who taught him the rudiments of his art. He likes his lonely province where Dutch influence is strong. Original and active, he founds the "Norwich School", then a local academy which he directs himself. Crome's work, which Turner held in high esteem, completes the liberation of the landscape. It already belongs to the 19th century.

But on the borders of these well-characterised representations, other types have used the landscape as a pretext and been linked directly with it. The proverbial English love of animals, allied with the progress of zoology, makes the English school a chosen place for animal painting. A passion for anatomy, a sense of precise detail and admiration for the landscape masters serve as links between several painters of animals, particularly horses, which are shown in vast backgrounds of greenery. The best known, George Stubbs*, professes a vibrant admiration for Wilson. From his studies there emerges a very fine work accompanied by engraved plates on *The Anatomy of the Horse*. He turns the noble animal into the thoroughbred adornment of delightful landscapes and gives rise to a host of animal and landscape painters of whom the best is Samuel Scott, who has left particularly worthy paintings of the London of his day.

At this time neo-classicism has won the whole of the European schools over to its cause. The English school, making great strides, stands up to the pretensions of the Roman school. The "grand style" hardly rallies any but secondary artists, most often from abroad. However, a special place must be reserved for an excellent painter whose horror of sophisticated life condemned him to an unobtrusive position. From a modest family, and self-taught, John Opie* had the good fortune to please the all-powerful Reynolds. But he preferred the then very uncertain career of historical painter to the brilliant prospects of portraitist. He deals with national subjects, such as *The Poisoning of Arthur* or *The Murder of James I of Scotland* without ever achieving fame that was remunerative.

On the eve of the new century two visionaries of genius assure the transition. Like the neo-classicists, Fuseli* and William Blake* show a bewildered admiration for Michelangelo and Raphael. More designers and poets than painters, they dip into Shakespeare, Dante or Virgil for strange worlds peopled by gnomes, goblins and monsters which incontestably link them with romanticism.

The Other Schools

In most other countries art is dormant. Often, as in Spain or Holland, the memory of a colossal genius—Rubens, Rembrandt, Velasquez—paralyses ambition. Elsewhere, in Russia, in Scandinavia, full of foreign artists, national schools hardly begin to be formed. But everywhere there is an immense demand for art. Even the countries that are poorest in indigenous art have princely or aristocratic art patrons. Also a study of these countries will show an important place for expatriates, particularly Italian and French, who are largely responsible for the orientation of the different European schools.

Switzerland, however, has a quite original artistic position by reason of its political, religious and linguistic characteristics. An independence too young to be anything but fragile and a political regime in advance of its time leave it on the edge of the European movements for a long time. A long Calvinist history, aided by sumptuary ordinances, has paralysed artistic inclinations of all kinds. But in becoming rich the Swiss citizen tends to ignore the law. In 1739 the ordinance which forbids "all busts or statues intended to adorn the exteriors or interiors of houses" seems quite an anachronism. Protestant migrants bring into their exile a little French levity. The European *avant-garde* begins to regard this model republic, which offers its hospitality to the redoubtable Voltaire, with curiosity and sympathy. Then in Geneva, Basle and Berne rich houses spring up. It only remains to decorate them. The Rococo, the court style, ventures only very cautiously into this field. At first all the grace and colour of the century takes refuge in the portrait. Then the country where Rousseau was born offers its mountain sites to the new-born tourism and to a new type of painting, the alpine landscape. Geographical and linguistic peculiarities of the country give this growing art a different complexion depending on whether it has started in the French-speaking cantons, and thus is open to French influence, or in the German part, where it is more prone to the teachings of Mengs and Winckelmann.

The talent of a pastellist, Jean-Etienne Liotard*, in particular illustrates the art of Geneva. This most brilliant representative of the French-speaking Swiss school belonged to the category of travelling artists whom no voyage deterred. At first he is in Paris,

where he has the patronage of a future Duke de Lauzun. There he meets Montesquieu, Voltaire and the Marquis de Puisieux, French Ambassador to Naples, who takes him to Italy. In Rome portraits of James Stuart and several cardinals win him recognition. Lord Bessborough takes him to Constantinople and he stays there for five years under the patronage of Mehemet Aga. Apart from local princes, he paints delightfully all the city's inhabitants, Armenian, Jew or Greek, in a manner deeply sensitive to their warmth and colour, and the seething diversity of the place. He returns through Hungary and Vienna, where he captivates the court of Maria Theresa, and Venice, where Algarotti buys his *Belle Chocolatière*. Hardly stopping at Geneva, he hurries to Paris where, at the Opera, in the salons and the cafés he wears a huge beard, a fitting accoutrement to help maintain his reputation as the "Turkish painter". Crebillon, Marivaux and Mademoiselle de Montauban pose for him. Maurice de Saxe introduces him to the court, where he paints the royal princesses. His paintings fetch unheard-of prices. Embittered by a setback at the Académie, Liotard takes himself off to England to seek the compliments of Horace Walpole and British high society. Up to the age of more than seventy-five, his craze for

79

George Stubbs
Liverpool 1724-London 1806
Mares and Foals in a Landscape
London, Tate Gallery

travel takes him again and again through Paris, London, Vienna and Geneva, where he finally dies. During this period he is working on a *Treatise of Principles and Rules for Painting*. Now he paints fruit, powdery and coloured, as if to follow Chardin's footsteps in reverse. A curious person, this Liotard! Walpole calls him "greedy beyond all imagination" and reproaches him for "too much finish and retouching" in his art. Like the period in which he lives, he is at the same time serious and playful, ambitious for success but human, and rakish but paternal. Among his immense production are some very beautiful pieces, such as the celebrated portrait of Madame d'Epinay, and a number of miniatures on enamel. Liotard is neither a La Tour nor a Chardin. Too careful of detail to reach the virtuosity of the former, he lacks the tenderness of the latter. His work, like his life, is an adventure in the exotic and in colour.

The more modest art of Jean Huber*, nephew of the celebrated Abbé Huber, may be ascribed to "society talent". The rakishness and wealth of the century permeate the writing, painting or drawing of the liveliest gentleman of the moment. In the entourage of Voltaire and Madame d'Epinay it nurtures the pastimes in vogue in Paris society, where

Anton Graff
Winterthur 1736-Dresden 1813
Portrait of Chambellan von Beust, 1780
Oil on canvas 2′6″ × 2′0″
Winterthur, Reinhart Collection

Jean-Etienne Liotard
Geneva 1702-89
Portrait of the Artist as an Old Man
Geneva, Museum of Art and History

the fashion of " shadow portraits " has made a name for M. de Silhouette. Huber invents the art of the cut-out and spends his time making caricatures of his friend the philosopher. Hence the delectable series, *Voltaire automédon*, *Voltaire falling at the Knees of the Clairon*, Voltaire in the costume of his roles, with his peasants. . . . The pastime becomes profitable. Huber excuses himself with the quip, " Doesn't Voltaire play comedy in castles built with tragedy? " The author of the *Treatise on Tolerance* savours the joke less and less. A certain *Petit Lever*, embellished with a very irreverent text by an unscrupulous engraver, brings the crowning irritation. " My Voltairism is incurable," asserts the man who from then on is called only " Huber-Voltaire ". The eagerness of Grimm to spread the cut-out throughout Europe assures the author of a notoriety proportionate to the subject and its surrounding frivolity.

German-speaking Switzerland, for its part, turns more towards Berlin or Rome than Paris. Installed in Zurich, Anton Graff* is appointed court painter in Dresden in 1765 after his fame has spread there. He becomes the most sought-after portraitist of both the aristocracy and the middle class, whose powers by now are about equal. From then on he divides his time painting aristocratic sophistication or middle-class industriousness in Dresden, Leipzig and Winterthur, tirelessly painting all the leading intellectuals such as the Schillers*, Wieland, Lessing and Schulzer, his future father-in-law. The subtle elegance of Stanislaus Potocki or Urbanowski stems solely from the simple, almost nonchalant attitude. Trappings vanish, and the face speaks for itself. Switzerland also has Angelica Kauffmann, a pleasant portraitist, but she more often uses her talents in Rome or London than in her native country.

Rustic scenes by Johann Ludwig Aberli*, published as engravings, have a picturesque charm which secures him renown and a comfortable living. But the strongest personality in Berne art circles is without doubt Sigismund Freudenberger*. His friendly relations with several members of the French school—Boucher, Aved and Greuze—broaden his following. His rare ability to integrate the new naturalism with an atmosphere still essentially gay smoothly and firmly sets the seal on the alpine landscape.

From the Rhineland to Poland, from the Baltic to the frontiers of a Venice incessantly threatened by Austrian pretensions, some 350 German principalities form a sort of giant crossroads in the heart of Europe. The genius of Handel, Bach, Haydn, Mozart and Glück spreads the fame of German music throughout Europe. On the scrolls of literary fame are the names of Kant, Wieland, Lessing, Schiller and Goethe. Schluter, Neumann and Zimmermann bring an international standing to German architecture. In such a context painting, which has no Dürer nor Cranach, seems to fall back on foreign talents. In fact Germany begins by receiving more than she gives. Italian and French influences invade German territory before neo-classicist feeling, instigated by Mengs and Winckelmann, shakes off this foreign yoke. Apart from the universal form, the portrait, the greater part of German talent is devoted to decorative painting.

The most fruitful influence comes from Italy. It floods the Catholic territories of southern Germany and Austria and goes as far as Bohemia and even Saxony. Proximity, community of religion and the prestige of Tiepolo partly explain this phenomenon, which is helped by the mobility of the artists from the peninsula. The visits to Germany by Sebastiano Ricci, Amigoni, Pellegrini and Canaletto, among others, assume great importance. Longer stays in Dresden and Warsaw by Bellotto, by the "Divine Bacciarelli" at the Polish court, and particularly by the Tiepolos at Wurzburg, play a decisive role. In such wildly Baroque cities as Prague, Munich and Vienna, Tiepolism finds a choice field at a time when, alone among European countries, southern Germany goes through a revival of religious fervour. The Benedictines and the Premonstrants build monasteries and pilgrimage churches in which Rococo ornamentation shows possibilities for hitherto undreamed-of audacity. Following Tiepolo sacred painting places its scrolls and twirls in the centre of a delirious interlacing of stuccos and gold. The theatre, from which it originates, comes to the rescue of religious sentiment. The Germans have excelled in this gaudy conception of religious themes which makes their churches the framework for Biblical scenes on a spectacular scale. Edifices remarkable for their uniformity grow out of the collaboration of the Asam brothers*, of whom Cosmas Damian is the painter and Egid Quirin the architect-decorator. One example of their work is the Church of Saint-John Nepomuk in Munich, where they have established themselves. The fame of Cosmas Damian, court painter to the Prince-Bishop of Freising, wins him numerous commissions in the Tyrol, Bohemia and Switzerland. The knowledge of illusionism, before the arrival of Tiepolo, brings to Germany vast perspectives which disappear into the centre of tumultuous ceilings. In Munich he finds an emulator and collaborator in Matthaus Gunther*, who is to dominate the German school. This indefatigable decorator of Tyrolian and Bavarian churches, of those in Neustif, Mitten-wald and Rott-am-Inn, accentuates even more the illusionist effect of his cupolas in gradually lessening the colours in his dizzy heights.

With J. W. Baumgartner* in Augsburg, J. M. Frantz* in Eichstaat and J. B. Zimmermann*, brother and collaborator of the architect, more or less irreligious heavens come into view throughout the century. It needs all the suppleness of the Catholic religion to tolerate this showy style!

A Swabian painter, F. A. Maulbertsch, is to give its most perfect expression to this type. Established in Vienna, where he carried out his studies, Maulbertsch works in the Austrian provinces of Moravia, Bohemia and Hungary. About 1750 he begins decorating religious or princely buildings with great asymmetrical compositions in which flowing browns and reds are in sumptuous contrast with neighbouring light tones. The art of capturing a face in a stream of colour constitutes one of the aspects of his virtuosity, which also permits of bold foreshortening and stridently shredded flights into tints of saffron and lilac. The sensitiveness of his line recalls Sebastiano Ricci, who spent some time in Vienna. The quality of his Assumptions likens him to Piazzetta and Tiepolo although he seems never to have been acquainted with them. In a score of years Maulbertsch pours the most Baroque part of his genius into vast frescoes painted for Jesuits and others, then at the Vienna City Hall, Ebenfurth Castle, in the Heiligenkreuz Church and the Carthusian monastery at Brno. Often constructed on a diagonal, his

Antoine Pesne
Paris 1683-Berlin 1757
Portrait of Frederick II, King of Prussia
c. 1739-40
Oil on canvas 2'7" × 2'0"
Paris, Furstenburg Collection

strongly contrasting compositions integrate light and shade with the splendour of Tiepolo. After 1770, no doubt under the influence of neo-classicism, Maulbertsch's work tends to become more down to earth and loses some of its enormity.

But this is also a general phenomenon. An edict in 1770 advises a return to "noble simplicity" and the Archbishop of Salzburg bans all "theatrical representation contrary to the pure veneration of God". Austerity triumphs again. The spectacle is finished.

As for French influence, it is soon brought to the Rhineland and into Prussia by Protestant emigrants and gradually infiltrates as far as Poland. In the whole of Germany not a Prince is to be found now who is more "Francophile" than Frederick II of Prussia, whose agents in Paris—Count Rothenburg, Voltaire and D'Argens—choose for him the best works of Watteau and his school for the castles of Sans Souci and Charlottenburg. Antoine Pesne*, nephew and pupil of Charles de Lafosse, arrives in Berlin at the beginning of the century. During his long career in the service of the first three kings of Prussia he inculcates into Berlin portraitists his sense of the noble attitude and shimmering of rare tints. Frederick II, of whom he has left a very full iconography, entrusts him with the work of decorating his residences. After him, Amédée Van Loo is to remain for twenty years at the Prussian court. The court of Saxony, for its part, successively has Louis de Sylvestre*, who decorates the Zwinger, and Charles Hutin*. But local talents are discovered and then the Tischbein dynasty record the greatest successes. Some of them are particularly influenced by the French. Johann Heinrich, a pupil of Carle Van Loo and Boucher, paints portraits with tinges of precosity and naturalness at the court of Hesse-Cassel. The most German of the Tischbeins, Johann Heinrich Wilhelm, a protégé of the Duke of Gotha, has had an eventful career as sophisticated portrait painter but it has not satisfied his ambition. His stays in Rome, where he studied Raphael and the ancients, affirm his desire for the "grand style". His fundamental work, *Conrad of Swabia playing Chess with Frederick of Austria after their Condemnation to Death*, arouses the enthusiasm of David, who cites it as an example to his Roman competitors. It makes concrete the return to classicism which two Germans,

86

Francisco José de Goya y Lucientes
Fuentodos (Saragosa) 1746-Bordeaux 1828
Boys Climbing a Tree, 1791-2
Cartoon for a Tapestry
Madrid, Prado

Dimitri Gregoriovich Levitzky
Kiev 1735-St Petersburg 1822
Portrait of Diderot
Oil on canvas 1'11" × 1'7"
Geneva, Museum of Art and History

Anton Rafael Mengs
Aussig 1728-Rome 1779
The Marquise de Llano
Oil on canvas 6′8″ × 5′1″
Madrid, San Fernando Academy

Alexander Roslin
Malmoe 1718-Paris 1793
The Dauphin, Son of Louis XV
London, National Gallery

Mengs and Winckelmann, are to go off and preach to the limit in other countries: Carstens* handles it in such a way as to arrive at total abolition of colour.

In Warsaw the patronage of the Potockis, Radziwill and Czartoryski encourages art. Stanislaus-August sends Alexander Kucharski* to Paris to Van Loo and Vien in the hope of making him an historical painter. But the former page, seduced by the atmosphere of Paris, insinuates himself into Paris society. His sophisticated art has only one trace of the historical, the portrait of Marie-Antoinette at the Temple.

Although to all appearances less central than Germany, Scandinavia is the natural staging point for those going from France to Russia.

The Denmark of Christian VI, Frederick V and Christian VII and the Sweden of Charles XII, Louisa-Ulrica and Gustav III, artistically barely emerged from the Middle Ages, are still dependent on foreign influences. Gradually France supplants Holland there. Painting academies, supplied with French teaching, send their best pupils to perfect art in Paris.

Sweden is still surrounded by the aura of a hegemony which made the Baltic a Swedish sea. Up to the middle of the 17th century there everyone was either a warrior or a navigator. Queen Christina, gathering together the first collection, initiates her country into fine arts. A considerable flourishing of artistic talent appears suddenly but it is even more French than other European movements. Count Tessin, ambassador to Paris about 1740, goes about persuading French artists to leave for Stockholm: Pater and Oudry decline but a pupil of Lemoine, Taraval, makes Sweden his second home and plants there the blue and pink mythologies and the podgy Cupids of the Boucher school.

As for local artists they borrow, according to age, from the successive waves of French art. The Hamburg portrait painter, D. von Krafft, learns the secret of the formal portrait from Rigaud and Largillière. After becoming official portraitist to the Swedish court, he paints such a unique likeness that Charles XII consents to let him paint his august person. His pupil, Gustav Lundberg, has previously gone through an identical training in Paris. The Stockholm Academy is to make such courses mandatory for his successors. Numerous pastel portraits of Louis XV, Maria Leczinska, Natoire and Boucher make him the favourite portraitist of high society in his own country.

Swedish painters show a marked predilection for the Rococo. The most notorious of these are so French-looking that Paris often claims them for her own. Princely patronage has already opened the doors of the French court to Alexandre Roslin*. His charm, wealth and ability to paint materials raise his prestige even higher with the aristocracy. He becomes a member of the Académie, marries a French artist and leads a most sophisticated life. He takes advantage of a trip to St Petersburg in 1774 to stop in Stockholm where he paints several portraits of Gustav III and the royal family.

His contemporary Nicolas Lafrensen*, miniature painter at the Swedish court, gallicises his name to Lavreince and comes to Paris to work under the direction of Baudouin. After the manner of his master he paints a string of little gouaches, somewhat insipidly licentious, which bring him easy success until the Revolution forces him to return to his own country.

The modest place which Russian painting occupies in the 18th century is not a true pointer to its importance. The Petrovian era in effect sees a veritable revolution in plasticity. When Peter the Great mounts the throne, icon painting is the only type practised and its working skills have been handed down from generation to generation since the distant Middle Ages. The builder of St Petersburg shatters tradition by appealing to foreign artists. Among the French artists approached, the most illustrious, like Nattier and Oudry, back out. The *fête galante* enters Russia with Jean Pillement*. But it is a man of good will from Marseilles, Louis Caravaque*, who over a period of forty years initiates the Russians into secular painting while keeping for himself a sort of monopoly as imperial artist.

In the middle of the century Elisabeth, daughter of Peter the Great, draws freely on Western tastes. She is a little confused between elegance and flashiness or pleasure and debauchery, but St Petersburg is indebted to her for its Rococo when the architect Rastrelli decks it out with new buildings. Catherine II, a contemporary of neo-classicism and an admirer of Diderot, hardly appreciates this profusion of colours and ornaments. Under the successive reigns of the two Empresses the new city acquires enough prestige to interest Western masters in travelling there. For a long time to come they furnish all the painting for the court. Italy sends Pietro Rotari, who adorns the Peterhof *Cabinet des modes et des grâces* with some 300 feminine portraits. A Fine Arts Academy is founded in 1758. Apart from Stefano Torelli, decorator of the Chinese Palace of Oranienbaum, mostly French artists of the second half of the century such as Lagrenée*, Doyen and Lorrain provide the instruction for the young Russian school. The school also draws more freely on Vien than on Watteau. Tocqué, who came to paint a portrait of Elisabeth, exerts a deep influence on young local portraitists. Roslin teaches them the secret of painting velvety or silky materials. Others like J.-B. Le Prince* come without being asked, attracted by this new country. Le Prince finds among the peasants the material for a new exotism that is to find a warm welcome in France. Right at the end of the century J.-B. Lampi*, from the Tyrol, fights for prime position against the English influence with the slightly showy elegance of his court art. He paints several official portraits of Catherine and her entourage.

By dint of effort, a national school is born in the time of Catherine II. But, obsessed with admiration for the West, the " Empress of All the Russias " does not grasp the importance of this event. Paris and Rome have shaped the first Russian painter, Anton Pavlovich Losenko*. After fruitless incursions into the " grand style ", he shows in his portraits of poets and actors qualities which would have been enough to ensure him a decent living. The French sculptor Falconet takes advantage of an audience granted him by the Empress to intervene in his favour. But in vain. The munificent Catherine, who would pay ransom prices for the most prestigious European collections, lets Losenko die in poverty at the age of thirty-six.

The portrait provides the greater part of Russian painting of the time. Born of the common people, most of the painters have never left their own country. They have

Cornelis Troost
Amsterdam 1697-1750
Family in an Interior
Oil on canvas 3'1" × 2'8"
Amsterdam, Rijksmuseum

worked at St Petersburg with foreign artists on whom they are more or less dependent. After Antropov*, pupil of Caravaque, and Rokotov*, talented enough to collaborate with Rotari in decorating the *Cabinet des modes et des grâces*, Russia finally can proudly boast her own portrait master in the person of Dimitri G. Levitski*. Very impressionable, this pupil of Antonov and Lagrenee assimilates the qualities of Tocqué and Roslin, but also the faults of Lampi. His appointment as court painter in 1780 puts the seal of Imperial recognition on indigenous art. It results in a series of official allegories glorifying Catherine. But Levitski appears more at ease with the less formal type of portrait. That of Diderot, now in Geneva, is an eloquent example. A series of seven paintings showing inmates of the Smolny convent confirms that Russian art has embraced the taste of the West.

In an era when all living European art takes some sustenance from Rubens, Belgium remains fixed in its admiration for him. The 17th century lingers on in the portrait, the intimate scene or the religious painting.

J. P. Verhagen, who is barely twenty years old in 1750, gets his taste for great rhythmical and coloured compositions from Rubens. The boldness of his drawing, the tonalities of ochre, blue and pink, sometimes recall Tiepolo, whose works he has seen in Italy. He also goes to France and Austria, where he becomes painter to the court of Maria Theresa. Verhagen sees the sacred through theatrical and lively eyes, well in tune with the century. His *Feasts of Herod* or *Balthazar* are fairy-storyish and emphasise the distance between him and his brother Jean-Joseph Verhagen*, whose predilection for kitchen interiors earns him the nickname of " Potteken". It is also this sort of realism, intimate or rustic, that characterised and united the numerous small Antwerp masters. P. Snyers*, Verbruggen*, Bosschaert* and C. Bigee* pile up fruits and flowers in a style also practised in Holland and Spain and inspired by the same decorative realism. However, the style of the eclectic B. Beschey* lasts into the Empire period. At the end of the century Léonard Defrance of Liège, a friend of Fragonard, devotes himself enthusiastically to great revolutionary themes such as *Abolition of Slavery* or *Suppression of Monastic Orders*.

During the same period Amsterdam and The Hague publish political writings that by their revolutionary nature are suppressed in France. In the field of art, however, no country is more conservative than Holland. Since the disappearance of Rembrandt painting is immobilised in his tradition. As impervious to the grace of the Rococo as it is to the doctrine of neo-classicism, it sticks obstinately to that over-subtle heaviness which weighs down the assemblies of Regents or learned professors of J. M. Quinckhardt*. Or else they are the scrupulously perpetuated everyday gestures of families that seem uniform and ageless. The still-life becomes a painting of fruit and flowers which finds a virtuoso in Van Huysum*. His passion for perfection in optical illusion assures him of a renown that stems more from his technical prowess than his undeniable qualities as a painter. The sole attempt at Rococo in Holland comes from J. de Witt*. But his friezes of chubby Cupids painted in *trompe-l'œil* are only pallid reflections of the Boucher school.

Francisco de Goya
Blind-man's Buff
Cartoon for Tapestry
Oil on canvas 8'10" × 11'6"
Madrid, Prado

The work of a humorous chronicler, Cornelis Troost*, has the greatest place in Dutch painting of the century. More than his portraits of bewigged local officials, it is his zest for burlesque which makes him the most sought-after member of the 18th-century Dutch school. The passion for the theatre at the time explains the success of his comic scenes which pass directly from farce into his paintings, complete with accessories and costumes. His technique itself, in which he mixes pastel, water-colour and gouache, makes him original. This flash of imagination is extinguished in 1750, leaving Holland in a state of torpor.

A tragedy in the heart of the century in Portugal, the Lisbon earthquake of 1755, engulfs numerous works from past centuries and justifies the precedence given to architecture and decoration in the reign of Joseph I.

His predecessor, John V, had made a particular appeal to Italians. Dupra*, V. Baccarelli* and Trevisani even had a small local lineage in A. Lobo, J. de Silva* and others. France had sent an imitator of Watteau, A. Quillard*, who, after becoming court painter, carries out several aristocratic portraits before his untimely death in 1733. In the

94

second part of the century the delicate Jean Pillement, master of Vieira Portuense*, proves to be more influential.

When the death of Quillard leaves the post of Painter to the Chamber vacant, John V chooses Francesco Vieira de Matos*, better known as Lusitano, to succeed him.

Having gone to Rome in the entourage of the Portuguese Ambassador at a very young age, Lusitano returns to Lisbon seven years later and exercises his talents at first in the convent of the "Paulistas", where he has taken refuge after a series of amorous adventures that have made him a sort of legendary hero. A great part of his decorative work here seems to have vanished in the earthquake.

But in fact it is a pupil of Pillement, Francesco Vieira Portuense, who best illustrates this period. Almost all of his too-short life is spent in travel. Different plastic streams flow in his work, in which the influence of English portraitists comes up against traces of Correggio and even some inclinations towards the neo-classic. The brief lustre of Portuense closes out the century in Portugal.

The art situation is analogous in adjoining Spain. Bringing the Bourbons to power, the accession of Philip V, grandson of Louis XIV, opens up the country to foreign influence. The King has the Granja built for himself and in it tries to recreate the atmosphere of Versailles. The glory of Spain after the Treaty of Utrecht deeply feels the need for a new "Golden Century". Thus court art is to be French and decorative painting Italian until local talent is discovered. In fact, despite some glimmerings of hope, Spain seems to lapse into memories of Velasquez and the expectation of Goya.

At the beginning of the century Michel-Ange Houasse* and Jean Ranc* bring the grace of French pastorals and the slightly starchy elegance of princely portraits to a point that wins them the coveted title of "Pintor de Camara".

In 1737 Louis-Michel Van Loo succeeds Ranc as court portraitist. Philip V, the whole of whose family has been painted by Van Loo in a vast collective portrait with formal trappings, keeps him in his service for fifteen years and entrusts him with the task of establishing the San Fernando Academy, of which Van Loo is to become director on its inauguration in 1751.

The decoration of churches and palaces, however, is handed over to the Italians, A. Procaccini* and D. M. Sani*, whose talents prove to be somewhat dull. In this connection the choice of Ferdinand VI is more fortunate than that of his father. G. Amigoni and C. Giaquinto follow at his court. The latter particularly paints frescoes with admirable fluidity and movement in the salons and the grand staircase of the royal palace. In 1761, however, Giaquinto prefers to step down in the face of the neo-classic movement.

Less prudent, Tiepolo arrives in Spain in 1762, several months after the redoubtable A. R. Mengs has become established there. In bringing together in his court the two undisputed leaders of tendencies so incompatible as Rococo and neo-classicism, Charles III no doubt has satisfied his vanity. But it is painful to think of the old Tiepolo still agreeing to leave his own country to paint an apology for the Spanish monarchy

95

which has placed him in the unhappy position of being present to witness the triumph of a rival style preached by an opponent much less great than himself.

Mengs exerts an almost dictatorial influence on the new generation in Spain. He enjoys such renown that the Spanish court, from 1761 to 1776, becomes the rendezvous for the European art world. Mengs takes advantage of this to charge exorbitant prices and lead the life of a prince. As technically perfect as they might be, his frescoes painted for the royal palaces are far too lacking in feeling. In his portraits, on the other hand, this perfection does not exclude gracefulness and his portrait of the *Marquise de Llano* is very characteristic of the century.

His most faithful follower, M. S. Maella*, who represents the most academic element of the Spanish school, is highly regarded at the court, where he is to be made principal painter in 1799, an honour equal to that bestowed on Goya. Mengs also takes under his wing the young Francisco Bayeu* y Subias, future brother-in-law of Goya, who under this patronage becomes "Pintor de Camara", then director of the San Fernando Academy. An indefatigable decorator of royal palaces and religious buildings Bayeu also paints a number of portraits and cartoons for the insatiable Santa Barbara tapestry works where the young Goya makes his debut.

Of the three Gonzalez-Velasquez* brothers, Antonio particularly has achieved great renown. He has been the master of the "Spanish Watteau", the likeable Luis Paret* y Alcazar. Not suited for great flights into decorative painting, Paret makes himself a chronicler of the royal carnivals and equestrian entertainments dear to the heart of Charles III. There is perhaps a little of the French artists B.Ollivier and C.-F.de La Traverse, whom he met in Madrid, in that breeziness which is apparent in the ceremonial of the King's luncheon and in his small figures with their glowing red garb. He is also responsible for a series of "Ports of Spain" and several pretty paintings of flowers. But it is Luis Melendez* who provides the best example of naturalism with his *bodegones* (still-lifes). These still-lifes, as exceptional in Spain as those of Chardin in France, resemble those of the Dutch and mark him as belonging to the 18th century in Spain.

In reality Spanish painting, firmly under foreign influence and caught in the crossfire of two opposing art forms, awaits the redemption of a genius. Francisco Goya y Lucientes is born in the middle of the century, in Aragon. Too original to fit in with academic surroundings, he is rejected in the San Fernando Academy competition and is no luckier at Parma, where the despotism of Mengs also prevails. Italy shows him its colour and light. From 1776 to 1791 he paints forty-three cartoons for the Santa Barbara tapestry works. It is the ascensional period of his life, a period of optimism which gradually brings him success. Under the patronage of Jovellanos, later to become a Minister, Goya gains admission to the entourage of the grandees; then come his aristo-cratic portraits in which a fanciful turn balances out dignity of attitude, and popular anecdotes in which the lack of self-consciousness and spontaneity of his little characters in their striking costumes fit in so well with living Spain. For original as they may appear in a Spanish context, these works are still bound up with the 18th century.

Evidence and Documents

Decline of Religion in the 18th Century

If our religion were not a sad and dull psychology; if our priests were not stupid bigots; if this abominable Christianity had not been built up on murder and blood; if the joys of our Paradise were not reduced to an irrelevant beatific vision of goodness knows what, beyond comprehension or understanding; if our Hell offered anything else but gulfs of fire, hideous Gothic demons, howling and gnashing of teeth; if our paintings could be anything else but scenes of atrocity, a man scorched, a man hanged, a man roasted, a man grilled, a disgusting slaughter; if all our saints were not veiled up to the tip of the nose; if our ideas of decency and modesty had not proscribed the sight of arms, thighs, breasts, shoulders, of all nudity; if the feeling of mortification had not withered up these breasts, softened these thighs, emaciated these arms and torn these shoulders; if our artists were not shackled and our poets hedged in by the frightening words of sacrilege and profanity; if the Virgin Mary had been a mother through pleasure or indeed, Mother of God, if it had been her beautiful eyes, her beautiful breasts or her lovely thighs which had attracted the Holy Spirit to her and if that had been written into her story; if the Angel Gabriel were vaunted to her by his fine shoulders; if Mary Magdalen had had some amorous adventure with Christ; if at the wedding at Cana Christ, tipsy and slightly nonconformist, had eyed the bosom of one of the bridesmaids and the buttocks of St John, not certain whether he would remain faithful or not to the Apostle with the chin shaded by a light down: then you would see what our painters, poets and sculptors might have become; in what tone we would have spoken of those charms, which would have played so great and marvellous a role in the history of our religion and our God; and the manner in which we would have regarded the beauty to which we owe the birth, the incarnation of the Saviour, and the blessing of our Redemption.

> Diderot
> *Essays on Painting*

Diderot and the Salons

On Chardin

You come in time, Chardin, to refresh my eyes. There you are again, then, great magician, with your mute compositions! How eloquently they speak to the artist! All that they tell him about the imitation of nature, science of colour and harmony! How the air flows about these objects! The light of the sun does not conceal the disparity of things any more than it lights them up. Here is one who is little acquainted with friendly colours or hostile colours!

If it is true, as the philosophers say, that nothing is real but our sensations; that neither the emptiness of space nor even the solidity of bodies may have nothing in itself of what we feel; then let them tell me, these philosophers, what difference they find, looking at your paintings, between the Creator and you. (Salon of 1765.)

This man is the premier colourist of the Salon, and perhaps one of the leading colourists of painting. I cannot forgive this impertinent Webb for having written a treatise on art without naming a single Frenchman. I cannot pardon Hogarth to any greater degree for having said that the French school had not even a mediocre colourist. You have lied about it, Mister Hogarth; on your part it is ignorance or servility. I am well aware that your nation has the habit of scorning an impartial author who dares to speak of us with praise; but must you so basely pander to your fellow-citizens at the expense of the truth? Paint, paint better if you can. Learn to draw and do not write. We have, the English and ourselves, two very different ways of doing things. Ours is to overrate English productions; theirs is to underrate ours. Hogarth survives after two years. He stayed in France; and Chardin has been a great colourist for thirty years. (Salon of 1765, on number 49: *A Basket of Plums*.)

I am aware that Chardin's models, the inanimate nature which he imitates, change neither in place, shape or colour; and that with equal perfection a portrait by La Tour has more merit than a piece of genre by Chardin. But time will leave nothing to justify the reputation of the former. The precious dust will lift from the surface of the canvas, partly dispersed in the air and partly attached to the long plumes of old Saturn. One will talk about La Tour, but one will see Chardin. O La Tour! *memento, homo, quia pulvis es et in pulverem reverteris*. (Salon of 1767, on number 38.)

On Greuze

First, the type pleases me; it is moral painting. What! Has not the painter's brush been devoted too long to debauchery and vice? Must we not be pleased at last to see it compete with dramatic poetry to move us, instruct us, correct us and invite us to be virtuous? Take heart, my friend Greuze, put a moral into your painting and do it always like that! (Salon of 1763.)

A very fine portrait. It has the brusque and hard appearance of Wille; it is his rugged build; it is his small, keen, startled eye; they are his blotchy cheeks. How well the hair is done! How fine is the drawing, how bold the manner! . . . I should be pleased to see this portrait beside a Rubens, a Rembrandt or a Van Dyck. I should have pleasure in feeling what our painting might have to gain or lose. When one has seen this Wille, one turns one's back on the portraits by the others, even on those by Greuze. (Salon of 1765, on the *Portrait of the Engraver Wille*.)

On Michel Van Loo

. . . Very lifelike; it is its mellowness with his vividness; but too young, head too small, pretty as a woman, ogling, smiling, with a girlish air, pouting, simpering; nothing of the wisdom of the *Cardinal of Choiseul*; and then a superfluity of clothing enough to ruin the poor writer if the tax collector came to levy on his wardrobe. . . . He is seen full-face; he is bareheaded; his grey forelock, with that effeminate look, makes him look more like an old coquette still trying to charm; the position of a Secretary of State and not a philosopher. . . .

My pretty philosopher, you will ever be to me a worthy mark of the friendship of an artist, an excellent artist and more excellent man. But what will my grandchildren say when they come to compare my dreary works with this laughing, delicate, effeminate old coxcomb? . . . (Salon of 1767 on *Portrait of Diderot*.)

On Vernet

. . . You know his merit. It is all there in fourteen or fifteen paintings. The seas become rough or calm at his will; the sky darkens, the lightning flashes, the thunder rumbles, the storm rises; vessels are ablaze; one hears the crash of the waves, the cries of those who perish; one sees . . . one sees everything that pleases him. (Salon of 1759.)

. . . France may boast about her Vernet with as much justification as Greece about her Apelles or Zeuxis and Italy about her Raphaels, her Correggios and her Carracci. He is a truly astonishing painter. (Salon of 1763.)

Diderot

The Salons, Ed. Garnier, Paris

The French School

On Boucher

F. Boucher, principal painter to the King and who brings so much honour to our French school, told me in 1767 that he was sixty-three years old and that, although it was true that he had studied under Lemoine, he had not profited very much from a master who took so little care of his pupils and with whom he had not stayed very long. . . . M. Boucher assured me he had not spent more than three years with M. Lemoine. Whose disciple, then, is he? . . .

. . . He took little time in making the acquaintance of M. de Julienne who, wanting to engrave the drawings of Watteau, handed some of them to Boucher, who acquitted himself perfectly well. His light and lively hand seemed to be made for this work. . . .

On Chardin

The ordinary man gets pleasure from seeing things that go on daily under his eyes, in his household, and without hesitation prefers them to loftier subjects which require some study to be understood. I certainly do not want to go into whether this is detrimental to taste; I shall confine myself to saying that, rightly speaking, M. Chardin's art is only a new version of that of the Le Nain brothers. Like them he has chosen the most simple and unsophisticated subjects and, in truth, his choice is even better. He has caught attitudes and characters very well and he does not lack expression. That in itself I believe is what has contributed most so far to the vogue for his paintings and won them a place alongside the Teniers and other Flemish painters who worked in somewhat similar style, although his works and theirs are quite some distance apart. For, it must be admitted, M.Chardin's paintings give the impression too much of fatigue and effort. His touch is heavy and not at all varied. There is no facility in his brushwork; he expresses everything in the same manner and with a sort of indecision that makes his work too cold. . . .

On Desportes

. . . It is not that he puts the same finish into his works as is found in those of Mignon, J.van Huysum and other Flemish painters who are distinguished in the same field. His appear only as rough outlines compared with theirs, yet his have still more freshness and truth, and are more effective. It is because M.Desportes had a good knowledge of his art, because he knew how to use his brushwork to good effect and knew how to characterise each object as it suited him that his compositions are put together in a manner in which some parts add to the value of the others. . . .

On Greuze

. . . After having painted the Dauphin, this prince, kindness itself, believed he could not do anything more flattering or obliging than to ask him for a portrait of the Dauphine. She was present and, without thinking what he was saying, Greuze asked to be excused saying, "I am not able to paint such heads." He wanted to criticise the rouge which disfigured the princess's cheeks, but left it unsaid. They shrugged their shoulders and looked at the painter with pity.

On La Tour

He has not the freshness in his colour which Rosalba puts into hers, but he draws better. He goes into very great detail and has the particular talent for getting a perfect resemblance. But his mood is odd and his behaviour with an infinity of people . . . does not do him honour. . . .

Here is an example. He was painting the portrait of Madame de Pompadour; the King was present and the conversation turned to buildings which the King had had built; La Tour, without being asked, spoke up and had the impertinence to say that that was very good, but some warships would be more useful. It was at the time when the English had destroyed our fleet and we did not have a single warship to put up against them. . . .

On J.M. Nattier

. . . (He) soon gave up his historical talents and applied himself solely to portraiture, certain that his manner of painting would be pleasing particularly to women, whose knowledge of painting extended only to the colours and the finish. Nattier was not wrong; he became the fashion. Women, beautiful or ugly, came in droves to be painted by him, and all of them left with the satisfaction of carrying in their hands portraits shining with roses and lilies.

On Watteau

. . . This painter put finesse into his drawing without ever having been able to draw in the grand manner. His brushwork, the same as his pencil work, is most lively, the shapes of his faces most pleasant, his expressions common enough but very graceful, his work frothy. He had one misfortune, that was to become too easily dispirited with what he had done. He has been seen wiping out parts of a painting that were well conceived and as well executed, only to substitute for them other things that sometimes were very much inferior. He was not at all meticulous about painting cleanly and that, together with his too great use of a heavy oil, did great harm to his paintings. . . .

Paul-Jean Mariette
Abécédaire

The Italian School

On Batoni

... At first he was a jeweller by profession; he made jewellery and snuffboxes, engraving and tooling them. Someone happened to give him the order for a snuffbox and sent him a miniature to set in it. Batoni looked at the miniature and took it into his head to copy it; by dint of hard work he succeeded so well that the copy was taken for the original. Thus encouraged, he draws, he paints ... he realises that he is a born painter, that it is his vocation; he applies himself to painting and in a relatively short time makes his name and becomes one of the best painters in Italy. ...

On Bellotto

... He is a Venetian like his uncle; he is also painter of views. He seeks to be the perfect imitator of his master in all his work. The King of Poland, the Elector of Saxony, unable to secure his uncle, summon the nephew to Dresden and have him paint the principal views of the city, and then have him make engravings of them. This is done in 1752; one might have thought them to be the work of Antonio Canal himself so much do they resemble the handiwork of the latter in Venice. They have the same firm hand; and exception may even be taken to too much similarity of touch, and graduations of light that are not sensitive enough. ...

On Canaletto

He has become distinguished in the field of painting views and for a long time has painted pictures of this type, so much so that the finesse of his manner, the faithfulness of his work and the singular nature of his views has made his work sought-after by foreigners, particularly the English, for whom he has done much work. ...

On Carriera

... Vleughels, a friend of Rosalba, told me that before she began painting this scholarly girl had nothing else to do but design patterns for lace called "Venetian points", and when these went out of fashion she was financially embarrassed since she had to live and neither she nor her parents had any means. In this distressing position a French painter named Jean Steve, who painted snuffboxes, which had become fashionable, persuaded her to do likewise. ... Thus do great things come out of little ones. ...

On Giaquinto

C. Giaquinto is summoned to Spain and there occupies the post of principal painter to the King, which Louis-Michel Van Loo had held. It was said to be an underhand affair in which the influence of the musician Farinelli played a great part. M. Cochin, in his *Italian Voyage*, has him painting several ceilings in the palace of the King of Sardinia in Turin and represents him immediately afterwards as chevalier and disciple of Solimena. But I think he is mistaken and that he attributes to the Count de Corrado what belongs to F.de Mura who, in fact, painted a number of ceilings in this palace. . . .

On Longhi

. . . He got a taste for conversational subjects, festivals and masquerades and, in brief, for everything that went on in private life. He was able to sum himself up and decide that he would never succeed himself as a painter of history in the grand manner. So he restricted himself to these and was relished; he became another Watteau and received very many commissions. . . .

On Pellegrini

. . . He was a practician who would undertake to paint a vast ceiling as another might have undertaken a small easel painting. He was only able to draw on nature, as much for form as for colour. He had some successful moments, but they were rare. Time was to efface very quickly what he produced and nothing remains to remember him by except the fact that he was Rosalba's brother-in-law.

On Piazzetta

. . . In 1711 he was admitted to the college of painters and since that time has never ceased to be occupied on churches and private houses. . . . He draws with the same facility as he paints. . . . He also made an infinite number of life-sized heads which he drew from the model and which were almost all done in black stone and brought up with white on blue paper. They were much sought-after and highly paid. He could hardly meet the demand. . . .

On Ricci

When I knew him he was living in an apartment in the Procuratorship, and living grandly. His genius was of a very fine order. His compositions were always successful and always rich; his colouring striking and agreeable; all he lacked was a better taste in design. . . .

On Tiepolo

. . . He was barely more than sixteen when he was doing drawing exercises. Since then he has fathered compositions in which the richness of his genius shines, but it is none the less true that this facility harmed his correction and he may be reproached for having neglected this while giving way too much to the enthusiasm of his imagination. He was not very careful about the accuracy of his tints. His colouring is not true, seductive as it may be. He was never able to paint graceful heads. . . .

Paul-Jean Mariette
Abécédaire

Boucher

Boucher is one of those men who stand for the taste of a century, who express it, personify it and are its incarnation. The French taste of the 18th century is manifested in him in all the peculiarity of his character: Boucher remains not only its painter but its witness, its representative, its type.

. . . While the century of Louis XV succeeds the century of Louis XIV, when elegant France evolves from ostentatious France, and when around a royalty that is more human things and men become smaller, the ideal of art remains a meretricious and conventional ideal; but from majesty this ideal descends to entertainment. Everywhere there spreads a refinement of elegance, a delicate voluptuousness, what the period calls "the quintessence of the attractive, the colouring of charm and grace, the embellishment of festivals and love "…. The pretty thing—in those hours of fickle history there was the symptom and the seductiveness of France. The pretty thing is the essence and the formula of its spirit. The pretty thing is the school for its fashions. The pretty thing is the soul of the age—and the genius of Boucher.

. . . Boucher was the first to turn drawing into a commercial proposition for the artist, who launched it into publicity and who brought down on himself wealth, taste and fashion. The sheets of paper on which he strewed his studies and his whims were to come out of the boxes of amateurs and exclusive collectors of drawings to adorn apartments, figure on panels, enter into the decoration of the richest interiors. They assumed a familiar place in the boudoir, the salon, the bedchamber or alongside a table. Women were to want them; the Joullains and the Basans were to buy them: it was a mark of distinction to have them.

E. et J. de Goncourt
Art of the 18th Century
Flammarion and Fasquelle, Paris

The Analysis of Beauty

Therefore in the year 1745 I published a frontispiece to my engraved works in which I drew a serpentine-line lying on a painter's pallet with these words under it: "The Line of Beauty". The bait soon took; and no Egyptian hieroglyphic ever amused more than it did for a time; painters and sculptors came to me to know the meaning of it, being as much puzzled with it as other people, till it came to have some explanation; then indeed, but not until then, some found it out to be an old acquaintance of theirs, though the account they could give of its properties was very near as satisfactory as that which a day-labourer, who constantly uses the leaver, could give of that machine as a mechanical power. (Preface.)

The principles I mean are fitness, variety, uniformity, simplicity, intricacy, and quantity—all which co-operate in the production of beauty, mutually correcting and restraining each other occasionally. . . .

Yet in my mind odd numbers have the advantage over the even ones (in works of art) as variety is more pleasing than uniformity. . . . Nature, in all her works of fancy, if I may be allowed the expression, where it seems immaterial whether even or odd numbers of divisions were preferred, most frequently employs the odd; as, for example, in the indenting of leaves, flowers, blossoms, etc. . . .

Intricacy of form, therefore, I shall define to be that peculiarity in the lines, which compose it, that leads the eye a wanton kind of chase, and from the pleasure that gives the mind, entitles it to the name of beautiful; and it may be justly said that the cause of the idea of grace more immediately resides in this principle than in the other five, except variety; which indeed includes this, and all the others. . . .

It is to be observed that straight lines vary only in length, and therefore are least ornamental. That curved lines, as they can be varied in their degrees of curvature, as well as in their lengths, begin, on that account, to be ornamental. That curved and straight lines, joined, being a compound line, vary more than curves alone, and so become somewhat more ornamental. That the waving line, or line of beauty, varying still more, being composed of two curves contrasted, becomes still more ornamental and pleasing, insomuch that the hand takes a lively movement in making it with the pen or pencil.

And that the serpentine line, by its waving and winding at the same time different ways, leads the eye in a pleasing manner along the continuity of its variety, if I may be allowed the expression; and which, by its twisting so many different ways, may be said to enclose (though but a single line) varied contents; and therefore all its variety cannot be expressed on paper by one continued line, without the assistance of the imagination, or the help of a figure; see where that sort of proportioned winding line, which will hereafter be called the precise serpentine line, or *line of grace*, is represented by a fine wire properly twisted round the elegant and varied figure of a cone. . . .

I am apt to believe that the not knowing nature's artful and intricate method of uniting colours for the production of the variegated composition, or prime tint of flesh, hath made colouring in the art of painting, a kind of mystery in all ages; insomuch that it may be fairly said, out of the many thousands who have laboured to attain it, not above ten or twelve painters have happily succeeded therein: Correggio (who lived in a country village, and had nothing but the life to study after) is said almost to have stood alone for this particular excellence. Guido, who made beauty his chief aim, was always at a loss about it. Poussin scarcely ever obtained a glimpse of it, as is manifest by his many different attempts: indeed France hath not produced one remarkable good colourist. Rubens boldly, and in a masterly manner, kept his bloom tints bright, separate, and distinct, but sometimes too much so for easel or cabinet pictures.

William Hogarth
Analysis of Beauty

Gainsborough, as seen by Reynolds

However, it is certain, that all those odd scratches and marks which, on a close examination, are so observable in Gainsborough's pictures, and which even to experienced painters appear rather the effect of accident than design, this chaos, this uncouth and shapeless appearance, by a kind of magic, at a certain distance assumes form, and all the parts seem to drop into their proper places; so that we can hardly refuse acknowledging the full effect of diligence, under the appearance of chance and hasty negligence. . . . The slightness which we see in his best works cannot always be imputed to negligence. However they may appear to superficial observers, painters know very well that a steady attention to the general effect takes up more time and is much more laborious to the mind than any mode of high finishing or smoothness without such attention. His handling, the manner of leaving the colours, or in other words the methods he used for producing the effect, had very much the appearance of the work of an artist who had never learned from others the usual and regular practice belonging to the art; but still, like a man of strong intuitive perception of what was regular, he found a way of his own to accomplish his purpose. . . . It must be allowed that this hatching manner of Gainsborough did very much to contribute to the lightness of effect which is so eminent a beauty in his pictures, as on the contrary, much smoothing and uniting the colours is apt to produce heaviness. Every artist must have remarked how often that lightness of hand which was in his dead-colour, or first painting, escaped in the finishing, when he had determined the parts with more precision; and another loss he often experiences, which is of greater consequence; whilst he is employed in the detail, the effect of the whole together is either forgotten or neglected. The likeness of a portrait, as I have formerly observed, consists more in preserving the general effect of the countenance than in the most minute finishing of the features, or any of the particular parts. Now Gainsborough's portraits were often little more, in regard to finishing, or determining the form of the features, than what generally attends a dead-colour; but as he was always attentive to the general effect, or whole together, I have often imagined that this unfinished manner contributed even to that striking resemblance for which his portraits are so remarkable.

Reynolds
14th Discourse to Students
of the Royal Academy

Reynolds' Discourses to Students of the Royal Academy

2nd Discourse (11 December 1769)

. . . When you have clearly and distinctly learned in what good colouring consists, you cannot do better than to have recourse to nature herself, who is always at hand, and in comparison of whose true splendour the best coloured pictures are but faint and feeble.
    . . . Style in painting is the same as in writing, a power over materials, whether words or colours, by which conceptions or sentiments are conveyed. And in this Ludovico Carrache (I mean in his best works) appears to me to approach the nearest perfection.

3rd Discourse (14 December 1770)

For in the same manner and on the same principles, as he has acquired the knowledge of the real forms of nature, distinct from accidental deformity, he must endeavour to separate simple, chaste nature from those adventitious, those affected and forced airs or actions, with which she is loaded by modern education. . . . Beauty and simplicity have so great a share in the composition of a great style that he who has acquired them has little else to learn.
    Even in the portrait grace, and I dare to say, resemblance consist more in capturing a general impression of physiognomy than copying each feature.

4th Discourse (14 December 1770)

Thus figures must have a ground whereon to stand; they must be clothed; there must be a background; there must be light and shadow; but none of these ought to appear to have taken up any part of the artist's attention. They should be so managed as not even to catch that of the spectator. . . .

6th Discourse (10 December 1774)

. . . We must trace back the art to its fountain-head; to that source from whence they drew their principal excellences, the monuments of pure antiquity. All the inventions and thoughts of the Ancients, whether conveyed to us in statues, bas-reliefs, intaglios, cameos or coins are to be sought after and carefully studied; the genius that hovers over these venerable relics may be called the father of modern art.

9th Discourse (16 October 1780)

The Art which we profess has beauty for its object; this it is our business to discover and to express; the beauty of which we are in quest is general and intellectual; it is an idea that subsists only in the mind . . . it is an idea residing in the breast of the artist, which he is always labouring to impart, and which he dies at last without imparting; but which he is yet so far able to communicate as to raise the thoughts and extend the views of the spectator; and which, by a succession of art, may be so far diffused that its effects may extend themselves imperceptibly into public benefits, and be among the means of bestowing on whole nations refinement of taste; which, if it does not lead directly to purity of manners, obviates at least their greatest depravation, by disentangling the mind from appetite, and conducting the thoughts through successive stages of excellence, till that contemplation of universal rectitude and harmony which began by Taste, may, as it is exalted and refined, conclude in Virtue.

12th Discourse (10 December 1784)

The art of seeing Nature, or in other words the art of using models, is in reality the great object, the point to which all our studies are directed. . . .

Our neighbours the French are much in this practice of extempore invention, and their dexterity is such as even to excite admiration, if not envy; but how rarely can this praise be given to their finished pictures!

The late Director of their Academy, Boucher, was eminent in this way. When I visited him some years since in France I found him at work on a very large picture, without any drawings or models of any kind. On my remarking this particular circumstance, he said, when he was young, studying his art, he found it necessary to use models; but he had left them off for many years. . . .

. . . He often had grace and beauty, and good skill in composition; but, I think, all under the influence of a bad taste; his imitators are indeed abominable.

Sir Joshua Reynolds
Extracts from Discourses
Delivered to Students of
the Royal Academy

The Salons of 1751 and 1753

Salon of 1751

... M. Tocqué has exhibited portraits in which touch, finish, composition and fidelity to nature appear undestroyed: each Salon adds to the reputation of this painter. The greatest compliment that can be paid to the ten pastels of M. de La Tour is to say that they are superior to those of preceding years. The enlightened public have very much admired the great parts of painting set out in these pieces. We are struck by the very great art of the painter in surmounting very considerable difficulties in the portrait of Madame de La Reynière, those of preserving the brilliance of colours in her attire and of catching the likeness of a pretty woman without doing her an injustice. The portrait of M. de La Reynière is a speaking likeness. The fleshiness and effects in the head of M. Wille present nature in a way to delight art lovers. M. Perronneau in fourteen pastels has given proof of his facility and the pleasure of his colour. M. Vernet, so well known for his talent in seascapes and landscapes, has sent us three from Italy where his tastes, and perhaps his circumstances, have kept him. ...

Salon of 1753

Never has the Salon been so brilliant, so beautiful, so varied and so numerous; everything in it responds to the reputation of the arts and the care of M. de Vandières, whose knowledge, acquired in two years' travelling in Italy, has perfected a natural taste. ...

Gathered together are the noble and the elegant, the austere and the playful, history and fable, heroic and pastoral, battle and allegory; nothing is lacking that has drawing as its principle and basis, nothing that can please the eye, the mind or the imagination. ...

M. Carle Van Loo, in six paintings of different sizes and absolutely varied composition, shows all the grace of his brush and the fertility of his mind: action, repose, devotion, the great machine, easel paintings, even the portrait, everything is striking proof of superior merit. M. Boucher has continued to delight with his gracefulness and the pleasure of his composition in the paintings of Thetis and the Sun, in overdoors for Bellevue and in the " Seasons " painted for a ceiling at Fontainebleau; his style, which is beloved and followed, warrants the welcome it receives.

Comte de Caylus
Œuvres, Ed. Laurens

"La Lecture" by Fragonard

. . . A man reads, and as suits the reader, and perhaps also the author of a novel (be it only that of his own existence!), he turns his back squarely on reality. It is his dream on the contrary which unfolds and is presented to us, but quite full-face, in this young girl seated: I speak of that dress with its broad folds and lustrous reflections, but the attention of the pensive one, who shows only an obliterated profile, is quite complete, over there, behind, focused on an imaginary spot which she hesitates to join or leave. On her elbow, and as if leaning on the railing of an invisible lake. But the reader has ceased to read, he is asking questions and the lines have disappeared from the little book he is holding in his hands, and the sonority of an unspoken phrase fills the whole scene.

They are sad paintings, those to which it is impossible to lend an ear!

Paul Claudel
L'Œil écoute, Gallimard

Watteau

Let us remember that Watteau is the great innovator among 18th-century painters, that it is he who, at the beginning of this extraordinary period in which the world is to turn on its hinges, invents new themes and new poetry which are to reign until the fall of the Bastille, and that it will take all David's Greeks and Romans to make us forget the *bal capricieux* for a single moment. Let us remember that all that comedy in the Italian style, " Cythera ", the " Enseigne " and " Signature of the Contract ". . . all that is a break with academic subjects as laid down in the sun of Versailles, with the wig of the Great King, that black wig which the packers are carrying out in front of us and that the porters look at in bantering manner before taking it away. Let us remember that Watteau is a youthful denial of Madame de Maintenon and the bigotry of the final years of the Grand Century. And at thirty-seven, still young but already dying, Watteau abandons decoration and the charms in which he excels to press, beyond his own poetry, an investigation of the world by painting; he guesses at and discovers in the depths of the near future the strength and novelty of realism, all the equivocacy of middle-class comedy with its porters on the side, and he paints this picture which, thirty years before the *Encyclopaedia*, is singularly prophetic of Denis Diderot.

Aragon
L'Enseigne de Gersaint
Ides et Calendes, 1946

(A propos of *L'Indifférent*)
No, no, it is not that he might be indifferent, this mother-of-pearl messenger, this herald of Aurore; rather let us say that he is poised between flying and walking, and not only is he already dancing, but with one arm outstretched and the other broadly spreading a lyrical wing, he holds a balance in which weight, more than half countered, is only the least element. He is ready to go or to come, he listens, he waits for the precise moment, he seeks it in our eyes, from the quivering tip of his fingers. . . . Half-fawn, half-bird, part feeling and part talk, half-poised but already half-relaxed! Sylph, marvel, and the giddy pen ready to draw a flourish!

Paul Claudel
L'Œil écoute, Gallimard

Watteau, Recorder of the Ephemeral

What a mystery is a great artist! Whether Watteau wished it or not, his sentimental comedy in the eternity of nature is the image of existence of us all, seen by an ardent nature across his bitter destiny. He is the confronting, without respite and with admirable love, of life too short and of the infinite desired. Trembling soul, adoring soul—the burned-out pinks and the pale blues quiver like his poor soul. He feels that he is going to die. Between two flutters of an eyelid which mark the awakening of consciousness and the repose which comes too soon, he expresses the happy appearances and the poignant realities of the adventures to which he is condemned.

The resigned pessimism of the Italian farce, the cruel reality which prowls through the masquerade and masks itself with black velvet, came at their destined hour to afford distraction to a dying aristocracy and to the profound man who hides this death struggle under flowers. The whole century will feel it; Tiepolo, Cimarosa, Guardi and Longhi will reply, later on, to Watteau, from the centre of the fête; and from Spain herself, sombre, ruined, and seeming almost dead, comes the bantering laugh of Goya. But with Watteau it is the prelude, intimate, delicate, drunk with tenderness, wildly desirous of making the illusion endure. He listens to the wind. He wanders and chats with the comedians. Like them he embroiders upon any canvas. Never did subject have less importance in itself. It is always the same, like the relationship of man and woman with love and with death. Since that is so, how monotonous! The groups posed on the moss, like leaves torn dying from the trees, or like ephemeral butterflies, will be carried away by the breeze which hurries them on to the abyss, with the forgetfulness and the phantoms, the plaint of the violoncellos, the sigh of the flutes, the perfumes, and the sound from the jets of water. When one isolates from its frame the talk of all these charming creatures, dressed in satin, powdered, rouged, having nothing in life to do but make love and music, everything expresses the joy of the instant seized on the wing. Here is nothing but prattle, rockets, and cascades of laughter, and an intricate crossfire of gallantries and confessions. The round dance turns, innocent games are organised and, when the concert begins, the flute and mandolin scarcely cause voices to be lowered. Why does the ensemble give that sensation so near to sadness? The spirit of the poet is present. Slow steps and swayings, scattered words, necks that turn aside to seize a phrase of gallantry, throats bending to escape or offer themselves, inclined and laughing faces resembling flowers only half-open, all will pass, all will pass! How quickly a society appears and disappears under trees a hundred years old which, themselves, will die one day! Nothing is eternal but the sky, from which the clouds will disappear. The costumed comedy reveals a terrible ennui with life; it is only the song of the sonorous instruments which can cradle the despair of those who have nothing to do but amuse themselves. None of us will fix the impalpable instant when love transfixed him, and he who comes to tell of it with tones which penetrate one another and lines which continue one another, still burns with a desire that he will never satisfy.

To tell all this, he had therefore placed that which is the most fleeting amid that which is most durable among the things seen by our eyes—space and the great woods. He died at Nogent, under the fog and the trees, quite near the water. He had brought back from his Flemish country, and from a visit he had made to England, the love of moist landscapes where the colours, in the multiplied prism of the tiny suspended drops, take on their real depth and their splendour. Music and trees, the whole of him is in them. The sonorous wave, rising from tense strings, itself belongs to the life of the air, with the light vapour which sets its azure haze around the scattered branches, the slender trunks which space themselves or assemble in clusters near the edge of the deep forests, and the luminous glades away toward the distance and the sky. The sound does not interrupt the silence, but rather increases it. Barely, if at all, a whispered echo reaches us from it. We do indeed see the fingers wandering upon the strings; the laughter and the phrases exchanged are to be guessed from busts leaning over or thrown back, and from fans that tap on hands—the actors in the charming drama are at a distance from their painter, and scattered to the depth of the clearings which flee toward the horizon, whose blue grows deeper, little by little. And the genius of painting resolves into visual harmonies the sound of the instruments which hovers over the murmur of the voices. The green, the red or the orange of the costumes of comedy or of parade, and the dark and silky spots made by the groups of people conversing, are mingled with the diffused silver which trembles and unites the tips of the nearby leaves with the sunny spaces which stretch away among the dark trunks.

Elie Faure
Histoire de l'Art: L'Art Moderne I
Jean-Jacques Pauvert, Paris 1964

The Leafy World

The assembly of the gods is held in the boudoir of the favourites. All the good sculptors of the century, old Coyzevox first of all, in whom Puget is still felt, and already Clodion as well, and then Lemoine, Pajou, Pigalle, Falconet, the brothers Adam, and Bouchardon, will not be quite themselves until they introduced into the fashionable Olympus, Chubby Eros or Venus at her toilet, like a lady of elegance well-versed in matters of love. And Nattier will paint the princesses of the blood as rustic divinities, almost disrobed at times, their arms and their feet bare, and with flowers garlanded on their dresses, around their fingers, and in their hair. Rose bushes grow among the yews and the trimmed boxwood of Versailles.

These roses, moreover, do not lose their petals as soon as they are plucked. They will be applied all along the walls, they will encircle the sofas and the ladies who chat there, they will be around mirrors and chandeliers and will be suspended from the canopies of beds. Everyone, like Coypel and Caylus, for example, talks of " imitating nature ". But upon condition that it submit to the caprice of the society least prepared to feel it living in man, and to experience its mystic intoxication, without which art loses the sole cause of its eternal character. Watteau is a king of the spirit whom the aristocracy of France will obey. But it will take its revenge, in its turn, by giving its orders to those who will succeed Watteau. " Nature " will reduce itself to a kind of *objet d'art* placed on a shelf, and destined for the usage of fashion set by those who possess favour and money which, by the way, they employ with extreme elegance.

Watteau being dead, the 18th century is aesthetically bankrupt of taste. The entire élite is furnished with an intense art education, which rises and broadens in it in the measure that creative force declines and shrinks in the souls of the artists, its servitors. It is drawing-room art, which does not pass the limits of the drawing-room. The exhibitions of paintings are themselves " Salons ". Painters, sculptors, engravers, jewellers, gold-smiths, cabinet-makers, hairdressers, tailors and bootmakers all contribute to surround the fine flower of a highly-developed culture with this frail and creeping frame which brings out its splendour, but which tightens around it, gradually causes its natural origins to be lost to view, and exhausts itself in satisfying a spirit which is fading and dying of ingenuity and ennui. Everywhere, around the conversationalist and the coquette, in crystal, unglazed porcelain, marble and tapestry, from the glass cabinet for bibelots to the tableware, from the carriage to the sedan chair, and from the antechamber to the alcove, this charming art repeats and reflects the words exchanged about love, about new-born science, about Persia, about China, about the spectacles of the day, and about the countryside seen from an opera box. A fashionable art, which uses up and completely drains the amiability of artist, scatters it with the flights of the Amors and the flowers which are strewn about, disperses it through a thousand toilet articles, and debases it through those same surroundings.

François Boucher is its soul. Fashion insinuates itself and fixes itself around his easy fecundity which everywhere, on ceiling, screens, carriage panels and small friezes above doors, on caskets and fans, scatters its monotonous subjects—shepherdesses and pastorals. Charming in manner, generous, one who loved enjoyment and who is adored by men and women, ceaselessly exchanging with his century that which they both need in order to love and be loved, he stands, with the mistress of the King, at the centre of his own revolving circle of winged loves and of flowers woven in garlands, which he is quite free—as artists of his race alone are—to bring forth in greatest profusion and to hang up wherever it pleases the alert and spontaneous fantasy of his desire, which is ever in accord with his requirements. In order to yield to the flexible grace of this world, where philosophic and gallant conversation flows on sinuous lines, and makes delicate detours, everything adapts itself without effort to the forms imagined by the architect and the cabinet-maker of society, forms tending constantly toward the circular. The fat, soft roundnesses turn with the woodwork and the frames; there are chubby shepherds, beribboned shepherdesses, and serving maids whom the painter raises to the dignity of goddesses by disrobing them, to show their full-blooded young flesh, their smiles, their dimples, and the elastic and quickly-swelling curve of their buttocks and their breasts. The plump children of Bouchardon, the sculptor, are swept into the dance. Fragonard is prefigured; and Boucher, through his savory master Lemoyne, through Watteau, and through the world of decorators and artisans inspired by him, links the whole fragile setting of the French aristocracy with the supreme teaching of the Italian fête which Tiepolo, at the same time with him, is unfurling over the ceiling of Venetian bedchambers and drawing-rooms. Almost freed from form, the aerial harmonies sprinkle, with the rouge of cheeks and the powder from puffs, light skies, where the whirl of the clouds effaces itself little by little in the diffused rose and silver.

Unfortunately, the twisted and serpentine line prevents the decorator from making a complete escape into space and ever recalls him to labour for the tyrannous world of fashion, for which he was born. He remains the prisoner of the prince. For the first time the artist is admitted to the drawing-room and the table, with the critic who dictates rules, the writer who explains and the scientist who diffuses knowledge and the philosopher who destroys. It is the painter and the sculptor who lose most through these contacts; they are ill at ease between rationalistic analysis and sentimental abstraction; they forget, little by little, the life of the profound volumes and of the colours steeped in rain and in light, when they enter upon moral considerations, where they very quickly lose their way. The only one who gains is the newsmonger of plastics, who grows up somewhere between the rhymer of epigrams and the indiscreet confidant—the engraver of anecdotes of gallantry and of spicy gossip, who pretends that he was present, concealed behind a screen, at the disrobing of the bride, at the consultation of the marquise, and at the vicomte's or the abbé's capture by assault of the chambermaid. The genius for gossip, rendered sharp and subtle by a century of the life of fashion, overflows the drawing-rooms, the suppers, and the teas in the English style, and sweeps over everything that is expressed by pen, pencil and modelling tool. Cochin, Beaudoin, Moreau the Younger, Eisen, Leprince, and the Saint-Aubins, create a chronicle of fashion peculiar to this country and this period. Conversations are carried on in exquisite style with a pastel crayon, a luminous engraving, pretty as a blonde—that one finds on turning the pages of a tale of gallantry or of a classic tragedy, or in a delicate, powdered head on a translucent medallion a quarter the size of one's hand. Everything is conversation—letters to the ladies, the article in the *Encyclopaedia*, the short story by Voltaire, and the critique by Diderot. A witty word shakes a world, and a hundred thousand such words are struck off every day.

Elie Faure
Histoire de l'Art: L'Art Moderne I
Jean-Jacques Pauvert, Paris 1964

Chronology

Date	Political Events	Arts	Literature, Philosophy, Theatre and Music	Science and Technology
1700	Peter the Great at war with Sweden. 1700-14: Spanish War of Succession.	Birth of Natoire.		
1701	Frederick I, King of Prussia.			
1702	Fourth War of Louis XIV.			
1703	Foundation of St Petersburg.	Birth of Boucher.		
1704	British at Gibraltar.	Birth of Quentin de La Tour.	Translation of *Arabian Nights*.	
1705	Condemnation of Jansenism.	Birth of Carle Van Loo.		Englishman Thomas Newcomen develops fir steam engine.
1706		Hardouin-Mansart completes Dome of Invalides.		
1707			Birth of Buffon.	
1708		First porcelain in Europe, invented by Bottger.		
1709	Polish revolt against Stanislas.		Berkeley's *Principles of Human Knowledge*.	
1710		Robert de Cotte and Hardouin-Mansart complete chapel of Versailles Palace begun in 1699. Messein porcelain.		
1712	Destruction of Port-Royal.	Birth of Guardi.	Birth of Rousseau. Corelli: "Concerti Grossi".	
1713	Frederick-Wilhelm succeeds Frederick I. Treaty of Utrecht.		Birth of Diderot. Leibniz: *Monadologie*. Stradivarius makes violins in Cremona.	
1714		Birth of Vernet.	Lesage: *Gil Blas*.	Fahrenheit thermomete
1715	Death of Louis XIV; accession of Louis XV.		Vivaldi: Concertos for Violin.	
1716	Law founds the General Bank.		Fénelon: *Letter to the Academy*.	
1717		Watteau: *Embarkation for the Island of Cythera*.	F. Couperin revives art of the clavichord.	
1719	Peter the Great expels Jesuits.		Defoe: *Robinson Crusoe*. Voltaire: *Œdipus*.	

Date	Political Events	Arts	Literature, Philosophy, Theatre and Music	Science and Technology
720	Law flees; riots in Paris.	Watteau: *Enseigne de Gersaint.*		
721	Creation of Holy Synod in Russia.	Death of Watteau. *c.* 1721: Hôtel de Matignon in Paris.	Montesquieu: *Persian Letters.* Bach: *Brandenburg Concertos.*	
722			Defoe: *Moll Flanders.* Bach: *Well-tempered Clavier* (first part). Rameau: Modern harmonic system.	
723	Louis XV comes of age.	Birth of Reynolds.	Bach: *Passion of St John.*	
724	Russia: Tariff protection. Foundation of Paris Bourse.		Birth of Kant.	
725	Death of Peter the Great.	Birth of Greuze.	Vico: *Philosophy of History.*	
726		1726-7: Tiepolo frescoes in Udine.	Swift: *Gulliver's Travels.*	
727	Quakers against slavery.	Birth of Gainsborough.		
728		Chardin: *La Raie ouverte.* Birth of Mengs. Dom. Rossi: Jesuits' Church in Venice. 1728-41: Château de Rohan in Strasburg.	J. Gay and Pepusch: *Beggars' Opera.*	
729			Bach: *Passion of St Matthew.*	
731			Voltaire: *Charles XII.*	
732		Birth of Fragonard.	Birth of Haydn.	
733	War of Succession in Poland.	Frescoes by Asam brothers and Zimmermann at Weltenburg. Birth of Hubert Robert. Hogarth: *Harlot's Progress* and *Rake's Progress.*	Pope: *Essay on Man.* Abbé Prevost: *Manon Lescaut.* Pergolese: *The Maidservant Mistress.*	Demonstration by Dufay of positive and negative electricity.
734		Birth of Romney.	Rameau: *Castor and Pollux.*	
735	Turkish war against Austria and Russia.	Salvi: Fountain of Trevi. Lancret: *The Ham Luncheon.*		

Date	Political Events	Arts	Literature, Philosophy, Theatre and Music	Science and Technology
1736		Death of Pater.	First Chinese drama translated in Europe by P. Prémare.	
1737		Inauguration of "Salon" of painting.	Scarlatti: Sonatas for clavichord.	
			F. Algarotti: *Newtonianism for Women*.	
1738		Boucher: *The Luncheon*.		
1739		Chardin: *Grace, The Governess*.	Hume: *Treatise on Human Nature*.	Réaumur thermometer.
			Frederick II: *Anti-Machiavel*.	
1740	Death of Frederick-Wilhelm; succession of Frederick II.			
	War of Succession in Austria.			
1741		La Tour: *President de Rieux*.	Performance of Handel's *Messiah* in London.	
		Birth of Fuseli.		
1742			Young: *Night Thoughts on Life, Death and Immortality*.	Celsius thermometer.
1743		Death of Lancret.		
		Death of Rigaud.		
1744	Louis XV declares war on England and Austria.		Birth of Herder.	
1745	Battle of Fontenoy.	Hogarth: *Marriage à la Mode*.	Rameau: *Temple of Glory*.	
		Mengs: *Portrait of Madame Thiele*.		
1746		Birth of Goya.	Vauvenargues: *Maxims*.	
		Death of Largillière.	Condillac: *Essay on the Origins of Human Knowledge*.	
1747	Franco-Dutch War.	Completion of Sans-Souci Palace in Potsdam.	La Mettrie: *Man-Machine*.	
1748	Treaty of Aix-la-Chapelle.	Ruins of Pompeii discovered.	Montesquieu: *Esprit des Lois*.	
		1748-50: Gainsborough: *Portrait of Robert Andrews and his Wife*.		
1749			Swedenborg: *The Heavenly Arcana*.	
			Fielding: *Tom Jones*.	
			Birth of Goethe.	

ate	Political Events	Arts	Literature, Philosophy, Theatre and Music	Science and Technology
750		Tiepolo : frescoes at Labia Palace in Venice. 1750-3 : Tiepolo : decoration of Archbishop's palace at Wurzburg.	Goldoni : *Venetian Dramas.* Death of J.-S. Bach. Richardson : *Clarissa.*	Invention of planing machine by Focq.
751	Abolition of slavery in Pennsylvania.		Voltaire : *Century of Louis XIV.* First volume of *Encyclopaedia* (1751-72).	
752	Condemnation by High Court of *L'Encyclopédie.*	Boucher : *Girl on a Couch.*	Rousseau : *Discourse on Inequality.*	Invention of lightning conductor by Benjamin Franklin.
753		Boucher : *Sunrise.* Oudry : *The White Swan.* Foundation of British Museum.		
754			Condillac : *Treatise on Sensationism.*	
755	Anglo-French Colonial War. Lisbon Earthquake.	Greuze : *Father of the Family.* Death of Oudry. La Tour : *Marquise de Pompadour.*	Death of Montesquieu.	Discovery of carbonic gas by Black.
756	Seven Years War (France, Austria and Russia against England and Frederick II).	Piranesi : Roman engravings.	Birth of Mozart. Voltaire : *Essay on the Morals and Spirit of Nations.*	
757		Birth of William Blake. 1757-91 : Soufflot : The Pantheon, Paris.	Diderot : *Illegitimate Son.* Publication of *Nibelungen.*	
758			Helvetius : *Of the Mind.*	
759			Voltaire : *Candide.* Death of Handel. Birth of Schiller.	
760		Reynolds founds the Society of Artists. Reynolds : *Portrait of Miss Nelly O'Brien.* Birth of Hokusai.	Macpherson : *Songs of Ossian.* 1760-1 : Diderot : *The Nun, Nephew of Rameau.*	
761	France evacuates India.	Greuze : *L'Accordée de Village.*	Rousseau : *Nouvelle Héloïse.*	

Date	Political Events	Arts	Literature, Philosophy, Theatre and Music	Science and Technology
1762	Catherine II seizes power in Russia.		Rousseau: *Social Contract*, *Emile*. Glück: *Orpheus*. Goldsmith: *Chinese Letters*.	
1763	Treaty of Paris.	Gabriel builds the Petit Trianon at Versailles.	Winckelmann: *History of Art*.	
1764	Bengal revolt crushed by British.	Hogarth: *Finis*, or *The Bathos*. Death of Hogarth.		
1765		Archbishop of Paris demands removal of Baudouin's works from Salon because of immorality.	Sterne: *Sentimental Journey*.	
1766	Lorraine reunited with France.	Fragonard: *The Swing*. Death of Nattier.	Goldsmith: *Vicar of Wakefield*. 1766-8: Lessing: *Laocoon*.	Cavendish isolates hydrogen.
1767			Lessing: *Minna von Barnhelm*. d'Holbach: *Christianity Unmasked*.	
1768	Russo-Turkish War.	Death of Canaletto. Foundation of Royal Academy.	Birth of Chateaubriand.	
1769	Birth of Bonaparte.	Birth of Lawrence.		Watt's steam engine.
1770		Death of Boucher. Death of Tiepolo. Gainsborough: *Blue Boy*.	d'Holbach: *System of Nature*. Birth of Beethoven.	Joseph Cugnot produce first steam-driven carriage. Cook in Oceania.
1771	Dissolution of Parliament by Louis XV.	Houdon: Bust of Diderot.		
1773			Diderot: *James the Fatalist*. Herder: *Eulogy of the Gothic*. Goethe: *Werther*.	
1774	Death of Louis XV; accession of Louis XVI.		Glück: *Iphigenia in Aulis*.	
1775	American War of Independence.	Gainsborough: *The Watering Place*. 1775-80: Victor Louis: Bordeaux Theatre.	Beaumarchais: *Barber of Seville*. Spencer: *The Real Rights of Man*.	English scientist Edware Jenner discovers vaccine

Date	Political Events	Arts	Literature, Philosophy, Theatre and Music	Science and Technology
1776	British colonies in America revolt; Independence for United States.	Fragonard: *Festival of St Cloud.* 1776-80: La Scala, Milan.	Gibbon's *Decline and Fall of the Roman Empire.*	
1777		Death of Natoire.	Restif de la Bretonne: *Perverted Peasant.*	Laplace and Lavoisier invent the calorimeter.
1778		Goya: *The China Seller.*	Death of Rousseau. Death of Voltaire.	
1779	Suppression of serfdom in French royal estates.	Death of Chardin. Death of Mengs. 1779-82: Construction of the Odéon in Paris.	Schiller: *The Robbers.*	
1780			Lessing: *Nathan the Wise.* Wieland: *Oberon.* Gluck: *Iphigenia in Tauris.*	Foundation of modern chemistry by Antoine-Laurent de Lavoisier.
1781			Kant: *Critique of Pure Reason.*	Herschel discovers planet Uranus.
1782			Laclos: *Dangerous Liaisons.*	
1783	Treaty of Versailles.		d'Alembert: *Miscellany of Philosophy, History and Literature.*	Montgolfier brothers invent first aerostatic balloons.
1784	Pitt's India Act: British Dominion in India.		Rivarol: *On the Universality of the French Language.* Death of Diderot. Grétry: *Richard Cœur de Lion.*	
1785		Louis David: *The Oath of the Horatii.*	Sade: *One-hundred-and-twenty Days.* Mozart: *Marriage of Figaro.*	Watt's double-action steam engine. Englishman Edmund Cartwright invents power loom.
1786	Affair of the Queen's Necklace.	Guardi: Venetian "vedute" and "capriccios". Reynolds: *Duchess of Devonshire and her Daughter.*		Modern stenography.
1787	American Constitution. Second Russo-Turkish War.		B. de Saint-Pierre: *Paul et Virginie.* Schiller: *Don Carlos.* Mozart: *Don Giovanni.*	First iron-hulled ship.

Date	Political Events	Arts	Literature, Philosophy, Theatre and Music	Science and Technology
1788		Death of Quentin de La Tour. Vigée-Lebrun: *Portrait of the Painter Hubert Robert*.	Death of Buffon. Kant: *Practical Reason*. Cherubini: *Iphigenia in Aulis*.	
1789	Storming of Bastille: Declaration of Rights of Man.	David: *Oath of Jeu de Paume*. Death of Vernet.	Goethe: *Tasso*.	The German Martin Heinrich Klaproth discovers uranium.
1790			Blake: *Marriage of Heaven and Hell*. Birth of Lamartine.	
1791	French Constitution.		Mozart: *Requiem*. Death of Mozart.	Industrial production of synthetic soda by Nicolas Leblanc. The metre, basic metric unit.
1792	Fall of French Monarchy; first republic. France at war with Prussia and Austria.		Goethe: *Roman Elegies*. Rouget de Lisle: *La Marseillaise*. Birth of Rossini.	Lighting from coal gas, by the Englishman Murdock.
1793	Execution of Louis XVI. 1793-5: Vendée War.	Death of Guardi.	Condorcet: *Progress of the Human Mind*.	
1794	Executions of Danton and Robespierre.		Chenier: *Iambes*. Haydn: English symphonies. Fichte: *Bases of Science*.	Father Claude Chappe creates an aerial telegraph.
1795	Babeuf: Manifesto of Equality. 1795-9: The Directory.		Schiller: *Letters on Aesthetic Education*.	
1796	Failure of Babeuf Plot. Risorgimento in Italy. Wars of the Directory. Death of Catherine II; accession of Paul I.	Birth of Corot.	J. de Maistre: *On the French Revolution*.	Englishman Joseph Bram produces the hydraulic press. Discovery of lithography by the German Aloys Senefelder.
1797	Vendée pacified by Hoche.		Tieck: Fantasy Tales. Hölderin: *Hyperion*. Birth of Schubert.	

Date	Political Events	Arts	Literature, Philosophy, Theatre and Music	Science and Technology
798	Wars of French Empire. Nelson's victory at Aboukir.	Goya: *Portrait of F. Guillemardet*.	Coleridge and Wordsworth: *Lyrical Ballads*.	Machine of continuous production of paper invented.
799	Bonaparte, first Consul.		Birth of Balzac. Beethoven: *Pathétique Sonata*.	Coal-gas lighting by the Frenchman Lebon.
800			Schiller: *Maria Stuart*. Cherubini: *The Water Carrier*.	The Italian Volta invents the electric battery.
801	Concordat between Pope and Bonaparte.		Haydn: *The Seasons*.	American Robert Fulton conceives first idea of a submarine. Jacquard's mechanical loom. Manufacture of beet sugar.
802	Bonaparte, Consul for life.	Death of Romney.	Chateaubriand: *Spirit of Christianity*. Birth of Victor Hugo.	First steam-driven locomotive built by Trevithick.
803			Maine de Biran elaborates his philosophy. Birth of Berlioz.	Robert Fulton's steamship.
804	Napoleon's coronation.		Schiller: *William Tell*. Death of Kant.	
805	Napoleon, King of Italy.	Death of Greuze.	Chateaubriand: *René*. Death of Schiller. Beethoven: *Fidelio*.	
806	End of Holy Empire.	Death of Fragonard. Ingres: *La Belle Zélie*.	Hegel: *Phenomenology of the Mind*.	
808		Goya: *3 May 1808*. Death of Hubert Robert. Beginning of construction of the Paris Bourse.	Goethe: *Faust*. Beethoven: *Pastoral Symphony*.	
809			Death of Haydn.	
810		1810-18: Goya: *Disasters of War*.		First food canning.
811	Birth of the King of Rome.			Mechanical printing press by the German König.

Museums

Artist	City	Museum	Title	Date	Material	Dimensions
Boucher, François (1703-70)	Leningrad	Hermitage	*The Bridge*		Canvas	1'11" × 2'5"
	Leningrad	Hermitage	*Head of a Woman*		Canvas	1'2" × 11"
	Munich	Pinakothek	*Recumbent Girl*	1752	Canvas	1'11" × 2'5"
	Paris	Louvre	*The Mill*		Canvas	2'2" × 2'9"
	Paris	Louvre	*The Odalisk*	c. 1743	Canvas	1'9" × 2'1"
	Paris	Louvre	*Diana leaving the Bath*	1742	Canvas	1'10" × 2'5"
	Paris	Louvre	*The Painter in his Studio*		Wood	11" × 9"
	Rome	National Museum of Ancient Art	*Morning*		Canvas	2'2" × 2'8"
	Rome	National Museum of Ancient Art	*La Petite Jardinière*		Canvas	2'0" × 1'6"
	Rotterdam	Boymans-Van Beuningen Museum	*Chinoiserie*		Canvas	1'3" × 1'8"
Chardin, Jean-Baptiste-Simeon (1699-1779)	Berlin	Kaiser-Frederick Museum	*Lady sealing a Letter*	1733	Canvas	4'9" × 4'9"
	Berlin	Kaiser-Frederick Museum	*Young Man drawing*	1737	Canvas	2'8" × 2'1"
	Berlin	Kaiser-Frederick Museum	*La Pourvoyeuse*	1738	Canvas	1'6" × 1'3"
	Berlin	Kaiser-Frederick Museum	*La Pourvoyeuse*	1739	Canvas	1'6" × 1'3"
	Berlin	Kaiser-Frederick Museum	*La Ratisseuse*	c. 1739	Canvas	1'4" × 1'1"
	Florence	Museum Uffizi	*La Petite Fille au Volant*		Canvas	2'8" × 2'2"
	Glasgow	Hunter Museum	*Lady drinking Tea*	1736	Canvas	2'8" × 3'3"
	Glasgow	Hunter Museum	*Tavern Waiter*	c. 1738	Canvas	1'6" × 1'2"
	Glasgow	Hunter Museum	*The Cleaner*	c. 1738	Canvas	1'6" × 1'2"
	Munich	Picture Gallery	*Woman scraping Turnips*	c. 1739	Canvas	1'6" × 1'3"
	Paris	Louvre	*Jar of Olives*	1760	Canvas	2'4" × 3'3"
	Paris	Louvre	*Copper Fountain*	1733	Wood	11" × 9"
	Paris	Louvre	*Dessert*	1763	Canvas	1'7" × 1'10"
	Paris	Louvre	Self-portrait with green shade	1771	Pastel	1'6" × 1'3"
	Paris	Louvre	*Portrait of Madame Chardin*	1775	Pastel	1'6" × 1'3"

tist	City	Museum	Title	Date	Material	Dimensions
	Paris	Louvre	*Young Man with Violin*		Canvas	2′2″ × 2′5″
	Paris	Louvre	*Child with Top*		Canvas	2′2″ × 2′5″
	Paris	Louvre	*House of Cards*		Canvas	2′6″ × 2′3″
	Paris	Louvre	*The Industrious Mother*		Canvas	1′7″ × 1′3″
	Paris	Louvre	*Grace*		Canvas	1′7″ × 1′3″
	Paris	Louvre	*La Pourvoyeuse*	1739	Canvas	1′6″ × 1′3″
	Paris	Louvre	*Le Singe Antiquaire*	Before 1740	Canvas	2′7″ × 2′1″
	Paris	Louvre	*Le Singe Peintre*	Before 1740	Canvas	2′4″ × 2′0″
	Paris	Louvre	*Attributes of Art*	1765	Canvas	3′0″ × 4′9″
	Paris	Louvre	*Attributes of Music*	1765	Canvas	2′11″ × 4′8″
	Paris	Louvre	*La Raie*	1728	Canvas	3′9″ × 4′7″
	Paris	Louvre	*The Buffet*	1728	Canvas	6′3″ × 4′2″
	Paris	Louvre	*Le Souffleur*	1734	Canvas	4′11″ × 3′3″
	Stockholm	National	*The Fountain*	1733	Wood	1′3″ × 1′5″
	Stockholm	National	*The Tapestry Worker*		Canvas	7″ × 6″
	Stockholm	National	*Le Dessinateur*		Canvas	7″ × 7″
	Stockholm	National	*La Blanchisseuse*	1737	Canvas	1′2″ × 1′5″
	Stockholm	National	*The Industrious Mother*	Before 1741	Canvas	1′7″ × 1′3″
	Stockholm	National	*Grace*	Before 1741	Canvas	1′7″ × 1′3″
	Stockholm	National	*Le Négligé*	Before 1741	Canvas	1′7″ × 1′3″
	Stockholm	National	*Les Amusements de la Vie privée*	Before 1746	Canvas	1′5″ × 1′2″
	Stockholm	National	*L'Econome*	1747	Canvas	1′5″ × 1′2″
agonard, n-Honoré 32-1806)	Amiens	Picardy Museum	*Les Lavandières*	1761-5	Canvas	1′7″ × 2′2″
	Amiens	Picardy Museum	*Autumn Landscape*	1765-72	Canvas	8″ × 1′1″
	Barcelona	Museum of Modern Art	*Abbé St Non in Spanish Dress*	1748-52	Round wood	Diam. 2′6″
	Besançon	Museum	*Venus Triumphant*	1754-5	Canvas	13′1″ × 9′10″

Artist	City	Museum	Title	Date	Material	Dimensions
	Grasse	Cathedral	*Jesus washing the Feet of his Apostles*			
	Leningrad	Hermitage	*The Furtive Kiss*	*c.* 1790	Canvas	1′6″ × 1′10″
	Leningrad	Hermitage	*The Peasant Family*	1745	Canvas	1′8″ × 2′0″
	New York	Metropolitan Museum	*The Lost Stakes*	1761-5	Canvas	1′7″ × 2′0″
	New York	Metropolitan Museum	*The Waterfall*	1773-6	Canvas	11″ × 9″
	New York	Metropolitan Museum	*The Thicket*	1773-6	Canvas	11″ × 9″
	New York	Metropolitan Museum	*Family Scene in an Italian House*	1773-6	Canvas	1′7″ × 1′11″
	New York	Metropolitan Museum	*Billet Doux*	1773-6	Canvas	2′9″ × 2′2″
	New York	Metropolitan Museum	*Profile of a Young Girl*	1773-6	Canvas	2′3″ × 1′10″
	New York	Metropolitan Museum	*The Two Sisters*	1777-9	Canvas	2′4″ × 1′9″
	Orleans	Museum of Painting	*Invocation to Love*	1780-8	Canvas	1′6″ × 1′2″
	Paris	Ecole des Beaux Arts	*Jereboam sacrificing to the Idols*	1752	Canvas	3′9″ × 4′9″
	Paris	Cognac-Jay Museum	*Portrait of Madame Bergeret de Norinval*	1780-8	Oval canvas	2′0″ × 1′8″
	Paris	Cognac-Jay Museum	*Portrait of Young Man with Collar*	1789-1806	Oval canvas	1′6″ × 1′3″
	Paris	Jacquemart-André Museum	*The New Model*	1765-72	Oval canvas	1′8″ × 2′0″
	Paris	Louvre	*The Hay Waggon*	1761-5	Canvas	2′5″ × 3′2″
	Paris	Louvre	*The Warrior's Dream of Love*	1761-5	Canvas	2′0″ × 1′8″
	Paris	Louvre	*High Priest Coresus sacrificing Himself to save Callirhoe*	1765	Canvas	10′2″ × 13′3″
	Paris	Louvre	*The Explosion*	1761-5	Canvas	1′3″ × 1′5″
	Paris	Louvre	*Little Cascades at Tivoli*	1761-5	Canvas	2′5″ × 2′0″
	Paris	Louvre	*Young Woman holding a Child*	1761-5	Oval canvas	1′7″ × 1′1″

Artist	City	Museum	Title	Date	Material	Dimensions
	Paris	Louvre	*Les Curieuses*		Wood	6″ × 5″
	Paris	Louvre	*Music*	1769	Canvas	2′8″ × 2′2″
	Paris	Louvre	*La Chemise enlevée*	1765-72	Canvas	1′2″ × 1′5″
	Paris	Louvre	*The Bathers*	1765-72	Canvas	2′2″ × 2′8″
	Paris	Louvre	*Inspiration*	1765-72	Canvas	2′7″ × 2′2″
	Paris	Louvre	*The Music Lesson*	1765-72	Canvas	3′5″ × 3′11″
	Paris	Louvre	*Portrait of the Abbé St Non*	1765-72	Canvas	2′7″ × 2′2″
	Paris	Louvre	*The Song*	1769	Canvas	2′7″ × 2′2″
	Paris	Louvre	*Blind-man's Buff*	1773-6	Canvas	1′2″ × 1′6″
	Paris	Louvre	*Love Call*	1780-8	Wood	9″ × 1′1″
	Paris	Louvre	*Bacchant Asleep*		Canvas	1′6″ × 1′10″
	Rouen	Museum	*Dream of Plutarch*	1748-52	Canvas	9″ × 1′0″
	Rouen	Museum	*Mountain Landscape with Thatched Cottage*	1761-5	Oval canvas	1′0″ × 10″
	Rouen	Museum	*The Washerwomen*	1773-6	Canvas	1′9″ × 2′3″
	Troyes	Fine Arts Museum	*Repose of the Holy Family*	1748-52	Canvas	6′2″ × 4′1″
	Washington	National Gallery	*Love's Folly*	1765-72	Oval canvas	1′9″ × 1′6″
	Washington	National Gallery	*Love on Guard*	1765-72	Oval canvas	1′9″ × 1′6″
	Washington	National Gallery	*Le Cheval fondu*	1773-6	Canvas	3′10″ × 2′11″
	Washington	National Gallery	*La Main chaude*	1773-6	Canvas	3′9″ × 3′0″
	Washington	National Gallery	*The Swing*	1773-6	Canvas	7′0″ × 6′1″
	Washington	National Gallery	*Blind-man's Buff*	1773-6	Canvas	7′0″ × 6′6″
	Washington	National Gallery	*Visit to the Nurse*	1777-9	Canvas	2′4″ × 2′11″
Gainsborough, Thomas (1727-88)	Bologna	Liceo Musicale	*J.-C. Bach*	1776	Canvas	11″ × 9″
	Dublin	Trinity College	*Anne, Duchess of Cumberland*	1766	Canvas	1′0″ × 10″
	London	National Gallery	*Wooded Landscape with House*	1774-88	Canvas	7″ × 8″
	London	National Gallery	*Two Dogs*	1777	Canvas	1′1″ × 1′5″

Artist	City	Museum	Title	Date	Material	Dimensions
	London	National Gallery	*An Old Horse*		Canvas	9″ × 10″
	London	National Gallery	*The Painter's Daughters chasing Butterflies*	1755-6	Canvas	3′6″ × 3′5″
	London	National Portrait Gallery	*Lord Amherst*		Canvas	1′0″ × 10″
	London	National Portrait Gallery	*John, Duke of Bedford*	1768	Canvas	1′0″ × 10″
	London	National Portrait Gallery	*George Colman*	1785	Canvas	11″ × 1′1″
	London	Tate Gallery	*The Baillie Family*	1784	Canvas	3′3″ × 2′11″
	London	Tate Gallery	*Sir William Blackstone*	1774	Canvas	1′0″ × 10″
	London	Tate Gallery	*The Market Cart*	1786-7	Canvas	2′5″ × 2′0″
	London	Tate Gallery	*Child leading Cattle*	1774-88	Canvas	9″ × 1′0″
	London	Tate Gallery	*Gipsies around a Fire*	1770	Canvas	1′7″ × 1′10″
	London	Tate Gallery	*A Servant* (Unfinished)	1782-6	Canvas	3′3″ × 1′11″
	London	Tate Gallery	*Nymph at the Bath*		Canvas	2′5″ × 2′0″
	Melbourne	National Gallery	*Mouth of the Thames*	1783	Canvas	2′0″ × 2′6″
	Melbourne	National Gallery	*An Officer*	1770	Canvas	2′11″ × 1′11″
	New York	Metropolitan Museum	*Charles Rousseau Burney*	1770	Canvas	1′0″ × 10″
	New York	Metropolitan Museum	*Nathaniel Burrough*		Canvas	1′0″ × 10″
	New York	Metropolitan Museum	*Queen Charlotte*	1782	Canvas	9″ × 7″
	New York	Metropolitan Museum	*Upland Hamlet with Figures and Stream*	1783	Canvas	1′7″ × 1′11″
	New York	Metropolitan Museum	*Cottage Children*	1787	Canvas	1′11″ × 1′6″
	Paris	Louvre	*Lady Gertrude Alston*	1760	Canvas	2′11″ × 2′2″
	Paris	Louvre	Man and Woman in a Landscape	1746	Canvas	1′10″ × 10″
	Paris	Louvre	*Conversation in a Park*		Canvas	2′5″ × 2′3″
Greuze, Jean-Baptiste (1725-1805)	Leningrad	Hermitage	*Paralytic tended by his Children*	1767	Canvas	3′1″ × 3′10″
	Leningrad	Hermitage	*Young Woman smiling*		Canvas	1′4″ × 1′1″

Artist	City	Museum	Title	Date	Material	Dimensions
	Leningrad	Hermitage	*Portrait of a Boy*		Canvas	2′2″ × 1′9″
	Leningrad	Hermitage	*Young Man with Tricorn*		Canvas	2′0″ × 1′8″
	Metz	Museum	*Bacchant*		Canvas	1′10″ × 1′3″
	Metz	Museum	*Young Boy*		Canvas	1′5″ × 1′3″
	Metz	Museum	*Count d'Angivillers*	1763	Canvas	2′2″ × 1′8″
	Montpellier	Museum	*Young Girl with Basket*		Oval canvas	1′6″ × 1′3″
	Montpellier	Museum	*The Little Mathematician*		Canvas	1′6″ × 1′3″
	Montpellier	Museum	*Young Girl*		Wood	1′3″ × 1′0″
	Montpellier	Museum	*Young Girl at Prayer*		Canvas	1′6″ × 1′2″
	Montpellier	Museum	*Head of a Child*		Canvas	1′3″ × 1′0″
	Montpellier	Museum	*Paralytic's Head*		Canvas	2′1″ × 1′9″
	Paris	Louvre	*The Emperor Severus reproaching Caracalla*	1769	Canvas	4′1″ × 5′3″
	Paris	Louvre	*Danaë*		Canvas (sketch)	1′1″ × 1′4″
	Paris	Louvre	*L'Accordée de Village*	1761	Canvas	2′11″ × 3′10″
	Paris	Louvre	*The Ungrateful Son*	1767	Canvas	4′3″ × 5′4″
	Paris	Louvre	*The Son Punished*	1767	Canvas	4′11″ × 5′4″
	Paris	Louvre	*The Broken Pitcher*		Oval canvas	3′7″ × 2′9″
	Paris	Louvre	*La Laitière*		Canvas	3′6″ × 3′1″
	Paris	Louvre	*Young Girl*		Canvas	1′4″ × 1′1″
	Paris	Louvre	*The Dead Bird*	1800	Canvas	2′6″ × 1′9″
	Paris	Louvre	*Dr Duval*		Canvas	1′6″ × 1′3″
	Paris	Louvre	*Fabre d'Eglantine*		Canvas	2′0″ × 1′7″
	Paris	Louvre	*Armand Gensonné*		Canvas	1′10″ × 1′6″
	Paris	Louvre	*J.-B. Greuze*	1763	Canvas	2′5″ × 2′0″
	Paris	Louvre	*Etienne Jeaurat*	1769	Canvas	2′8″ × 2′2″
	Paris	Louvre	*Jupiter and Aegina*		Canvas	1′1″ × 1′4″
	Tournus	Museum	*Young Girl*		Canvas	1′10″ × 1′4″
	Tournus	Museum	*J.-B. Greuze*		Canvas	1′8″ × 1′5″

Artist	City	Museum	Title	Date	Material	Dimensions
	Tournus	Museum	*Canon Piot*		Canvas	2′5″ × 1′9″
	Tournus	Church of the Madeleine	*St Francis of Assisi*		Canvas	6′7″ × 3′2″
	Versailles	National Museum	*Napoleon Bonaparte*	1789	Canvas	1′10″ × 1′6″
Guardi, Francesco (1712-93)	Berlin	Kaiser-Frederick Museum	*Departure of Balloons over the Lagoon*	1784	Canvas	2′2″ × 1′8″
	Berlin	Kaiser-Frederick Museum	*Roman Ruins*		Canvas	1′9″ × 2′4″
	Copenhagen	Museum of Art	*Return of the " Bucentaur "*		Canvas	3′3″ × 4′6″
	London	National Gallery	*Pesaro Palace on the Grand Canal*		Canvas	3′1″ × 4′4″
	London	National Gallery	*San Marco Square*		Canvas	2′4″ × 3′11″
	London	National Gallery	*Tower and Lagoon at Mestre*		Canvas	8″ × 1′4″
	London	National Gallery	*Venice and the Doges' Palace*		Canvas	1′10″ × 2′5″
	London	Victoria and Albert Museum	*Ruins with a Church*		Canvas	3′1″ × 2′4″
	Milan	Poldi-Pezzoli Museum	*The Grey Lagoon*		Canvas	9″ × 1′3″
	Munich	Pinakothek	*Gala Concert in Venice*	1782	Canvas	2′3″ × 3′0″
	New York	Metropolitan Museum	*The Grand Canal*		Canvas	1′4″ × 2′4″
	New York	Metropolitan Museum	*Landscape with Ruins*		Canvas	5′1″ × 8′11″
	Paris	Louvre	*The Doge on the " Bucentaur " on Ascension Day*	1763	Canvas	2′2″ × 3′3″
	Rome	National Museum of Ancient Art	*Giudecca Canal*		Canvas	1′8″ × 2′7″
	Toulouse	Museum	*Departure of " Bucentaur "*		Canvas	2′2″ × 3′3″
	Venice	Museum of the Academy	*Island of San Giorgio*		Canvas	2′4″ × 3′2″
	Venice	Ca'Rezzonico	*Visiting Room in the Monastery of San Zaccaria*		Canvas	3′6″ × 6′8″
	Venice	Ca'Rezzonico	*Il Ridotto* (The Casino)		Canvas	3′6″ × 6′8″
	Venice	Ca'Rezzonico	*The Lagoon Frozen*	*c.* 1789	Canvas	3′2″ × 4′5″
	Venice	Ca'd'Oro	*Market before the Royal Palace*		Canvas	1′6″ × 2′4″
	Venice	Labia Palace	*Aurora*		Fresco	13′9″ × 6′9″

rtist	City	Museum	Title	Date	Material	Dimensions
	Vienna	Albertina	*Old Tower in San Marco Square*		Canvas	2′1″ × 2′11″
	Vienna	Albertina	*Grand Canal with Santa Lucia and the Scala Church*		Canvas	2′1″ × 2′11″
	Vienna	Albertina	*San Giorgio Maggiore*		Canvas	2′4″ × 2′8″
	Vienna	Albertina	*Santa Maria della Salute*		Canvas	2′4″ × 2′8″
	Vienna	Albertina	*Piazzetta and Doges' Palace*		Two canvases	2′4″ × 2′8″ 2′5″ × 2′8″
	Vienna	Kunsthistorisches Museum	*Entrance to Venice Arsenal*		Canvas	11″ × 1′6″
	Vienna	Kunsthistorisches Museum	*Dnieper*		Canvas	3′11″ × 5′8″
	Vienna	Kunsthistorisches Museum	*San Marco Square*		Canvas	1′0″ × 1′6″
ogarth, William 697-1764)	Geneva	Museum	*Portrait of Viscountess de la Valette*		Canvas	2′6″ × 2′1″
	London	National Gallery	Self-portrait	1745	Canvas	2′11″ × 2′3″
	London	National Gallery	*Portrait of the Actress Lavinia Fenton*	1740	Oval canvas	2′5″ × 1′11″
	London	National Gallery	*Ann Hogarth*	1740	Canvas	
	London	National Gallery	*James Quin*	1740	Canvas	2′5″ × 2′0″
	London	National Gallery	*Marriage à la Mode* (series of six)	1740	Canvas	1′2″ × 1′5″
	London	National Gallery	Self-portrait of the Painter with his Dog	1745	Canvas	2′11″ × 2′3″
	London	National Gallery	*The Gate of Calais*	1749	Canvas	2′7″ × 3′1″
	London	National Gallery	Portrait of Servants		Canvas	2′0″ × 2′6″
	London	National Gallery	*The Shrimp Girl*		Canvas	2′1″ × 1′8″
	London	National Gallery	*Breakfast*		Canvas	1′4″ × 3′0″
	London	National Portrait Gallery	*Hogarth painting the Muse of Drama*	1758	Canvas	3′4″ × 1′3″
	London	National Portrait Gallery	*Bishop Benjamin Hoadley*	1743	Canvas	4′10″ × 3′3″
	London	Sir John Soane's Museum	*Rake's Progress* (eight plates)	1732-3	Canvas	1′0″ × 1′3″
	London	Sir John Soane's Museum	*The Election* (four plates)	1755	Canvas	1′4″ × 1′9″

Artist	City	Museum	Title	Date	Material	Dimensions
	London	South London Art Gallery	*The Wanstead Assembly*	1728	Canvas	2′3″ × 2′11″
	London	Tate Gallery	*Scene from the Beggars' Opera*	1731	Canvas	1′10″ × 2′5″
	London	Tate Gallery	*The Graham Children*	1742	Canvas	5′3″ × 5′11″
Lancret, Nicolas (1690-1743)	Chantilly	Condé Museum	*The Ham Luncheon*	1735	Canvas	5′11″ × 4′0″
	Leningrad	Hermitage	*La Camargo*	c. 1730	Canvas	1′6″ × 1′5″
	Leningrad	Hermitage	*The Kitchen*		Canvas	1′4″ × 1′1″
	Paris	Louvre	*The Italian Theatre*		Wood	10″ × 9″
	Paris	Louvre	*Innocence*		Canvas	2′11″ × 2′11″
	Paris	Louvre	*The Music Lesson*		Canvas	2′11″ × 2′11″
	Rome	National Museum of Ancient Art	*Rendezvous*		Canvas	11″ × 8″
	Rome	National Museum of Ancient Art	*Family Portrait*		Wood	1′4″ × 1′1″
	Rome	National Museum of Ancient Art	*The Fire*		Canvas	1′4″ × 1′1″
	Rotterdam	Boymans-Van Beuningen Museum	*Pastoral Dance*		Canvas	1′9″ × 2′3″
Largillière, Nicolas de (1656-1746)	Algiers	National Museum	*Study of Hands*		Canvas	2′2″ × 1′8″
	Grenoble	Museum	*Jean Pupil de Craponne*	1708	Canvas	2′9″ × 2′3″
	Leningrad	Hermitage	*Commemoration of the Entertainment given for Louis XIV by the Paris Magistrates in 1687*	1687	Canvas	2′3″ × 6′7″
	Lille	Museum	*Jean Forest*	c. 1704	Canvas	4′2″ × 2′10″
	Paris	Louvre	Portrait of the Artist with his Wife		Canvas	4′10″ × 9′11″
	Paris	Louvre	*Portrait of Le Brun*	1686	Canvas	7′7″ × 6′2″
	Paris	Louvre	Portrait presumed to be Fermier-Général de Laage		Canvas	4′8″ × 3′6″
	Rotterdam	Boymans-Van Beuningen Museum	*Portrait of Jeanne de Robais*		Canvas	2′8″ × 2′2″
	Versailles	National Museum	Self-portrait	1711	Canvas	2′7″ × 2′2″

rtist	City	Museum	Title	Date	Material	Dimensions
	Vienna	Kunsthistorisches Museum	*Boucher d'Orsay, Provost of Paris Merchants*		Canvas	4'6" × 3'6"
a Tour, Maurice uentin de 704-88)	Geneva	Museum	*Isabelle Van Zuylen*	1766		
	Geneva	Museum	*The Negro*	1741	Pastel	2'2" × 1'6"
	Paris	Louvre	*Portrait of d'Alembert*	1753	Pastel	1'10" × 1'6"
	Paris	Louvre	*Mademoiselle Dangeville*		Pastel	1'0" × 1'9"
	Paris	Louvre	*Louis XIV*	1748	Pastel	1'1" × 9"
	Paris	Louvre	*Louis, Dauphin of France*	1748	Pastel	2'1" × 1'9"
	Paris	Louvre	*Marie-Josephe de Saxe*	1761	Pastel	1'1" × 9"
	Paris	Louvre	*Madame de Pompadour*	1752-5	Pastel	5'9" × 4'2"
	Paris	Louvre	*Jean Restout*	1746	Pastel	1'4" × 1'0"
	Paris	Louvre	*Maréchal de Saxe*	1747	Pastel	2'11" × 2'11"
	Paris	Louvre	*Chardin*	1760	Pastel	1'11" × 1'7"
	Paris	Louvre	Self-portrait		Pastel	1'10" × 1'6"
	Saint-Quentin	Museum	*Portrait of d'Alembert*	1753	Pastel	1'1" × 8"
	Saint-Quentin	Museum	*Marquis d'Argenson*	1753	Pastel	2'1" × 1'8"
	Saint-Quentin	Museum	*Madame Boëte de Saint-Léger*		Pastel	1'1" × 9"
	Saint-Quentin	Museum	*La Camargo*		Preparatory sketch	1'1" × 9"
	Saint-Quentin	Museum	*Mademoiselle de Lagrange*		Pastel	1'3" × 1'0"
	Saint-Quentin	Museum	*Ch. Jacques Collin*		Pastel	1'1" × 9"
	Saint-Quentin	Museum	*Marquise de Courcy*	1740	Preparatory sketch	1'0" × 9"
	Saint-Quentin	Museum	*Crebillon*	1761	Preparatory sketch	1'0" × 9"
	Saint-Quentin	Museum	*Charles Pinot Duclos*	1748	Pastel	1'5" × 1'2"
	Saint-Quentin	Museum	*Don Peuche*	1739	Pastel	2'0" × 1'8"
	Saint-Quentin	Museum	*Father Emmanuel*	1757	Pastel	1'4" × 1'3"
	Saint-Quentin	Museum	*Madame Favart*		Preparatory sketch	1'1" × 9"

Artist	City	Museum	Title	Date	Material	Dimensions
	Saint-Quentin	Museum	*Marie Fel*	1757	Pastel	1'1" × 9"
	Saint-Quentin	Museum	*Duverger de Fourbonnet*		Pastel	1'4" × 1'0"
	Saint-Quentin	Museum	*Garnier d'Isle*		Pastel	1'5" × 1'2"
	Saint-Quentin	Museum	*Jean de Julienne*		Pastel	1'1" × 9"
	Saint-Quentin	Museum	*Le Riche de La Pouplinière*	1742	Pastel	1'11" × 1'7"
	Saint-Quentin	Museum	*Antoine-Gaspard Grimod de La Reynière*	1751	Pastel	2'7" × 2'5"
	Saint-Quentin	Museum	*Marie-Josèphe of Saxony and the Duke of Burgundy*	1761	Pastel	5'2" × 3'9"
	Saint-Quentin	Museum	*Jean-Joseph Cassena de Mondonville*	1747	Pastel	2'2" × 1'10"
	Saint-Quentin	Museum	*Jean Mounet*	1756	Pastel	1'11" × 1'7"
	Saint-Quentin	Museum	*Jean Paris de Monmartel*	1746	Pastel	2'4" × 1'10"
	Saint-Quentin	Museum	*Charles Parrocel*	1743	Pastel	1'10" × 1'5"
	Saint-Quentin	Museum	*Marquise de Pompadour*	1753	Preparatory sketch	1'1" × 9"
	Saint-Quentin	Museum	*Mademoiselle Puvigny*		Preparatory sketch	1'1" × 9"
	Saint-Quentin	Museum	*Jean-Jacques Rousseau*	1753	Pastel	1'6" × 1'1"
	Saint-Quentin	Museum	*Count of Saxony*	1747	Pastel	1'7" × 1'0"
	Saint-Quentin	Museum	*Marie-Christine of Saxony*	1763	Preparatory sketch	1'1" × 9"
	Saint-Quentin	Museum	*Prince Clement-Wenceslas of Saxony*	1763	Pastel	2'0" × 9"
	Saint-Quentin	Museum	*Prince Xavier of Saxony*	1761	Preparatory sketch	2'1" × 1'9"
	Saint-Quentin	Museum	*Louis de Sylvestre*	1753	Pastel	2'0" × 1'8"
	Saint-Quentin	Museum	*Baroness de Tuyll*		Study	2'3" × 1'9"
Nattier, Jean-Marc (1685-1766)	Copenhagen	Academy of Fine Arts	*Portrait of Louis Tocqué*	c. 1739	Canvas	2'8" × 2'1"
	Florence	Uffizi	*Madame Henriette, as Flora*	1745	Canvas	3'1" × 4'2"
	Moscow	Pushkin Museum	*Battle of Poltava*	1717	Canvas	2'11" × 3'8"
	Paris	Louvre	*Portrait of a Woman*	1741	Canvas	

Artist	City	Museum	Title	Date	Material	Dimensions
Oudry, Jean-Baptiste (1686-1755)	Leningrad	Hermitage	*Still-life*	*c*. 1740	Canvas	3'3" × 2'5"
	Madrid	Prado	*Lady Maria Josefa Drumond, Countess of Castelblanco*		Canvas	4'6" × 3'9"
	Paris	Louvre	*Still-life with Violin*		Canvas	2'10" × 3'4"
Reynolds, Sir Joshua (1723-92)	London	National Gallery	*Dr Samuel Johnson*	1772	Canvas	2'5" × 1'9"
	London	National Gallery	*Lady Anne Lennox*	1759	Canvas	4'0" × 3'3"
	London	National Gallery	*Lord Heathfield*	1787	Canvas	4'8" × 3'8"
	London	National Gallery	*The Age of Innocence*	1788	Canvas	3'2" × 2'1"
	London	Royal Academy	Self-portrait	1773	Wood	4'1" × 3'4"
	Paris	Louvre	*Portrait of Master Hare*		Canvas	2'6" × 2'0"
	São Paulo	Museum	*The Children of Edward Holden Cruttenden*		Canvas	5'10" × 5'6"
	Selkirk (Scotland)	Bowhill	*Portraits of Elizabeth Duchess of Buccleuch and her Daughter Lady Mary Scott*	1772	Canvas	6'10" × 4'10"
Robert, Hubert (1733-1808)	Paris	Museum of Decorative Arts	*Le Génie du Tombeau*	1796	Canvas	1'8" × 1'3"
	Paris	Museum of Decorative Arts	*Banquet of the Five Hundred in the Museum Gallery*		Canvas	1'9" × 2'0"
	Paris	Ecole des Beaux Arts	*Port of the Ripetta in Rome*	1766	Canvas	3'11" × 4'9"
	Paris	Ecole des Beaux Arts	*Lavandières dans un Parc*		Canvas	1'11" × 1'6"
	Paris	Carnavalet Museum	*Demolishing the Bridge at Neuilly*	1775	Canvas	1'11" × 4'2"
	Paris	Carnavalet Museum	*View of the Fire at the Opera Theatre*	1781	Canvas	2'9" × 3'8"
	Paris	Carnavalet Museum	*Demolition of Houses on Notre-Dame Bridge in 1768*		Canvas	2'9" × 5'2"
	Paris	Carnavalet Museum	*Demolition of Houses on the Pont au Change and Tour de l'Horloge in 1768*		Canvas	2'10" × 5'2"
	Paris	Carnavalet Museum	*Demolition of the Bastille*	1789	Canvas	2'6" × 3'8"
	Paris	Carnavalet Museum	*Desecration of the Tombs of Kings at Saint-Denis*	1793	Canvas	1'9" × 2'1"
	Paris	Carnavalet Museum	*Prisoners in Saint-Lazare at Recreation*		Canvas	1'1" × 1'4"

Artist	City	Museum	Title	Date	Material	Dimensions
	Paris	Carnavalet Museum	*Interior of Saint-Lazare Prison*	1793	Canvas	1′4″ × 1′1″
	Paris	Carnavalet Museum	*Mausoleum of Jean-Jacques Rousseau*	1794	Canvas	2′2″ × 2′7″
	Paris	Carnavalet Museum	*Demolition of the Church of Saint-Jean en Grève*	1800	Canvas	2′0″ × 1′9″
	Paris	Louvre	*Ruins of a Temple*	1783	Canvas	4′9″ × 2′6″
	Paris	Louvre	*Temple of Diana at Nîmes*	1787	Canvas	7′11″ × 7′11″
	Paris	Louvre	*The Pont du Gard*	1787	Canvas	7′11″ × 7′11″
	Paris	Louvre	*Triumphal Arch at Saint-Rémy*	1787	Canvas	7′11″ × 7′11″
	Paris	Louvre	*The Maison Carrée, Arenas and Tour Magne at Nîmes*	1787	Canvas	7′11″ × 7′11″
	Paris	Louvre	*Cascatelles de Tivoli*		Canvas	2′5″ × 2′0″
	Paris	Louvre	*Inside a Park*		Canvas	4′8″ × 2′6″
	Paris	Louvre	*The Fountain*	1783	Canvas	5′6″ × 2′0″
	Paris	Louvre	*Wandering Singers*		Canvas	2′4″ × 1′10″
	Paris	Louvre	*Spiral Staircase*		Canvas	10″ × 1′1″
	Paris	Louvre	*Proposed Conversion of the Grande Galerie at the Louvre*	1796	Canvas	1′1″ × 1′5″
	Paris	Opera Museum	*Fire at the Opera* (Two paintings)		Wood	1′1″ × 9″
	Rome	National Museum of Ancient Art	*Monk preaching in the Ruins*		Wood	1′4″ × 1′1″
	Rome	National Museum of Ancient Art	*The Landing Stage*		Wood	1′3″ × 1′5″
	Rome	National Museum of Ancient Art	*The Monumental Fountain*		Canvas	1′4″ × 1′1″
	Rome	National Museum of Ancient Art	*The Maison Carrée at Nîmes*		Wood	1′1″ × 1′5″
Tiepolo, Giambattista (1692-1770)	Berlin	Kaiser-Frederick Museum	*Cathedral of Saint-Agatha*	1740-50	Canvas	6′0″ × 4′4″
	Berlin	Kaiser-Frederick Museum	*The Way up to Calvary*	1738	Canvas	1′8″ × 2′1″
	Berlin	Kaiser-Frederick Museum	*Rinaldo in the Garden of Armida*	1751-3	Canvas	1′3″ × 2′0″

Artist	City	Museum	Title	Date	Material	Dimensions
	Berlin	Kaiser-Frederick Museum	St Dominic institutes the Rosary	1737	Canvas	3'3" × 1'7"
	Berlin	Kaiser-Frederick Museum	Saint Roch	1730-5	Canvas	1'9" × 1'4"
	Berlin	Kaiser-Frederick Museum	Toilet of Venus		Canvas	3'7" × 4'8"
	Berlin	Kaiser-Frederick Museum	Twenty-two frescoes, including Death of Dido	1754	Frescoes	
	Chicago	Art Institute	Rinaldo and Armida surprised by Ubaldo and Guelfo	1751-3	Canvas	6'1" × 8'8"
	Chicago	Art Institute	Rinaldo bewitched by Armida	1751-3	Canvas	6'1" × 8'8"
	Chicago	Art Institute	Rinaldo abandoned by Armida	1751-3	Canvas	6'1" × 7'1"
	Chicago	Art Institute	Rinaldo and the Hermit	1751-3	Canvas	6'1" × 7'1"
	Chicago	Art Institute	Madonna with St Dominic and St Hyacinth	1730-5	Canvas	9'0" × 4'6"
	Chicago	Art Institute	St Jerome in the Desert	1722-5	Canvas	1'1" × 9"
	Leningrad	Hermitage	The Annunciation	1720	Canvas	1'6" × 1'3"
	Leningrad	Hermitage	Rape of the Sabines	1720-2	Canvas	9'5" × 19'3"
	Leningrad	Hermitage	Triumph of Scipio		Canvas	17'11" × 10'8"
	Leningrad	Hermitage	Volumnia and her Children before Coriolanus		Canvas	12'8" × 7'1"
	Leningrad	Hermitage	Fabius Maximus before the Senate of Carthage		Canvas	12'8" × 7'1"
	Leningrad	Hermitage	The Dictatorship offered to Cincinnatus		Canvas	12'8" × 7'1"
	Leningrad	Hermitage	Maecenas presents the Arts to Augustus	1743-4	Canvas	2'3" × 2'11"
	Leningrad	Hermitage	Alexander and Diogenes		Canvas	1'7" × 2'0"
	London	National Gallery	Marriage of Frederick Barbarossa	1751	Canvas	2'5" × 1'9"
	London	National Gallery	Two Bearded Orientals	1751-3	Canvas	5'2" × 1'9"
	London	National Gallery	Renaud	1751-3	Canvas	5'2" × 1'9"
	London	National Gallery	Two Turks	1751-3	Canvas	5'2" × 1'9"
	London	National Gallery	Man and Young Woman	1751-3	Canvas	5'2" × 1'9"
	London	National Gallery	Descent from the Cross	1750-60	Canvas	2'1" × 1'5"

Artist	City	Museum	Title	Date	Material	Dimensions
	London	National Gallery	*The Trojan Horse*		Canvas	1′3″ × 2′2″
	Madrid	Prado	*Olympus*		Canvas	2′10″ × 2′0″
	Madrid	Prado	*Translation of the Santa Casa of Loreto*		Canvas	4′0″ × 2′9″
	Madrid	Prado	*The Immaculate Conception*	1767-9	Canvas	9′2″ × 5′0″
	Madrid	Prado	*Angel Watching over the Eucharist*	1767-9	Canvas	6′1″ × 5′10″
	Madrid	Prado	*St Pascal Baylon*	1767-9	Canvas	5′0″ × 3′8″
	Madrid	Prado	*Triumph of Venus*	1762-70	Canvas	2′10″ × 2′0″
	Madrid	Prado	*St Francis of Assisi receiving the Stigmata*	1767-9	Canvas	9′1″ × 5′0″
	Madrid	Prado	*Abraham and the Angel*	1762-70	Canvas	6′6″ × 5′0″
	Milan	St Ambrose Church	*Presentation at the Temple*		Canvas	1′3″ × 1′8″
	Milan	St Ambrose Church	*Holy Bishop*		Canvas	1′5″ × 1′1″
	Milan	St Ambrose Church	Allegory with an Angel (two paintings)		Canvas	2′2″ × 1′9″
	Milan	St Ambrose Church	*The Bronze Serpent*		Canvas	3′10″ × 5′0″
	Milan	Poldi-Pezzoli Museum	*Joshua commanding the Sun*	1725-30	Canvas	11″ × 2′4″
	Milan	Poldi-Pezzoli Museum	*Madonna with Rosary*	1730-5	Canvas	5′10″ × 3′4″
	Milan	Poldi-Pezzoli Museum	*Death of St Jerome*	1732-3	Canvas	1′2″ × 1′6″
	Milan	Poldi-Pezzoli Museum	*Apotheosis of the Saints*	1734	Canvas	1′7″ × 11″
	Milan	Poldi-Pezzoli Museum	*Sts Gaetan, Antony and John the Baptist*	1740-50	Canvas	1′8″ × 11″
	New York	Metropolitan Museum	*Apotheosis of Francesco Barbaro*	1745-50	Canvas	8′3″ × 15′3″
	New York	Metropolitan Museum	*Miracle of Saint Theola*	1758-9	Canvas	2′7″ × 1′6″
	New York	Metropolitan Museum	*Neptune and Zephyr*	1762-70	Canvas	2′0″ × 2′0″
	New York	Metropolitan Museum	*Courage and Wisdom*		Canvas	1′9″ × 1′4″

tist	City	Museum	Title	Date	Material	Dimensions
	New York	Metropolitan Museum	*Esther and Ahasuerus*		Canvas	1′6″ × 4′3″
	Paris	Louvre	*Apollo and Daphne*	1740	Canvas	3′2″ × 2′7″
	Paris	Louvre	*The Last Supper*	1745-50	Canvas	2′7″ × 2′11″
	Paris	Louvre	*The Charlatan*		Canvas	2′7″ × 3′7″
	Paris	Louvre	*The Minuet*		Canvas	2′7″ × 3′7″
	Paris	Louvre	*Meekness and Humility*		Canvas	4′0″ × 2′10″
	Paris	Jacquemart-André Museum	*Arrival of the Emperor Henry III*		Canvas	13′2″ × 23′4″
	Paris	Jacquemart-André Museum	*Spectators on the Balcony*		Canvas	9′10″ × 3′8″
	Paris	Jacquemart-André Museum	*Fame announces the Arrival of the Emperor*		Canvas	32′10″ × 13′1″
	Paris	Jacquemart-André Museum	*Apotheosis of a Hero*	1730-40	Frescoes moved on to canvas	
	Paris	Jacquemart-André Museum	*Peace and Justice*	1735-40	Canvas	7′11″ × 6′7″
	Venice	Academy Museum	*Rape of Europa*	1720-2	Canvas	3′3″ × 4′5″
	Venice	Academy Museum	*Diana and Actaeon*	1720-2	Canvas	3′3″ × 4′5″
	Venice	Academy Museum	*Diana and Calypso*	1720-2	Canvas	3′3″ × 4′5″
	Venice	Academy Museum	*Apollo and Marsyas*	1720-2	Canvas	3′3″ × 4′5″
	Venice	Academy Museum	*Jesus healing the Paralytic*	1718-20	Canvas	2′1″ × 1′6″
	Venice	Academy Museum	*The Holy Family with St Gaetan*	1735-40	Canvas	4′3″ × 2′5″
	Venice	Academy Museum	*The Miracle of Loreto*	1743	Oval canvas	4′1″ × 2′9″
	Venice	Academy Museum	*Antia and Abrocome at the Feast of Diana*		Canvas	1′9″ × 2′4″
	Venice	Pinacoteca	*Portrait of Procurator Giovanni Querini*	c. 1750	Canvas	5′2″ × 7′7″
	Venice	Ca'Rezzonico	*Pierrots at Rest*		Canvas	6′6″ × 4′11″

Artist	City	Museum	Title	Date	Material	Dimensions
	Venice	Ca'Rezzonico	*In the Circus Camp*		Canvas	6′5″ × 5′3″
	Venice	Ca'Rezzonico	*Pierrots in Love*		Canvas	6′6″ × 4′11″
Vernet, Joseph (1714-89)	Moscow	Pushkin Museum	*La Vigne Pamphili*	1749	Canvas	2′6″ × 3′4″
	Paris	Louvre	*View of the Bridge and Sant'Angelo*	1745	Canvas	1′4″ × 2′6″
	Paris	Louvre	*View of the Remains of the Palatine Bridge, called "Ponte Rotto" in Rome*		Canvas	1′4″ × 2′6″
	Paris	Marine Museum	Fifteen views of French Ports	1753-62	Canvases	
Watteau, Antoine (1684-1721)	Angers	Museum	*Rural Concert*	1716	Canvas	2′2″ × 1′8″
	Berlin	Kaiser-Frederick Museum	*Love in French Comedy*	1718-20	Canvas	1′3″ × 1′7″
	Berlin	Kaiser-Frederick Museum	*Love in Italian Comedy*	1718-20	Canvas	1′3″ × 1′7″
	Berlin	Kaiser-Frederick Museum	*Assembly in a Park*	*c.* 1717	Canvas	3′8″ × 5′4″
	Berlin	Kaiser-Frederick Museum	*L'Enseigne de Gersaint*	1720	Canvas	6′0″ × 10′1″
	Chantilly	Condé Museum	*Pastoral Pleasure*	1712	Wood	1′0″ × 1′5″
	Chantilly	Condé Museum	*Le Donneur de Sérénades*	1712	Canvas	9″ × 7″
	Chantilly	Condé Museum	*The Anxious Lover*		Wood	9″ × 7″
	Dresden	Museum	*The Feast of Love*	1717-18	Canvas	1′9″ × 2′6″
	Edinburgh	National Gallery	*The Sparrow's Nester*	1715	Wood	3′3″ × 2′7″
	Edinburgh	National Gallery	*Venetian Festivals*	1719	Canvas	1′10″ × 1′6″
	Helsinki	Museum	*The Swing*	1712	Canvas	2′9″ × 2′5″
	Leningrad	Hermitage	*Le Camp volant*	1710	Canvas	1′1″ × 1′5″
	Leningrad	Hermitage	*The Halt*	1712-15	Canvas	9″ × 1′1″
	Leningrad	Hermitage	*Landscape with Waterfall*	1714-15	Canvas	2′4″ × 3′6″
	Leningrad	Hermitage	*The Embarrassing Proposal*	1716	Canvas	2′2″ × 2′9″
	Leningrad	Hermitage	*Return from the Ball*	1712-15	Wood	8″ × 10″
	Leningrad	Hermitage	*Rest during the Flight in Egypt*	1717-19	Canvas	4′3″ × 3′2″
	London	Dulwich College	*Pleasures of the Ball*	1719	Canvas	1′8″ × 2′0″
	London	National Gallery	*The Gamut of Love*	1716	Canvas	1′8″ × 1′11″

tist	City	Museum	Title	Date	Material	Dimensions
	Madrid	National Palace	*The Shy Lover*	1716	Canvas	1′4″ × 1′1″
	Madrid	National Palace	*The Singing Lesson*	1716	Canvas	1′4″ × 1′1″
	Madrid	Prado	*The Marriage Contract*		Canvas	1′7″ × 1′10″
	New York	Metropolitan Museum	*Mezzetin*	1719	Canvas	1′10″ × 1′5″
	New York	Metropolitan Museum	*French Players*	1720	Canvas	1′10″ × 2′5″
	Orleans	Museum	*Le Singe Sculpteur*	1712	Canvas	8″ × 9″
	Paris	Louvre	*L'Indifférent*		Wood	10″ × 8″
	Paris	Louvre	*La Finette*		Wood	10″ × 8″
	Paris	Louvre	*Gilles*	1719	Canvas	6′0″ × 4′11″
	Paris	Louvre	*Jupiter and Antiope*	1716	Canvas	2′4″ × 3′7″
	Paris	Louvre	*The Faux Pas*	1717-18	Canvas	1′8″ × 1′4″
	Paris	Louvre	*Assembly in a Park*	1717-18	Wood	1′1″ × 1′6″
	Paris	Louvre	*Embarkation for the Island of Cythera*	1718	Canvas	4′2″ × 6′4″
	Paris	Louvre	*The Judgement of Paris*	1720	Wood	1′7″ × 1′0″
	Potsdam	New Palace	*The Shepherds*		Canvas	1′10″ × 2′8″
	Potsdam	New Palace	*The Dance*	1720	Canvas	3′2″ × 3′7″
	Potsdam	New Palace	*Rustic Love*	1718	Canvas	1′10″ × 2′8″
	Potsdam	Sans Souci	*The Concert*	1717	Canvas	2′2″ × 3′0″
	Potsdam	Castle	*Italian Recreation*		Canvas	2′6″ × 3′1″
	Valenciennes	Museum	*Portrait of Antoine Pater*	1716	Canvas	2′7″ × 2′0″
	Washington	National Gallery	*Italian Actors*	1720	Canvas	2′3″ × 2′8″

Principal Exhibitions

Boucher

1723   Place Dauphine.
1734   Academy: *Rinald and Armida.*
1742   Salon: *The Hermit, or Brother Luce.*
1745   Salon: First exhibition—sale of red chalks.
1747   Salon: *Rape of Europa; Forge of Vulcan.*
1750   Salon: Nativity.
1753   Salon: *Thetis; Sunshine.*

Chardin

1728   Place Dauphine: *Le Buffet; La Raie.*
1737   Salon: *The Laundress.*
1739   Salon: *Girl Peeling Vegetables.*
1746   Salon: *Grace.*
1759   Salon: Still-lifes.
1763   Salon: Still-lifes.
1765   Salon: *Attributes of Science; Attributes of the Arts; Attributes of Music; Basket of Plums.*
1767   Salon: Still-lifes.
1770   Salon: Pastels.

Fragonard

1752   Academy: *Jeroboam Sacrificing to the Idols.*
1765   Salon: *Coresus and Callirhoe.*
1767   Salon: First erotic painting.

Gainsborough

1768   Royal Academy: First showing.
1783   Royal Academy: Portraits of the Royal Family.
1784   Schombert House.
1789   Schombert House: Posthumous Exhibition in Retrospect.

Greuze

1755   Salon: *Reading the Bible.*
1757   Salon: *Oiseleur qui, au retour de la chasse, accorde sa guitare; La Paresseuse Italienne; L'Œuf cassé; Une jeune Italienne congédiant avec un geste napolitain un cavalier portugais travesti.*
1761   Salon: *L'Accordée de Village.*
1765   Salon: Portrait of the engraver Wille.
1769   Academy: *The Emperor Severus reproaching Caracalla.*
1808   Posthumous exhibition of the painting *St Mary the Egyptian.*

Lancret

1738   Salon: *Winter.*

La Tour

1737   Salon: Portrait of Madame François Boucher; self-portrait.
1741   Salon: Portrait of President de Rieux; portrait of Mademoiselle Salle.
1745   Salon: Portraits of Louis XV, the Dauphin, Duval de l'Epinoy and of Orry de Vignory.

1746   Academy: Portrait of Restout; portrait of Dumont le Romain.
1747   Salon: Portrait of Jean-Joseph Cassanea de Mondonville.
1747   Versailles: Portrait of the Queen in the royal apartments.
1748   Salon: Portraits of Louis XV, Maria Leczinska, the Dauphin, Marshal de Belle-Isle, Marshal de Lowendal and Marshal de Saxe.
1751   Salon: Portraits of Monsieur and Madame de la Reynière; self-portrait.
1753   Salon: Portraits of d'Alembert, Jean-Jacques Rousseau and Manelli.
1755   Salon: Portrait of Madame de Pompadour.
1757   Salon: Portrait of Marie Fel.
1768   Salon: Portraits of Monsieur and Madame Restout.

Nattier

1725   Place Dauphine.
1748   Salon: Portraits of the Queen, of Madame Sophie holding her veil, and of Madame Louise holding flowers.

Oudry

1708   St Luke Academy: *Saint Jerome.*

Robert

1767   Salon: *View of the Port of Ripetta in Rome.*
1771   Salon: Drawings of Italian monuments.
1783   Salon: *Fire at the Opera Theatre.*
1784   Salon: *The Ancient Portico of Marcus Aurelius.*
1785   Salon: *The Portico of Octavius in Rome.*
1787   Salon: *The Triumphal Arch in Orange; The Maison Carrée and the Arena of Nîmes.*
1789   Salon: *The Antique Temple transformed into a Dovecote.*

Vernet

1743   St Luke Academy.
1747   Salon: Two marine views.
1748   Salon: *Moonlight; A Fire.*
1751   Salon: Italian landscapes.
1753   Salon: The Ports of France.
1755   Salon: *View of the Port of Dieppe; View of Marseilles.*
1763   Salon: *View of Rochefort; View of La Rochelle.*

Watteau

1709   Academy: *David accordant le pardon de Nobal à Abigail qui lui apporte des vivres.*
1712   Academy: *Retour de Campagne; Halte d'Armée; Jaloux.*
1717   Academy: *Embarkation for the Island of Cythera.*

Dictionary

A

Aberli, Johann Ludwig (1725-86)

Swiss artist, painter and engraver. Born at Winterthur, died in Berne. Aberli, a pupil of Felix Meyer, is known for his Swiss landscapes executed in a style that made him the originator of the mountain landscape, often imitated since. The Berne museum has several of this artist's works.

Alembert (Jean Le Rond d') (1717-83)

D'Alembert, French writer, philosopher and mathematician, natural son of Madame de Tencin, was born and died in Paris. After brilliant studies, was made a member of the Academy of Sciences when only twenty-three. D'Alembert was an important collaborator in the *Encyclopaedia* and took the idea of it into the salons of the Academy, which accepted it in 1754. He was the author of these scientific and literary works: *Report on the Destruc-*

tion of the Jesuits (1765) and *Miscellany of Philosophy, History and Literature* (1783). He contributed, for the *Encyclopaedia* "Preliminary Discourse", the article "Geneva" and articles on mathematics and physics.

Algarotti, François (1712-64)

Italian critic and poet, born in Venice, died in Pisa. Was a friend of Voltaire, who called him "The Swan of Padua". His work on dissemination of knowledge among the masses, *Il Newtonianismo per le Dame* (Newtonianism for Women), was a great success in the period. He also wrote the interesting *Letters on Painting*.

Amigoni, Jacopo (1675-1752)

Venetian painter and engraver, Amigoni was influenced by Ricci and Solimena. He went to work in Bavaria in the castles of Schlessheim and Nymphenburg, where he painted ceilings. In 1729 he travelled to London, where he painted numerous portraits. He returned to Venice in 1739. Ferdinand invited him to Madrid in 1747 and he stayed there until his death, having worked on decoration of the palaces of Aranjuez and Bien Retiro.

Angeli, Giuseppe (*c.* 1709-98)

Born and died in Venice, pupil of Piazzetta, Angeli was an historical painter and decorator of furniture. He also decorated monuments in Venice, Padua and Rovigo. His chief work was the cupola of San Rocco in Venice.

Antropov, Alexis (1716-95)

From the age of sixteen Antropov worked under Russian and foreign masters, particularly Louis Caravaque. He collaborated in the painting of the Anitschkoff Palace and the new Opera. The Leningrad and Moscow museums have some of his works.

Asam (The Brothers)
Cosmas Damian (1686-1739)
Egid Quirin (1692-1750)

The Asam brothers were the first architects of the Rococo style churches of Bavaria. From 1712 to 1714 they studied in Rome where Egid Quirin was influenced by Bernin. He began working in Germany in 1720. Their talents were divided particularly between the fresco (Cosmas Damian) and sculpture (Egid Quirin). Notable among their work is the church at Weltenburg with a statue of *St George slaying the Dragon* and a very beautiful bust of *Cosmas as a Cherub* by his brother. Osterhofen and Straubing were among their later masterpieces. In Munich, alongside the church of Saint-John Nepomuk which they built, stands the celebrated "House of the Asam Brothers" (1733-46), one of the major monuments of German Rococo where the decoration of the façade is treated like that of the interior of a church or a castle.

Audran, Claude (1658-1734)

Born in Lyons, died in Paris; son of the engraver Germain Audran. Appointed comptroller of the Palace of Luxemburg in 1704, he fostered through his stewardship at the palace a good number of young artists, among them Watteau. He took part in decorating the royal residences of Meudon, La Muette, Marly and the Versailles Menagerie. These works have not survived.

Aved (called The Batavian) (1702-66)

Aved was born at Douai, and after the death of his father served his first apprenticeship in the studio of François Boitard in Amsterdam. In 1721 he went to Paris and took lessons from the portrait painter Belle; he was joined by his contemporaries Carle Van Loo and Chardin. In 1734 he entered the Academy where he had exhibited portraits of Jean-François de Troy and de Caze. He showed works at the Salons of 1737 to 1759. In 1744 he became counsellor to the Academy and in 1764 became a Pensioner. His *Portrait of Louis XV* in 1744 won him the title of painter to the King, but he made his reputation with *Portrait of Mehemed Effendi* (Versailles Museum), which he exhibited at the Salon. Aved died in Paris in 1766.

Baccarelli, Vincenzo (1672-1745)

Florentine painter, pupil of Pietro da Cortona and of Gherardini. Summoned to the court of Saxony, he introduced there decorative painting in the style of Cortona. Most of his works are to be found in Florence and Leghorn.

Balestra, Antonio (1666-1740)

Italian painter and engraver, born and died in Verona, where he began his apprenticeship in the studio of Giovanni Zeffio. He worked in Venice, Bologna (in the studio of Antonio Belluci) and in Rome (in the studio of Carlo Maratta). He painted a large number of works for the churches of Venice, as well as those of Vicenza, Padua, Brescia, Bergamo and Cremona. But the great merit of this painter consists in having shaped such artists as Mariotti, Nogari and Rosalba Carriera.

Bar (Bonaventure de) (1700-29)

Parisian painter, pupil of Claude-Guy Halle. Was admitted to the Academy in 1728. Fell under the influence of Watteau and became one of his followers, as shown by the painting which gained him entry to the Academy: *Fête Champêtre* (Country Festival). This work is to be found today in the Louvre.

Batoni, Pompeo Girolamo (1708-87)

Italian painter, born at Lucca, died in Rome. Son of a jeweller, he began his apprenticeship in his father's works but learned the art of the miniature at the studio of Sebastiano Conca in Naples. He studied Raphael and the ancients. His paintings—highly successful in their day —are characteristic of the reversion to the ancients at the end of the 18th century. The church of Estrella and the cathedral of Evora in Portugal contain some of his works.

Baudouin, Pierre-Antoine (1723-69)

French artist and painter, born and died in Paris. Baudouin was the pupil of Boucher, whose younger daughter Marie-Emilie he married in 1758. Through his father's influence he was accepted into the Academy in 1763 with the presentation of his miniature *Phryne and the Aeropagus*, a work that summed up his artistic taste and which today is in the Louvre. The artist was sharply criticised in his time and pushed the boldness of his subjects too far. He showed, as did Boucher, an insufficiency in drawing and took the same pains to pander to the tastes of the day. Grimm was one of his most severe critics, saying: "Baudouin has made himself a petty type, lascivious and dishonest, with a strong appeal to our libertine youth." But despite criticisms also by Diderot and the Archbishop of Paris, who forced the withdrawal of some of his works from the Salon in 1765, Baudouin none the less remained one of the 18th-century painters with the greatest vogue. Many of his works have been reproduced as engravings.

Baumgartner, Johann Wolfgang (1712-61)

Born at Kufstein (Tyrol), died at Augsburg. Baumgartner was a painter of landscapes, architecture and frescoes. He was responsible for the decoration of the offices of Cardinal de Rodt at Meersburg, as well as frescoes for the churches of Gersthofen and Eggenhausen, near Augsburg.

Bayeu y Subias, Francisco (1734-95)

Born in Saragosa, died in Madrid. Francisco Bayeu was a pupil of Antonio Gonzalez-Velasquez in Madrid. At the request of Raphael Mengs he undertook the decoration of the new royal palace in Madrid. In 1764, as King's painter, he taught Goya, who became his brother-in-law around 1775. A member of the San Fernando Academy, he became the doyen of

the Academy in 1788. Bayeu painted frescoes at the royal palace in Madrid, at Aranjuez, San Ildefonso and in the Prado: he carried out the decoration of the cloisters of Toledo Cathedral as well as that of the Madona del Pilar. The Prado Museum has a large number of his works.

Beaumarchais (Pierre-Augustin Caron de) (1732-99)

French writer, born and died in Paris. Son of a King's watchmaker, Pierre-Augustin Caron added Beaumarchais to his name when he married a woman from the lesser nobility. He had a keen sense of business, as shown in his *Memoirs* (1774-5). Among his dramatic works, those at the beginning and the end may be disregarded; what was new theatrically in Beaumarchais was the introduction of political and social satire, as in the *Barber of Seville* and the *Marriage of Figaro*. It was the role of Figaro that really established Beaumarchais.

There is much life in his comedies but his gaiety is tinged with bitterness.

Beaumont, Claude-François (1694-1766)

Beaumont was born in Turin of a family from Montpelier; Charles-Emmanuel awarded him a grant which allowed him to study in Rome from 1716 to 1719. He pursued his career in Italy where he was made court painter in 1727, then became principal painter to the King and a Chevalier. He was an honorary member of the St Luke Academy in Rome and director of the Academy of Turin, where he set up a manufactory of tapestries. He left frescoes and tapestries in the royal palace at Turin, particularly scenes from the *Story of Aeneas*, in a gallery which bears his name. He also painted altars in churches in and around Turin.

Bellotto, Bernardo (called Canaletto) (1724-80)

Italian painter and engraver, born in Venice, died in Warsaw. He was nephew

and pupil of Antonio Canal, also called Canaletto. It is very difficult to distinguish the works of these two Venetian portraitists. They have been confused to the point where both are known by the same name, Canaletto. From the age of fifteen Bellotto was a pupil in his uncle's studio, where he met Pietro Longhi and Francesco Guardi. Bellotto's adventurous spirit took him in his early twenties to Verona, Pavia, Turin and Milan. He spent several years in England under the patronage of Horace Walpole and then installed himself in Saxony in 1747. He became King's painter to August III in Dresden. King Stanislas Poniatowski took him to Warsaw with the title of court painter and Bellotto spent the last years of his life there. The Dresden Museum still has a great many of his views of the city.

Bencovich, Federico (*c.* 1670-after 1740)

Dalmatian painter, died in Gorizia. Had as a teacher Carlo Cignani; worked in Italy, Germany and particularly Vienna from 1700 to 1740. He is known for his *St Peter of Pisa* (Saint-Sebastian, Venice) and a *St Andrew* (Santa Maria di Piombo, Bologna).

Benefial, Marco (1684-1764)

Italian painter, born and died in Rome. He was a pupil of Bonaventura Lamberti in 1698. In 1718 Pope Clement XI commissioned him to carry out decorative work in the churches of Saint-John Lateran and Saint-Peter's in Rome, which in 1746 won him admission to the St Luke Academy. Raphael Mengs was his pupil.

William Blake
*Good and Evil Angels Struggling for
Possession of a Child*
London, Tate Gallery

Berkeley, George (1685-1753)

Irish philosopher, born in Kilkenny, died in Oxford, best known as the author of *Treatise concerning the Principles of Human Behaviour* and Dialogue between *Hylas and Philonous.* He fought disbelief and materialism, trying to resolve the outside world in terms of pure, eternal ideas originating from idealistic and divine knowledge.

Beschey, Balthasar (1708-76)

Historical painter and portraitist from Antwerp. Studied under Pierre Strick and painted landscapes in the style of Bruegel. A great number of his works are to be found in museums at Wurzburg, Dessau, Mannheim, Potsdam and Liechtenstein. He was a director of the St Luke Academy in Antwerp and died in that city.

Bibiena, Giuseppe Galli (1696-1756)

Italian painter and architect, born at Parma, died in Berlin. Son and pupil of Ferdinando Bibiena, he was installed with his father in the court of Vienna in 1712. From 1717 onwards he replaced his father. He was responsible, with others, for the new Dresden Opera and other decorative works in Munich, Prague, Linz, Venice, Stuttgart and Berlin. He also carried out the decoration of the new Bayreuth Theatre. Several European museums, Vienna, Munich and Dresden, have drawings by this artist.

Bigari, Vittorio (1692-1776)

Historical painter, born at Bologna; became something of a celebrity during his lifetime. Several Bologna churches have his works, notably the Virgin in the church of Our Lady of Succour. He directed a painting school in his native city and had among his pupils his own three sons.

Bigee, Charles

Painter of flowers, born at Malines, working in the 18th century.

Blake, William (1757-1827)

Blake was born in London; little is known of his ordinary life and the preferred stories were those which attributed to this visionary poet and painter a suggestion of madness. (The originality of his nature earned him the soubriquet of " Mad Blake ".) The solicitude of a father of modest origins (he was a hosier) and his exceptional gifts in poetry and drawing won him an apprenticeship at the age of

151

fourteen with an engraver. He lived off his art, experiencing real difficulties, discouraging buyers with the fantastic nature of his compositions. His wife, Catherine Bouchez, helped him until she died, sustaining him in a difficult livelihood. She is everywhere in his work, even among his long figures of women.

Blake invented a colour engraving process which he used for the illustration of his poems. He also illustrated Young's *Nights* in 1797, the *Divine Comedy*, etc. His drawings and paintings are conserved in the National Gallery in London. Among his lyrical works must be listed: *Songs of Innocence* (1789) and *Songs of Experience* (1794); among his fantasy narratives: *The Book of Thel* (1789), *The Marriage of Heaven and Hell* (1790) and *Europe* (1794).

Bonito, Giuseppe (1705-89)

Italian painter and engraver, born and died at Castellamare. Was the pupil of Francesco Solimena, whose style he imitated. During his lifetime he enjoyed a great reputation as historical painter and portraitist. Bonito worked at the court of Naples. The royal palace of Naples has two groups of portraits by him, those of *The Ambassadors of Turkey* and *The Ambassadors of Tripoli*; the Prado has a copy of the former.

Bosschaert, Jean-Baptiste (1667-1746)

Floral painter, born and died in Antwerp. In 1685 he was a pupil of Jean-Baptiste Crépu, painter of flowers, in Antwerp and

in 1703 was a teacher in the same city. He was principally employed on painting flowers and fruit in the works of his contemporaries.

Boucher, François (1703-70)

François Boucher was born and died in Paris. His father designed patterns and made prints for embroidery. François at first studied under his father, then under Lemoine, whose style he succeeded in imitating perfectly. At 17 he finished his first picture, *Judgement of Susanna*, which left Lemoine overwhelmed at the early development of his pupil. Three months later Boucher was a pupil of the engraver Cars. There again he showed such ability that Julienne commissioned him to reproduce the works of Watteau for an average £24 a day. In 1723 his *Evilmerodach délivrant Joachim* won him the first prize at the Academy. His works, as the custom of the day permitted, were hung in the Place Dauphine along the route of the Corpus Christi procession. They were noticed and from then on Boucher was known. He realised his dream of perfecting his art in Italy and left for Rome with Carle Van Loo. During this stay, from 1727 to 1731, he painted religious or historical subjects. But it was *Venus commandant des Armes à Vulcain pour Enée* that established Boucher as a painter of elegant mythology. About the same time he interrupted his painting to illustrate Molière and La Fontaine. In 1734 he was received into the Academy where he had presented *Rinaldo and Armida*. In April 1733 he married Marie-Jeanne Buzot, a pretty Parisienne who became his favourite model. From this period onwards the art of Boucher is extraordinarily varied: he decorated interiors, furniture, ceramics and so on. From 1744 to 1748, as chief decorator to the Royal Academy of Music, he painted canvases generally on bucolic subjects. From 1740 he showed his canvases at the Salons; in 1745 he exhibited and successfully sold his drawings and red chalks. In 1752 the patronage of the Marquis de Marigny secured him a pension and lodgings at the Louvre. Three years later he succeeded Oudry as deputy inspector of the Gobelins Manufactory; in 1765 he was appointed principal painter to the King. From this moment, however, his renown, which had been established before he won this coveted title (the protection of Madame de Pompadour, in particular, had secured him a pension and a great number of official commissions) began a noticeable decline. His nomination as principal painter in fact was accompanied by a change in art fashion. From then on Greuze had all the esteem of Diderot, who

flayed Boucher in his *Salons*. Boucher resigned himself to a changing world. The deaths of Deshays in 1765 and Baudouin in 1769 were hard blows; it was no longer just his glory that was melting away but something more personal, a family and pupils.

Boyne, John (*c.* 1750-1810)

Irish painter, born in County Down, died in London. Caricaturist, water-colour painter and engraver, he was a pupil of the engraver Byrne. He exhibited at the Royal Academy from 1788 to 1809.

Buffon (Georges-Louis Leclerc, Count of) (1707-88)

French writer and naturalist, born at Montbard. He succeeded in putting the scientific knowledge of the day within reach of the masses. He was the author of *Natural History* and *Epochs of Nature*. He was received into the French Academy in 1753.

Canal, Antonio (called Canaletto) (1697-1768)

Canaletto was born in Venice where his father, theatre decorator Bernardo Canal, gave him his first instruction. In 1719 he went to study in Rome, where he appears to have known Giovanni Battista Panini. After two years he returned to Venice where Carlevaris and Ricci were then the masters of landscape painting. Despite such competition he quickly succeeded in making his own talent felt and rapidly became acknowledged as the premier landscape painter of Venice. At the same time his contemporaries Tiepolo and Longhi were stepping into fame, one as a fresco painter and the other as a painter of everyday patrician life. In 1741 Canaletto became involved in dealings with the British consul, J. Smith, and, receiving virtually no profit from Smith's sale of his engravings in England, went to London himself in 1746 and remained there for some time. He was in Munich about 1748 and summoned his nephew Bernardo Bellotto there. Then about 1751 he was back in London. In 1756 he returned to Venice and stayed there until he died. He became a member of the Academy in 1763. Canaletto canvases are to be found in all the European museums.

Caravaque, Louis (died 1754)

French portrait painter, thought to come from Marseilles. In 1715 he arrived in Russia with several French artists. He passed his life there, working at the court of St Petersburg, where he carried out several portraits of Peter the Great and other members of the Tsar's family.

Carlevaris, Luca (1665-1731)

Italian painter and engraver, born in Udine, died in Venice, called Casanobrio and also Luca da Ca'Zenobio (because he was the protégé of the Zenobio family). Several works of this landscape and seascape painter remain in the museums of Darmstadt and Dresden.

Carriera, Rosalba (1675-1757)

Italian painter, born and died in Venice. Daughter of a family of artists, Rosalba learned drawing from her father before

154

becoming a pupil of Balestra. She devoted herself to the miniature, an art in which she rapidly excelled. She also painted a number of oils on canvas, among them a *Portrait of August III*, King of Poland, who was to play an important role in her career. While he was passing through Venice in 1715 the financier Pierre Crozat made her promise to come to Paris. She went there in 1720 and has left a very detailed diary of her stay. She returned to Venice in 1721. In 1730 the Emperor Charles VI summoned her to Vienna to paint his portrait. In 1750 she lost her sight.

Carstens, Asmus Jacob (1754-98)

German painter and draughtsman, born near Schleswig, died in Rome. Began his apprenticeship, about 1776, at Copenhagen. In 1783 he left for Italy and the Tyrol then spent nearly five years at Lubeck. In 1788 he went to Berlin, where he painted the *Chute des Anges* (Fall of the Angels). He went back to Copenhagen but left again for Rome, where he spent the remaining years of his life. The Copenhagen Museum, and particularly that of Weimar, have a number of his works.

Casanova, François (1727-1802)

Italian painter, born in London, died at Bruhl. Was the pupil of Guardi and Francesco Simonini in Venice. After several years' study he began to travel: he stayed for a year in Paris (about 1751) then arrived in Dresden, where he spent six years. Back again in Paris he was accepted by the Royal Academy in 1763. From that date onward he showed regularly at the Salon. Later he went to Vienna to paint a series of works on the victories of Catherine II over the Turks.

Caylus
(Anne-Claude-Philippe de Tubières, Count of) (1692-1765)

French engraver and archaeologist, born and died in Paris. Son of the Countess de Caylus. He took part in the Spanish War of Succession. After the war he travelled in Italy, Greece and Asia Minor from whence he brought back archaeological treasures. Back in France he devoted himself to engraving. In 1731 he was received into the Royal Academy of Painting and Sculpture as honorary adviser; in 1742 he entered the Academie des Inscriptions et Belles Lettres. The Count de Caylus was a great patron of the arts.

Ceruti, Giacomo (active about 1750)

Painter in the Italian style, born in Milan or Brescia, dubbed " Il Pitocchetto " (The Little Beggar). We have little information on his life. He worked in Milan, Brescia and Padua. The Milan Pinacoteca has several of his portraits and still-lifes.

Chardin, Jean-Baptiste-Siméon (1699-1779)

Chardin was born 29 November 1699 in the Rue de Seine in Paris. His father, a

155

cabinet-maker, entered him at the age of nineteen into the studio of the painter Pierre-Jacques Cazes. His sojourn with Cazes had a certain importance for Chardin for it was there that he developed a taste for Dutch and Flemish painting. He became later the pupil of Nicolas Coypel. In 1728, employed as helper by Jean-Baptiste Van Loo to restore the frescoes of Primaticcio at Fontainebleau, Chardin painted a signboard for a surgeon. When it was put in place it was noticed and the attention of the Academy was drawn to the artist. In the same year he hung several paintings in the Place Dauphine, among them the famous *Raie Ouverte*. Largillière noticed the painting. He met the artist and advised him to present himself to the Academy. Chardin was accepted in 1728 as "painter of fruits and animals". Three years later he was married, at the church of Saint-Sulpice, to Marguerite Saintard. They had a son, Pierre-Jean, who was destined to become a mediocre painter and take his own life in Venice. Chardin's wife died in 1735. For some time Chardin continued to hang his work in the Place Dauphine. In August 1738 he exhibited for the first time at the Salon, where he presented still-lifes and interior scenes. Critics of the period found in his work an exactitude in painting objects (Diderot even had a good page on the "natural" quality of a misty film around a plate of fruit). But his interior scenes made less impression at the time; this kind of painting then was often classed as "bad taste". In 1744 Chardin married again, to Françoise-Marguerite Fouget, a wealthy but avaricious woman who seemed to be the epitome of all the bourgeois virtues. While his renown grew, Chardin continued

painting in the same painstaking way, never working on more than one canvas at a time and ignorant of riches that painting so intimate and subdued as his could not bring him. In spite of accommodation he received at the Louvre in 1757 he continued to associate with unassuming people. Towards the end of his life in 1770, his sight, now weaker, prevented him from using oil colours any longer: he set himself to paint with pastels. A portrait of his wife and three self-portraits are of this period. In 1774 he resigned from the post of treasurer of the Academy.

Collet, John (1725-80)

English landscape artist and caricaturist, born in London. All that is known of him is that he was a pupil of Lambert. Two of his water-colours are in the Victoria and Albert Museum in London.

Charles-Antoine Coypel
Self-portrait
Paris, National Library

Conca, Sebastiano (1676/80-1764)

Italian painter, born at Gaeta, died in Naples. He studied in Naples under Solimena. He left for Rome with his brother Giovanni and stayed there to perfect his drawing. After five years he turned to painting; he worked for Pope Clement XI for whom he decorated a church with frescoes. This work won him the title of Cavalière. Conca also worked for foreign princes, in Portugal, Spain, Poland and for the Elector of Cologne.

Condillac (Etienne Bonnot de) (1715-80)

French philosopher, born in Grenoble. He was a friend of Rousseau and Diderot. With his *Essay on the Origins of Human Knowledge* (1746) and his *Treatise on Sensationism* (1754), he defined a theory of empirical sensationism in knowledge. As a disciple of Locke he considered sensation to be the origin and basic principle of knowledge. This regularisation of the principle of knowledge by empirical sensationism was widely believed during the 18th century.

Coypel, Antoine (1661-1722)

French painter and engraver, born and died in Paris. At the age of eleven he was sent to Italy by Colbert with his father, Noël Coypel, then a celebrated painter who was going back to his post as director of the French Academy in Rome. Bernini became interested in the young Antoine, who remained in Italy for three years and rose to be laureate of the St Luke Academy. In 1681 he was approved by the Academy of Paris; he collaborated in the decoration of the Church of the Assumption and decorated a pavilion for the Grande Mademoiselle. The Duke of Orleans engaged him as principal painter. The Regent, who once was his pupil, established him as principal painter to the King. He then carried out a series of works for the Chateau of Meudon, the Palais Royal, decorated the house of Cardinal Dubois and, in 1709, the vault of Versailles Chapel. He died in 1722, having been director of Crown paintings and director of the Academy in 1714.

Coypel, Charles-Antoine (1694-1752)

French painter and engraver, born and died in Paris. Son of Antoine Coypel. On the death of his father in 1722 he was appointed director of Crown paintings

157

and premier painter to the Duke of Orleans, posts which his father had held. In 1747 he was appointed principal painter to the King and director of the Academy. His works are in the Louvre and in the museums of Besançon and Nantes. Charles-Antoine Coypel was also a remarkable literary man.

Coypel, Noël-Nicholas (1690-1734)

French painter and engraver, born and died in Paris. He was the pupil of his father, Noël Coypel, and his mother Françoise Perrin. While still quite young he painted two pictures for the church of Saint-Nicholas du Chardonnet in Paris. But Noël-Nicholas is best known for his mythological paintings, among which should be mentioned *Triumph of Galatea*, *Venus and Amor* and *Diana at the Bath*. He was received into the Academy in 1720.

Cozens, Alexandre
(beg. 18th century-1786)

Born in Russia, died in London, Cozens was the natural son of Peter the Great and an English girl, which explains why his work shows some traces of Slav influence. He studied painting in Italy. In 1746 he went to live in London where he remained until his death. Between 1769 and 1781 his works were shown at the Free Society of Arts and the Royal Academy.

Crespi, Giuseppe Maria (1665-1747)

Italian painter and engraver, born and died in Bologna, called " The Spaniard "

because of his predilection for Spanish costume. Was the pupil of Domenico Canuti and Carlo Cignani; Crespi improved his work particularly in copying the paintings of Carrachi, Guerchin, Baroccio, the Venetian masters and Correggio. He painted mythological and religious portraits and stylised subjects. He taught Piazzetta and Pietro Longhi.

Creti, Donato (1671-1749)

Italian painter, known as Donatino, born in Cremona, died in Bologna. Was the pupil of Pisanelli and worked in the churches of Rimini, Bergamo, Lucca and Palermo; the Bologna Gallery has his *Coronation of Charles V at Bologna*. For the Public Palace he painted works inspired by scenes from the *Life of Achilles*.

Crome, John (1768-1821)

English painter and engraver called " Old Crome ", born and died in Norwich. From a modest family, Crome had difficulties at the beginning of his career. He set up in his native city a school of painting which was successful enough to allow him to live by his art. From 1805 he organised exhibitions of the Norwich Society of Artists, which became an important landscape school. From 1806 onwards he exhibited regularly at the Royal Academy. In 1814 he travelled through Belgium and France. He carried out a series of engravings which were gathered together after his death under the title of " Picturesque Norfolk scenery ".

Jacques-Louis David
Head
Paris, Ecole des Beaux-Arts

D

David, Jacques-Louis (1748-1825)

French painter, born in Paris, died in Brussels. In 1769 he became the pupil of Vien and two years later won the second prize in Rome. He took the first prize in 1774 with *The Loves of Antiochus and Stratonic*. He went to Rome with Vien and stayed there until 1780. In 1783 he was made a member of the Academy. He became acquainted with Napoleon who, while he reigned as Emperor, named David as principal painter. But the post of official painter caused him to lose a great deal of his personality. On the fall of the Empire he exiled himself to Belgium and settled in Brussels. David's painting is cold and the movement of the revival of antiquity which he created is of little interest. But it was he who began to react against the mannered art of the 18th century; he exerted a strong influence during the first half of the 19th century.

Defoe, Daniel (*c.* 1660-1731)

English author, born in London; he wrote the world-famed story of castaway adventure *The Life and Adventures of Robinson Crusoe* (1719) and several pamphlets. His novel *Moll Flanders* dates from 1722.

Deshays, Jean-Baptiste Henri (1729-65)

French painter, born near Rouen, died in Paris. Was first the pupil of his father, then of Colin de Vermont, Carle Van Loo and of François Boucher, whose elder daughter he married in 1758. Painted religious and elegant subjects. Winner of the first prize in Rome in 1751, he was admitted to the Academy in 1759. In 1760 he was named deputy-professor. He exhibited with success in the Salons of 1759, 1761 and 1763. Diderot saw him as a pupil of Le Sueur, but his works show clearly the influences of his masters, Van Loo and Boucher, as, for example, in *Achilles protected by Vulcan and Juno*, which is in the Louvre.

Desportes, Alexandre-François (1661-1743)

Son of a farmer in Champagne, Desportes went to Paris at the age of thirteen. He was a pupil of the Antwerp painter Nicaise Bernard. He worked with Claude Audran on the decoration of the Château d'Anet and some décor in the theatre and the Menagerie at Versailles. In 1695 he left for Poland, summoned by King Sobieski, and became official portrait painter to the Polish court. On his return to France in

1696 he was named Hunting Painter to Louis XIV, was admitted to the Academy in 1699 and given the title of adviser in 1704. After a voyage to England in 1712 he worked on the decoration of the Château de la Muette, the Château de Chantilly and the Hôtel Bouillon. In 1735 he introduced Indian tapestries for the Gobelins factory. He died in Paris.

Diderot, Denis (1713-1784)

Diderot was born in Langres of a lower middle-class family. From the age of eight he was taught by Jesuits in his native town. He received a solid education but it was at the college of Harcourt in Paris, where his father took him, that he completed his studies. When these were finished he entered an attorney's office, but did not stay there long, preferring to lead an independent life and satisfy his intellectual curiosity. When his father cut off his allowance Diderot made translations and even wrote sermons. During this time he made the acquaintance of d'Alembert, Rousseau and Condillac. In 1746 he was presented to the bookseller Le Breton, who gave him the job of directing the *Encyclopaedia*. Up to 1773 Diderot devoted himself to this task, filling it out with his own personal work, the most important phases of which came from this period. After three months' imprisonment in the Bastille, caused by publication of his *Lettre sur les Aveugles* (Letter on the Blind), Diderot turned his attention to the theatre. Thus he wrote, in 1757 and 1758, *Fils Naturel* (Illegitimate Son) and *Père de Famille* (Father of the Family). In 1759 Grimm asked him for reports on the

Salons for the *Correspondance Littéraire*. Diderot was already familiar with the problems of aesthetics: in 1751 he had edited the article " Beau " for the *Encyclopaedia*; moreover, he frequented the studios of the painters and knew Greuze and Vernet. He accepted the commission, and from 1759 to 1781 produced the reports which were the origin of art criticism as we know it today. In 1760 and 1761 Diderot broke off his work as chief editor of the *Encyclopaedia* to write two novels, *La Religieuse* (The Nun) and *Neveu de Rameau* (Rameau's Nephew). His activity multiplied incessantly; he kept up a protracted correspondence with Sophie Volland, published novels and, in 1769, three philosophical works among which was *Rêve de d'Alembert* (D'Alembert's Dream), which defined a point of view of materialist philosophy. In 1773 Catherine II, with whom he had been in touch for a decade, summoned him to St Petersburg. He stayed there a year. *Le Paradoxe sur le Comédien* (Paradox on the Actor) and *Jacques le Fataliste* (James the Fatalist) date from the same year. He

François-Hubert Drouais
Petite Fille et sa Poupée
(Little Girl and her Doll)
Grenoble Museum

went back to Paris in 1774; from then on he worked for his own pleasure, enjoying a measure of comfort from the protection of Catherine II. In his last years Diderot withdrew from all literary activity and died in 1784 from apoplexy.

Dighton, Robert (1752-1814)

English portrait painter and caricaturist, died in London. Sometimes sent his works to the Royal Academy and the Free Society of Artists, but after the publication of his *A Book of Heads* in 1799 devoted himself almost entirely to caricaturing.

Diziani, Gasparo (1689-1767)

Italian painter and caricaturist, born in Belluno, died in Venice. Studied under Sebastiano Ricci and Gregorio Lazzarini, spent some time in Rome and in Germany and then settled in Venice. His works (religiously inspired) remain in Bergamo and Venice.

Doyen, Gabriel-François (1726-1806)

French painter, born in Paris, died in St Petersburg. His father was upholsterer to the King. A pupil of Carle Van Loo, Doyen won the Rome prize in 1746 and stayed in Italy for nine years. He was admitted to the Academy in 1759. He worked principally as a decorator: in 1767 he painted pictures for the church of Saint-Roch and for the vault of Saint-Gregory's Chapel at the Invalides. In 1777 he was appointed chief painter for the Count of Provence and the Count d'Artois. In 1789 he left for Russia at the invitation of Catherine II. There he decorated royal palaces until the time of Paul I, who entrusted to him the decoration of the Hermitage Palace. Doyen was one of the last representatives of the 18th-century school.

Drouais, François-Hubert (1727-75)

French painter, born and died in Paris. Son of a miniaturist and pastel painter, Hubert Drouais, who was known for his *Portrait de Madame de Pompadour*, François-Hubert took lessons from his father, from Carle Van Loo, Natoire and Boucher. A protégé of Madame du Barry, he was a portrait painter of repute, particularly of children's portraits, during the reign of Louis XV. Accepted by the Academy in 1755, court painter in 1756, he was in turn received into the Academy, appointed King's painter and to other members of the royal family. He took part in exhibitions at the Louvre from 1755 to 1775. His son Jean-Germain, born in 1763, who died at the age of twenty-five, was one of the first pupils of David.

161

Duplessis, Joseph (1725-1802)

Portrait painter, born at Carpentras, died at Versailles. His father, Joseph-Guillaume Duplessis le Vieux, who had given up his profession of surgeon, was his first teacher. Afterwards he studied under Imberg and Subleyras. Approved by the Academy in 1769, he was admitted in 1774 and became adviser to the Academy in 1780; appointed director of the Versailles Gallery, he became administrator of the museum that was installed there in 1794. After becoming court painter, he made portraits of Louis XVI and most of the personalities of the period.

Dupra, Giorgio Domenico (1689-1770)

Italian painter, born in Turin. After having studied in Rome, he was, like his brother Giuseppe, painter at the court of Charles-Emmanuel III of Savoy. It is difficult to say which painter was responsible for certain works, but several portraits signed by Giorgio Domenico are known.

Durameau, Louis-Jean-Jacques (1733-1796)

French painter, born in Paris, died at Versailles. Gained second prize in Rome in 1756, first in 1757 and was approved by the Academy in 1766, then admitted to the Academy in 1774. Durameau was painter to the King's chamber and offices and keeper of paintings for the Versailles authorities. From 1767 to 1789 he exhibited at the Salon. His works are particularly noted for beauty of design.

E

Encyclopaedia

The work of the *Encyclopaedia* lay at the very heart of the 18th-century intellectual movement and occupied an important place in the history of thought, though less important in the history of literature. Diderot got his first idea for the *Encyclopaedia* in translating Ephraim Chambers's *Cyclopaedia* from the English for a bookseller. Diderot's *Encyclopaedia* as we know it today was published in twenty-eight volumes from 1751 to 1772 and is the résumé of 18th-century knowledge of science, art, philosophy and literature. Generally it shows a feeling of scepticism. Diderot played the most active part in the work of this encyclopaedia. Among the most important contributors were: d'Alembert, mathematician; Condillac, representing the most important 18th-century sensual theory of knowledge; Farmer-General Helvetius, apostle of materialism; and the German d'Holbach, author of a treatise on *Système de la Nature* (System of Nature). Among secondary contributors were Marmontel for literary subjects, Voltaire, Buffon and Montesquieu, who furnished articles.

Fielding, Henry (1707-54)

English writer, born near Glastonbury. Best known for his earthy novel *Tom Jones: A Foundling*, which he wrote in 1749.

Fragonard, Jean-Honoré (1732-1806)

Fragonard was born on 5 January 1732 into a modest family in Grasse. At the age

of six he went with his parents to Paris, where his father was to work. While very young he worked as a clerk in a lawyer's office. Boucher, to whom he was offered as a pupil, sent him to Chardin but accepted Fragonard himself six months later. In his master's studio, subjected to the sole discipline of work, Fragonard studied anatomy, perspective and the technique of light and shade on engravings by Rembrandt, Rubens and Tiepolo. In 1752 Boucher entered his pupil for the Rome competi-

tion. Fragonard took the first prize with *Jéroboam sacrifiant aux Idoles* (Jeroboam sacrificing to the Idols). In 1753 he entered the royal school for aided pupils as a boarder. There he painted *Psyché*, which was shown to the King in March 1753. During the same period the Brotherhood of the Holy Sacrament in Grasse commissioned from him a holy picture: *Jesus washing the Feet of the Disciples*. In 1756 the Marquis de Marigny sent him to the Villa Medici. Little is known of the first part of his stay there, but in 1758 a letter from Natoire, then director of the French Academy in Rome, gave de Marigny an account of Fragonard's talent. In Italy in 1759 he met the Abbé St Non, of whom he painted a number of portraits. This art lover, himself an engraver, took Fragonard under his patronage and thus allowed the artist to prolong his stay in Italy. In the summer of 1760 Fragonard lived at the Villa d'Este with the abbé and Hubert Robert. Attributed to this period is Fragonard's *Tall Cypresses of the Villa d'Este*. After a trip to Naples Fragonard returned to France in May 1761 with the abbé. In March 1765, aspiring to the title of King's painter, he submitted *Coresus sacrificing Himself to Save Callirhoe*; it was accepted. The canvas, bought by de Marigny, was sent to the Gobelins to be executed in tapestry. Fragonard obtained lodgings in the Louvre and, for a reception piece, was instructed to execute a ceiling for the Apollo Gallery. Then, too busy with commissions that followed the success of his *Pastorales*, he renounced the project and consequently was never admitted to the Academy. In 1767 a painting inspired by the *Journal de Collé* won him the reputation of a libertine painter. Commissions flowed in, particularly from the Marquis de St Julien. In 1769 he married Marie-Anne Gerard, aged seventeen. In the same year he undertook important decoration work for Madame du Barry. Rejected, the work was returned to him with £18,000 as compensation. In 1773, on the recommendation of the Abbé Şt Non, Farmer-General Bergeret de Grancourt joined the Fragonard family in a trip across Italy to Vienna and Dresden. The two men did not get on together and Fragonard had to bring a lawsuit to recover from Bergeret the sketches he had made during the trip. Back in Paris he painted *Fête de Saint-Cloud* (Festival of St Cloud) and worked for the actress Adeline Colombe. It was then a period of full prosperity, but before long the Revolution took both his fame and his fortune. In 1789 the Fragonard family left for Grasse, where the painter sold to one of his relatives for a very low price the canvases which he regarded as compromising. Returning to Paris he sent his son Evariste to study under David, from whom Fragonard received various official commissions. These he lost a year before his death. His work sold badly but Fragonard appeared resigned to this mediocrity. He died on 22 August 1806 from congestion.

Frantz, Johann Martin

Painter on pottery at Kunersburg, Germany, in the 18th century. Also worked on the decoration of churches in the Arnstadt and Eichstaat regions.

Freudenberger, Sigismond (1745-1801)

Painter and engraver, born and died in Berne, pupil of Greuze and Boucher in Paris. In 1773 he settled back in Switzerland. Specialised in representing intimate scenes. His works remain in Geneva and Neuchâtel.

Fuseli, Jean-Henri (1741-1825)

Swiss painter, born in Zurich, died in Putney, London. First studied theology and English in his native town. Met Lavater and went with him to Vienna and Berlin. After having illustrated some of the works of Shakespeare, he took the advice of the British Ambassador to Prussia, Sir Robert Smith, and visited England. There he became acquainted with Reynolds, who insisted that Fuseli should go to Italy, where he studied the classics and joined Raphael Mengs and Winckelmann. He returned to London in 1779 where he exhibited at the Royal Academy. He was admitted to the Academy in 1788, elected in 1790 and from 1799 to 1804 was professor of painting. For six years a cabal in the Academy kept him out but in 1810 he was re-elected and continued to teach until his death.

Gainsborough, Thomas (1727-88)

Gainsborough was born into a large family in Sudbury, Suffolk, where his father was a tailor. He was remembered as a mediocre pupil, caring little for his studies. About 1742 he went to London and became the pupil of Gravelot, working on the restoration of paintings of the Dutch school. Later he entered St Martin's Academy. When he had obtained enough knowledge, Gainsborough returned to Sudbury and set himself up as painter of portraits and landscapes. At nineteen he married Margaret Burr and with the money she provided he was able to paint from then on without financial worry. In 1746 he went to live in Ipswich, then in 1758 at Bath, where he remained until 1774. This was the period of his portraits. The success of his work led him to increase his prices. In the same period he painted landscapes which were less appreciated. In 1766 he became a member of the Society of Artists and exhibited in London. In 1768 he was one of the founders of the Royal Academy. The number of his admirers in London never ceased to grow, and in 1774 he decided to settle in London, where he was undeniably a success. During this period there were numerous clashes between Gainsborough and Reynolds, neither of whom would concede to the other the title of the greatest portrait painter. In 1783 Gainsborough ceased exhibiting at the Academy after an incident with the hanging committee, which had refused to hang his *Portrait of the Royal Family* at the height demanded by the painter; but he did exhibit once more before his death. In 1787 he developed cancer and Reynolds came to see his old rival and be reconciled. Gainsborough died the following year.

Gersaint, Edmé-François (*c.* 1696-1750)

Engraver and art dealer in Paris; was a close friend of Watteau, who painted for him the celebrated signboard now to be found in the Berlin Museum.

Ghislandi, Vittore (1655-1743)

Italian portraitist, born at San Leonardo and died in Venice, also called Il Frate Paolotto (Friar Paolotto). Son of an artistic family, he entered a religious order at an early age and worked at the Convent of the Galgario order in Bergamo, then in Milan. In 1717 he became an honorary member of the Clementine Academy in Bologna. This painter was the last of the Bergamo school of portraitists.

Giaquinto, Corrado (*c.* 1690-1765)

Italian painter, born at Molfetta, died in Naples. Studied under Solimena in Naples and Sebastiano Conca in Rome. Became a member of the St Luke Academy in 1735. Is known to have worked for King Ferdinand VI of Spain in 1753.

Gillot, Claude (1673-1722)

Painter and engraver, born at Langres, died in Paris. Went to Paris at an early age and studied under J.-B. Corneille. Furnished décor and costumes for the Grand Opera. He met Watteau, with whom he became friends. He was Watteau's teacher and the two collaborated for five years. They separated in 1708 but the cause of their parting was never revealed. From this date Gillot is said to have abandoned painting to devote himself to drawing and his etchings. He was admitted to the Academy in 1715.

Gillray, James (1757-1815)

Painter, caricaturist and engraver, born and died in London. Drew numerous caricatures which made his reputation. His last works date from 1811. A prey to alcohol, he lived for several years in a state of degeneration before taking his own life in 1815.

Goethe, Wolfgang von (1749-1832)

German writer, born in Frankfurt, son of a jurist. Studied law in Leipzig from 1765 to 1770 and pursued his studies in Strasburg until 1771. In Strasburg at this time he met Herder and took over leadership of the literary "Sturm und Drang" movement. During a journey in Alsace, where he was gathering popular songs, he met a pastor's daughter who inspired some of his finest lyrics. As a doctor of law he returned to Frankfurt to carry on his profession from 1771 to 1775. It was a

period of boredom and frustration but an unfortunate love affair produced his *Sorrows of Young Werther*, which spread his reputation through Europe. The period also produced his dramas *Götz von Berlichingen* and *Clavigo*. In 1775 he settled in Weimar, entered the service of the Duke of Weimar and became interested in the politics of the Duchy. In 1782 he was raised to the nobility. He had begun *Egmont* some years earlier. At the court of Weimar he met Charlotte von Stein, with whom he corresponded from 1776 to 1826. In September 1786 he left the court and went to Italy, first to Verona, then Venice and Rome and in 1787 to Naples and Sicily. He returned later to Rome and completed *Egmont*. More than a year later he went back to Weimar, with some regrets about Italy. From this period came his *Roman Elegies* and *Torquato Tasso*. In 1805 Schiller died; Goethe had his *Theory of Colours* published. Not long afterwards he met Bettina, with whom he corresponded until 1811. In 1807 the meeting between Goethe and Napoleon took place. From these years came some of his main works: *Wilhelm Meister's Apprenticeship*, published in 1821 and 1829, *Hermann and Dorothea* and *Poetry and Truth*. At the age of eighty-three he completed *Faust*, on which he had worked since 1772. He died on 20 March 1832.

Goldoni, Carlo (1707-93)

Italian dramatist, born in Venice, died in Paris. Studied law and philosophy. From 1748 to 1752 he wrote plays for the Sant'Angelo theatre in Venice. He tried to reform the Italian theatre by freeing it from the traditional form of the Commedia dell'Arte. In 1762, despite his success, the criticisms of Gozzi, whose aesthetic beliefs were more conservative, forced him to leave for Paris. There he still fought against the partisans of the Commedia. He wrote several plays in French, including *Bourru Bienfaisant* (Rough Diamond) (1771) and *Memories* (1784-7). He was appointed Italian teacher to the royal princesses and was granted a pension, but this ended with the Revolution. He died in penury.

Goldsmith, Oliver (1728-74)

English writer, born at Pallasmore, Ireland, died in London. After studying medicine in Edinburgh he went to Leyden and then travelled through Europe. Back in England he practised medicine for some time in the poorer quarters of London, then worked for a bookseller. He launched a journal, *The Bee*, and entered the Literary Club of London. Although reckless and prodigal with money, his genius was undeniable and he soon came to the notice of Johnson and his circle. *The Traveller* in 1764 established him firmly as a poet and his chief prose work two years later, *The Vicar of Wakefield*, became one of the classics of the English language. His plays *The Good-natured Man* and *She Stoops to Conquer* have lived on down the ages of the theatre, and *The Deserted Village* ranks among the finest of English 18th-century poetry.

Gonzalez-Vélasquez, Antonio (1723-93)

Spanish painter, born and died in Madrid. A pupil of Corrado Giaquinto, he painted frescoes in various churches in Castille, Madrid and Saragosa. In 1765 he was appointed director of the Madrid Academy. From 1757, as court painter, he did frescoes in the royal palaces and completed a number of portraits.

Goya y Lucientes (Francisco José de) (1746-1828)

Goya was born on 31 March 1746, near Saragosa. In 1760 he went to the Saragosa school to study painting and in 1763 left for Madrid. He once said his teachers

were "Rembrandt, Velasquez and Nature" but he studied under Francisco Bayeu, painter to the King with Mengs and Tiepolo. In 1766 he went to Italy and the following year took the second prize for painting at the Parma Academy. He left Italy in 1771. Returning to Saragosa, he did his first important work, decorating the chancel of the church of Our Lady of the Pillar. In 1775 he undertook, in Madrid, a series of cartoons for the royal tapestry factory at Santa Barbara. He worked under the direction of Raphael Mengs with his instructor, Francisco Bayeu. In 1775 he married Bayeu's daughter, who bore him twenty children, almost all of them dying at a very young age. In 1780 he was received into the San Fernando Academy with his *Crucifixion*. For some time he had been presented at court and had become a celebrity; he painted the portraits of all the important people, including that of the King. In 1785 he was appointed deputy-director of the San Fernando Academy and from then on lived

an opulent life. He bought a house at San Isidoro where he received friends. In 1788 Charles III died. His heir, Charles IV, named Goya painter of the King's chamber. But at the same time Goya fell ill and remained incurably deaf. His liaison with the Duchess of Alba ended in 1802 when the Duchess was mysteriously poisoned. The Majas date from the period of this liaison. In 1800 Goya painted a collective portrait of the royal family. In 1808, horrified by the Napoleonic invasion, he painted *The Outbreak of May 3* and *May 3, 1808*. Later he made the engraving *Disasters of War*. About 1824 he fell out of favour with Ferdinand VII and went to Bordeaux. At the age of eighty he made a trip to Madrid, but returned to Bordeaux and died two years later.

Graff, Anton (1736-1813)

Portrait painter and miniaturist, born at Winterthur, where he studied, died in Dresden. In 1756 he went to Augsburg and then to Ansbach, where he became assistant to the court painter Schneider. In 1759 he painted portraits at Augsburg. He was painter to the court at Dresden from 1765 and member of the Vienna and Munich Academies.

Gravelot (known as Hubert-François Bourguignon d'Anville) (1699-1773)

French painter and engraver, born and died in Paris. Gravelot was best known for the books he illustrated (Boccaccio, Racine, Corneille, Marmontel, Ovid, etc.)

Studied art in Paris. In 1733 Claude du Bosc invited him to London to help with engraving. It was at this time that Gravelot published his *Treatise on Perspective*. Through the drawing school he opened in the Strand, Gravelot was able to exercise a certain influence over the English school. Notable among his pupils was Gainsborough. Gravelot was also one of the first caricaturists in England. In 1754 he settled in Paris where he made a great reputation as an illustrator; among his works are the engravings for Rousseau's *Nouvelle Héloïse*.

Greuze, Jean-Baptiste (1725-1805)

Greuze was born in Tournus, where his father was a slater. In his middle twenties he went to Lyons to learn painting in the

studio of the painter Grandon. About 1750 he was studying under Natoire in Paris. Very rapidly one of his paintings, *Father of the Family explaining the Bible to his Children*, was noticed and made his name. The Academy accepted him in June 1755; without delay Greuze exhibited at the Salon stylised scenes which, apart from some portraits, were to constitute the whole of his work. From September 1755 to April 1757 he travelled in Italy but this did not seem to have any effect on his work. Returning to Paris he exhibited in 1761 *Accordée de Village* (The Village Betrothed), which put the seal on his success; *Paix en Ménage* (Peace in the Household) and the *Paralytique soigné par ses Enfants* (Paralytic tended by his Children) were new successes. About this time Diderot noted in his *Salons* his preference for Greuze at the expense of Boucher. But then Greuze made an unfortunate error: trying to enter the Academy as an historical painter, he presented a canvas *L'Empereur Sévère reprochant à son Fils d'avoir voulu l'assassiner* (Emperor Severus reproaching Caracalla). The Academy committee gratuitously snubbed him on this and classified him as a genre painter on the basis of his previous work. From that moment Greuze refused to exhibit at the Salon and never again set foot inside the Academy. At the same time the popularity of his work began to dwindle. Stricken by all sorts of worries, he separated from his wife, who had almost ruined him, in 1785. The Revolution, which he welcomed enthusiastically, did nothing to restore him to favour. He exhibited at the Salon in 1800 and 1802 without marked success: his style had definitely ceased to please. He died on

169

21 March 1805, and by a strange quirk of fate left unfinished a *Portrait of the Emperor*, which his daughter was to complete.

Grimm (Frederick Melchior, Baron) (1723-1807)

German writer, born near Ratisbon, died at Gotha. He studied at the University of Leipzig, then went to France as attaché to the Prince of Saxe-Gotha. He was an intimate friend of the great writers. In 1753 he took over direction of a literary journal from the Abbé Raynal and his *Literary, Philosophical and Critical Correspondence* (seventeen volumes) appeared in 1812 and 1813. He also wrote for the *Encyclopaedia*.

Guardi, Francesco (1712-93)

Italian painter, born and died in Venice. He belonged to a family of painters: his sister married Tiepolo and his father had been a pupil of Sebastiano Ricci. Guardi began in the family " bottega ", then directed by his elder brother Gianantonio. At first he did decorative work and religious paintings for the church and then numerous paintings of Venice (*Rialto, St Mark's Square, The Church of the Salute*) which he repeated a number of times. He was accepted by the Academy in 1784 only as a painter of perspective. Francesco Guardi was one of the great Venetian painters of the 18th century. He is regarded as the forerunner of the romantic stream which led to French Impressionism and Tuscan " tachism ".

Guardi, Gianantonio (1698-1760)

Italian painter, born and died in Venice. Elder brother of Francesco, Gianantonio was the great Venetian painter's only instructor. In 1755 he made his name as historical painter at the Venice Academy of Arts. A follower of Sebastiano Ricci, he adopted the romantic and naturalist style. His most important work, *Death of St Joseph*, is in the Berlin Kaiser-Friedrich Museum. He collaborated with his brother Francesco and it is difficult to distinguish between some of their studio work.

Guglielmi, Gregorio (1714-73)

Italian painter, born in Rome, died at St Petersburg. At first he studied under Sebastiano Conca. They were together in Dresden (1753), Vienna (1755), Turin (1765) and then in St Petersburg. Guglielmi also carried out several works at Augsburg and for the Schönbrunn Castle; he painted several frescoes for the Hospital of the Holy Spirit in Rome. He is also known for ceiling sketches (now in the Nancy Museum) which he offered to Catherine II.

Günther, Matthäus Matha (1705-88)

Bavarian painter, born in Bisenberg, died at Hard. Was a pupil of Cosmas Damian Asam in Munich. Günther was director of the old Augsburg Academy, where he was installed in 1731. The Bavarian national museum in Munich has several portraits by this painter.

H

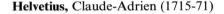

Hayman, Francis (1708-76)

English historical painter and illustrator, born in Exeter, died in London. Was a pupil of Robert Brown, and Gainsborough worked under his direction. He illustrated Pope, Milton, Cervantes and Shakespearean works. Hayman was one of the founder-members of the Royal Academy. A self-portrait is in the National Portrait Gallery. Hayman also made a number of etchings.

Helvetius, Claude-Adrien (1715-71)

Farmer-General and philosopher, born near Paris. Was one of the supporters of the *Encyclopaedia*. Helvetius developed and took to its extreme Condillac's sensualist theory of knowledge in two treatises: *Of the Mind*, which appeared in 1768, and *Of the Man*. The former caused a great indignation and controversy. Parliament, the Sorbonne and the Pope condemned the book; Rousseau and Voltaire declared themselves shocked. On the death of Helvetius, his widow opened a "philosophical" salon for intellectuals and artists who shared her husband's views.

Hogarth, William (1697-1764)

English painter, born and died in London. At fifteen he became an apprentice. At first his teacher was the engraver Ellis Gamble; later he studied under James Thornhill, whose daughter he married.

His first great work, a series of six engravings called *A Harlot's Progress*, appeared in 1732. It was followed three years later by *A Rake's Progress*. Ten years later came his masterpiece, *Marriage à la Mode*. From then on his works became more and more caricatured. In April 1764, shortly before he died, he painted a curious picture in which his own face appears behind the features of an old bearded man. In 1753 he published his celebrated *Analysis of Beauty*. A self-portrait with his dog appears in the National Gallery in London.

Holbach (Paul-Henri, Baron d') (1723-89)

French philosopher, born at Edesheim in the Palatinate. He ran in Paris a salon which was the rendezvous of the encyclopaedists. He wrote articles on chemistry and mineralogy for the *Encyclopaedia*. Fame came to him from his *Christianity Unmasked* (1767) and *System of Nature* (1770) which made him one of the most

171

intransigent, materialist atheists of his time.

Hoppner, John (1758-1810)

English painter and engraver, born and died in London. He was a natural son of the King and studied at the Royal Academy on a modest allowance from George III. He exhibited at the Academy from 1780. Although at first attracted by landscapes, he later painted numerous portraits of the peerage. In 1789 he became painter to the Prince of Wales and in 1795 a member of the Royal Academy. He painted numerous portraits of women and children.

Houasse, Michel-Ange (1680-1730)

French painter, born in Paris, died in Arpajon. He passed a great part of his life in Spain where he replaced his father, René-Antoine Houasse, as principal painter to King Philip V. In 1707 he was elected a member of the Academy of Paris. Several of his works, historical scenes and portraits, are in the Prado Museum in Madrid.

Huber, Jean (1721-86)

Swiss painter and engraver, known as "Huber-Voltaire", born in Chambéry, died in Lausanne. A great part of his work is devoted to the life of Voltaire. Some of his landscapes may be found in the Ariana and Rath museums of Geneva. Huber was also interested in ballooning and pub-

lished several works on this subject, as well as on the flight of birds, which earned him the nickname of "Hubert the Bird-catcher".

Huet, Christophe (died 1759)

French painter and decorator. To him are attributed the *Grande* and *Petite Singerie* at Chantilly, which for a long time were thought to have been the work of Watteau. Huet also painted Chinese motifs and other work at the Hôtel de Rohan. His *Dog pointing Partridges* is in the Nantes Museum.

Hume, David (1711-76)

English philosopher and historian, born and died in Edinburgh. He went to France, where he wrote *Treatise on Human Nature*. Returning to Scotland, he became librarian to the Corporation of Advocates in Edinburgh. In 1763 he went back to Paris, joined Rousseau for a time and returned to London, where he was for some time an Under-Secretary of State. He passed the last part of his life in Edinburgh. Hume was the founder of the "phenomenist" school of thought.

Hutin, Charles-François (1715-76)

French painter, sculptor and engraver, born in Paris, died in Dresden. He was pupil of François le Maux and won the Grand Prize for Painting in 1736. He stayed in Rome for seven years, concentrating on sculpture. In 1748 he was appointed instructor, then in 1764 director, at the Dresden Academy.

Huysum (Jan Van) (1682-1749)

Dutch painter, born and died in Amsterdam. Son of Juste van Huysum, a floral painter, he specialised in painting flowers, still-life and landscapes. He painted sculpted vases, marble consoles and bas-reliefs to emphasise the quality of his bouquets of flowers. His work was bought by the Kings of Poland and Prussia and the Duke of Orleans. In England his fame was spread by Horace Walpole.

Jeaurat, Etienne (1699-1789)

French painter, born at Vermenton, died at Versailles. Historical and genre painter, he worked with Nicholas Vleughel. In 1724 the latter was appointed director of the Rome Academy and took Jeaurat with him. Jeaurat was admitted to the Academy in 1733; he showed at the Salon from 1739 to 1769. In 1782 he also exhibited at the Correspondence Salon. Between 1737 and 1781 he held several important posts at the Academy and in 1767 was named King's painter and custodian of paintings at Versailles.

Jouvenet, Jean (1644-1717)

French painter, born in Rouen, died in Paris, studied under his father, Laurent Jouvenet. From 1661 he studied at the Royal Academy in Paris and was admitted to the Academy in 1675. He was a great success, and after the death of Mignard and Le Brun became the head of the French school. He carried out the decoration of the Rennes Parliament in 1695. Because of a stroke he lost the use of his right hand towards the end of his life, but quickly trained himself to use the left hand.

Juel, Jens (1745-1802)

Danish painter, born at Gamborg Figen, died in Copenhagen. Studied under Gehrmann in Hamburg, then took lessons at the Copenhagen Academy. After travelling to Rome, Paris and Geneva, he returned to Copenhagen in 1780, where he was appointed court painter and later director of the Academy. He was a great portraitist, as evidenced by his works which remain principally in the Copenhagen Museum.

Juvara, Filippo (1676-1736)

Italian architect and engraver, also called Juara or Ivara; born in Messina, died in Madrid. In Rome, Juvara studied under Carlo Fontana. In 1714 Victor Amadeus II summoned him to the court of Turin, where he worked for almost twenty years, interspersed with journeys abroad. He was responsible for several Turin churches (particularly the Superga Basilica), a royal palace and the plans for the Stupingi Castle. In 1735 he went to Madrid, where he died the following year.

Kant, Emmanuel (1724-1804)

German philosopher, of Scottish origin, born and died in Königsberg. Was professor of logic and metaphysics at the University of Königsberg from 1770 to 1797 and his later writings established him as the leading exponent of modern ideal philosophy, which had a great influence on modern philosophical speculation. His best-known work is *The Critique of Pure Reason*, written in 1781. The second part of his *Religion within the Limits of Pure Reason* was suppressed by the *Berlin Journal* in 1793 after it had published the first part, but the whole of the work was later published in Königsberg. Soon after this Kant retired and saw no one but intimate friends in the last years of his life.

Kauffmann, Angelica Catharina Maria Anna (1740-1807)

Born in Coire, Switzerland, died in Rome. Because she showed very great promise in drawing at a very early age, her father put her into boy's clothing so that she could attend classes at the Academy. She studied in Florence, Rome, Venice, had a great success in Italy and then at court in London where, in 1768, she became one of the original members of the Royal Academy. She painted a portrait of her great friend Sir Joshua Reynolds, later married the Venetian painter Antonio Zucchi and went to live in Rome. Her work was graceful and included portraits, mythology and allegories.

Kneller, Gottfried (1646-1723)

Portrait painter, of German origin, born in Lubeck, died in London. He succeeded Van Dyck as official portrait painter to the court in London. He first studied under the Dutch painter Ferdinand Bol, where he assimilated Rembrandt's technique. In 1672 he went to Rome as the pupil of Carlo Maratta and Bernini. After a stay of two years in Italy he returned to Germany, then went to London: here his success was considerable. He collaborated at the court with Peter Lely. A great number of his portraits are to be found in European museums.

Krafft (Per le Vieux) (1724-93)

Swedish portraitist, known as "The Swede", born in Arboga, died in Stockholm. He was professor of fine arts in Stockholm. At the Polish court he painted several portraits for King Stanislas-August. The Stockholm Museum has some of his portraits.

Kucharski, Alexander (1741-1819)

Polish painter, born in Warsaw, died in Paris. He studied in Italy and in Paris, where he painted a portrait of Marie Antoinette in 1780. Twice he found himself working in the Temple prison: he painted a new portrait of Marie Antoinette while she was being detained there.

Labille-Guiard, Adélaïde (1749-1803)

French portrait painter, born and died in Paris. She was the pupil of the painter Elie Vincent. The Academy admitted her at the same time as Madame Vigée-Lebrun in 1783. She made numerous portraits in oil and pastels of the principal figures of the day, from the old regime to the revolutionaries: *Mesdames of France* (daughters of Louis XV), *Comtesse de Clermont-Tonnerre*, *Robespierre*, etc.

Lafosse (Charles de) (1636-1716)

French historical painter, born in Paris. A pupil of Le Brun, he decorated several churches in Paris (Invalides) and stately homes in England. He was admitted to the Academy in 1673.

Lafrensen the Younger, Nicolas
(called Lavreince) (1737-1807)

Swedish painter, born and died in Stockholm. He studied under his father, the miniaturist Nicolas Lafrensen the Elder. On his father's death he went to Paris, where he stayed three years, visited Germany and then returned to Stockholm. He went back to Paris in 1771 but was recalled to Stockholm and was made a member of the Academy and King's painter. He returned to Paris again but was forced to leave when the Revolution broke out and went home to Stockholm, where he completed a suite of compositions on the history of Sweden.

Lagrenée, Louis-Jean-François
(1725-1805)

French painter, born and died in Paris. He
was a pupil of Carle Van Loo, won the
Rome prize in 1749 and was accepted by
the Academy in 1755. In 1760 he was
appointed director of the Fine Arts Academy at St Petersburg, but returned to
Paris three years later. In 1781 he became
director of the Rome school. On leaving
this school he received a pension from the
King and an apartment at the Louvre.

Lampi the Elder, Jean-Baptiste
(1751-1830)

Italian portraitist and historical painter,
born in Romeno, died in Vienna. Made
his studies at Salzburg and under Lorenzi
in Verona. In 1783 in Vienna he painted
portraits of the Potocki family. In 1787 he
became painter to the court of Warsaw
where he painted the portrait of King
Stanislas-August. In 1791 he left for
Russia but returned later to Vienna and
became a member of the Academy.

Lancret, Nicolas (1690-1743)

French painter, born and died in Paris,
son of a coachman. He first learned engraving as the pupil of Pierre Dulin. In
1702 he was expelled from an Academy
course and withdrew from the competition for the Rome prize after an early
setback. Studying under Gillot, he began
to imitate Watteau. On Watteau's advice
he applied himself to painting landscapes,
about 1717. He was admitted to the Aca-

demy in 1719 as painter of *fêtes galantes*,
the type in which he specialised. He re-
ceived many commissions from the great
European collectors, including Louis XV,
Frederick II and the Prince. He was
named adviser to the Academy in 1735.
He painted many decorative pieces for
Versailles, La Muette and Fontainebleau
and a series of paintings inspired by La
Fontaine's *Fables*.

Largillière (Nicolas de) (1656-1746)

French painter, born and died in Paris.
His parents went to live in Antwerp three
years after his birth and it was there that
he served his apprenticeship. Admitted as
master of the Guild in 1672. In 1674 he
worked in London under the direction of
Peter Lely. Persecution of the Catholics
brought him to Paris in 1678 where, as a
protégé of Le Brun, he built up a considerable reputation. In 1685 he went to London to paint a portrait of King James II
and the Queen. In 1686 he was admitted
as a member of the Royal Academy in

Paris (*Portrait of Le Brun*) and was named a director in 1728. He painted a great number of portraits of women, at which he was more gifted than his friend Hyacinthe Rigaud, and to whom, in return, he sent his male clients.

La Tour (Maurice Quentin de) (1704-88)

French painter, born and died at St Quentin. His father wanted him to be an engineer but La Tour rapidly proved his own talent. In 1722, after being refused several times, he succeeded in working with Spoede and Dupoch in Paris. In 1724 he was at Cambrai, where a diplomatic congress was being held. The British Ambassador offered him a place in London and La Tour remained there for two years. On his return he wanted to take advantage of the pro-British feeling of his countrymen in passing himself off as an English painter, but instead, on the advice of a contemporary, retired for two years to perfect his drawing and read scientific and literary works. In 1737 he was ac-

cepted by the Academy on presentation of two pastel portraits. He exhibited at the Salon from 1739 until 1765. His work fetched high prices at this time. In 1745 he exhibited at the Salon a *Portrait of the King and Dauphin*; the same year he received permission to live at the Louvre. He was admitted to the Academy in 1746 with a portrait of his master, J. Restout. In 1751 he was named adviser to the Academy. In 1753 his *Portrait of Queen Marie Leczinska* was exhibited at Versailles; the vogue of his work grew incessantly. *Portrait of Madame de Pompadour*, regarded as his masterpiece, was painted in 1755. In 1766 he travelled in Holland. Towards the end of his life La Tour sank into a delirium and his brother took him back to St Quentin, where his family had him certified. He died on the night of 16-17 February 1788. The St Quentin Museum has about eighty pastels, found in his studio at the time of his death.

Lawrence (Sir Thomas) (1769-1830)

English portrait painter, died in London. In 1787 he entered the Royal Academy in London as a pupil. Lawrence rapidly distinguished himself as a portrait painter and replaced Reynolds as an ordinary painter to the King in 1792. Made a member of the Royal Academy in 1794, he pursued a brilliant career as a portraitist. In 1814 and 1815 he painted the portraits of the Prince Regent and leading French personalities who were in London. In 1818 he went to Aix-la-Chapelle, Vienna and Rome and brought back portraits for the royal collection. He was made President of the Royal Academy

177

and made a portrait of Charles X in 1825. His works remain in Dublin, London museums and in the Louvre.

Le Lorrain, Louis-Joseph (1715-59)

French painter and engraver, born in Paris, died in St Petersburg. Was the pupil of Dumont le Romain. Won the first prize for painting in 1739, admitted as Academician in 1756. Two years later he was director of the Academy of Fine Arts at St Petersburg. In 1753, 1755 and 1757 he exhibited religious, mythological and decorative subjects at the Salon. He illustrated Le Fontaine's *Fables* and *Orlando Furioso*.

Lemoine, François (1688-1737)

French historical and genre painter, born and died in Paris. Won the Academy grand prize in 1711 and was admitted in 1718. In 1723 he travelled in Italy. Lemoine painted various pictures for the Chateau of Versailles and Saint-Sulpice Church in Paris (1729-31). In 1733 he was appointed professor at the Academy. From this date he began decorating the Hercules Salon at Versailles which gained him the title of King's principal painter in 1736. He took his own life the following year.

Lépicié, Michèle-Nicolas-Bernard (1735-84)

French painter, born in Paris of a family of painters and was a pupil of Carle Van Loo. In 1751 and 1753 he won prizes at the Academy and took the second prize in Rome in 1759. In 1764 he was accepted by the Academy and admitted in 1769. In the same year he was made King's painter and, in 1779, professor at the Academy. A religious crisis in 1783 caused him to modify his paintings and he devoted himself to scenes of rural life. At the end of his life he had Carle Vernet as a pupil.

Le Prince, Jean-Baptiste (1734-81)

French painter and engraver, born at Metz, died at St-Denis-du-Port. Historical painter, portraitist and painter of genre and landscapes. Because of the patronage of the Marshal de Bell-Isle, governor of Metz, he was able to enter the studio of François Boucher in Paris. He excelled above all in engraving. In 1758 he went to Russia to fulfil an order from the Tsar for decoration of several ceilings in the Imperial Palace, St Petersburg. Towards the end of 1764 he went back to Paris where he achieved great success with the drawings and engravings he brought back from his travels. He was admitted to the Academy in 1765. Diderot had a great admiration for Le Prince. Towards the end of his life, weakened by the Russian climate, he retired to live in the country.

Levitski, Dimitri Gregoriovitch (1735-1822)

Russian portrait painter, born in Kiev, died in St Petersburg. He enjoyed a considerable reputation and painted portraits of the Imperial family and leading

Pietro Longhi
Duck Hunters on the Lagoon
Venice, Querini Stampalia Gallery

Russian personalities. The Leningrad and Moscow museums have a number of these works.

Liotard, Jean-Etienne (1702-89)

Swiss painter, of French origin, born in Geneva. Went to Paris in 1723 where he worked for several princely families and for ecclesiastical circles. Of an adventurous nature, he undertook a number of journeys, to Rome (1736), to Constantinople, where he stayed five years, and to Moldavia. He was a great success in Vienna where, because of his Moldavian-style beard, he was called "The Turkish Painter"; from this period dates his greatest work, *The Chocolate Seller*, which is in the Dresden Museum. After Venice, Darmstadt and Lyons he went to Paris where his success was as great as in Vienna. Before settling in Geneva in 1758 he stayed in England, Holland, again in France and went several times to Vienna. In his latter days he produced a technical work, *Treatise on the Principles and Rules of Painting*. Liotard left for posterity pastels, miniatures, portraits and paintings on enamel.

Locatelli, Andrea (1693-*c*.1741)

Italian painter, born and died in Rome; painter of historical subjects, architecture, genre and landscapes. He imitated Claude Gellee and Francesco Zuccarelli and had a fairly great reputation in Rome. He taught Joseph Vernet.

Locke, John (1632-1704)

English philosopher. An adversary of the innate idea, he placed all man's knowledge in the category of resulting from experience and laid down the idea that all facts must be severely tested before being used as the basis for theories. He was also an ardent defender of liberalism. His famous *Essay concerning the Human Understanding* appeared in 1690.

Longhi, Alessandro (1733-1813)

Italian painter and engraver, born and died in Venice. Taking advantage of the popularity of his brother Pietro Longhi, Alessandro was able to paint portraits of Venetian society. He was a member and professor of the Academy. He also produced a *Life of Modern Venetian Artists* with portraits engraved by himself, which contained valuable information on Venetian painting of the time.

Longhi, Pietro (1702-85)

Venetian genre painter, pupil of Balestra and particularly of G. M. Crespi. Passed his life in his native city, with honours

179

heaped on him and a degree of wealth. He was the painter of the well-off middle class of Venice, whose private and public lives he put on canvas. The greater part of his works are in Venice in the Correr Museum, the Academy, the Palazzi Grassi and Albrizzi.

Losenko, Anton Pavlovitch (1737-73)

Russian historical painter, born in Glukhov, died in St Petersburg. After travelling in Italy and France he was made director of the St Petersburg Academy. A number of his works are in the museum of this city.

Loutherbourg, Jacques-Philippe II (1740-1812)

Landscapist and painter of battles, born in Strasburg, died in London. Served his first apprenticeship under his father, Jacques-Philippe Loutherbourg the First. He also studied under Tischbein and Casanova. He had a great reputation as a painter of animals and landscapes. In 1768 he was a member of the Academy, later painter to the King and in 1781 became a member of the Royal Academy. His works remain in London, Strasburg and Stockholm.

Lundberg, Gustav (1695-1786)

Swedish painter. Lived in Paris from 1717 to 1745, where he was admitted to the Academy. He is regarded in Sweden as the best portraitist of the Swedish 18th-century school. His works are to be found in the museums of Stockholm and Nancy.

Maella (Mariano Salvador de) (1739-1819)

Spanish painter, born in Valencia, died in Madrid. He was a pupil of Gonzalez. Maella was director of the San Fernando Academy and principal painter to the King. He painted historical scenes, landscapes and seascapes. The Prado Museum has several of his works.

Magnasco, Alessandro (called Lissandrino) (1667-1749)

Italian painter, born in Genoa. He worked in Milan with Abbiati. He painted great religious compositions which are regarded as having reached one of the peaks of Italian 18th-century painting (*Supper at Emmaus*). He was painter to the Grand Duke of Florence and his work is somewhat analogous to that of Callot and seems to point to that of Goya.

Marivaux (Pierre de Chamblain de)
(1688-1763)

French writer, born in Paris. The novelty
in Marivaux's theatrical work is the
importance given to love. From this
stemmed the importance of his feminine
roles and a certain lack of action strength.
In 1722 he achieved a great success with
his *Surprise of Love*. His best works,
which he wrote between 1730 and 1740,
were *The Game of Love and Chance*,
Indiscreet Vows, *The Fortunate Stratagem*,
The Legacy, *False Confidences* and *The
Proof*. In 1743 he was elected a member of
the French Academy.

Maulbertsch, Franz Anton (1724-96)

Austrian painter and engraver, born at
Langenragen on Lake Constance, died in
Vienna. Painted numerous frescoes in
Moravia, the Tyrol and Hungary, and
some portraits. Was admitted to the
Vienna Academy in 1759 and became
professor there in 1770. He travelled to
Dresden in 1775 and to Prague in 1794.
He is best known as the leading fresco
painter at the end of the Austrian Rococo
period. His works are to be found in the
museums of Graz, Berlin and Vienna.

Melendez (or Menendez), Luis (1716-80)

Spanish painter, born in Naples, died in
Madrid. Studied in Madrid with his
father, then went to Rome to perfect his
art. In Madrid he worked on miniatures
and painted the decorations for the choir-
books of the royal chapel. In 1773 he
painted the *Holy Family*, which won him
great success. He painted numerous pictures for the Aranjuez Palace. He was
found later to be a very great painter of
still-life, examples of which are in the
Escorial and the Prado in Madrid. The
Louvre has a *Self-portrait* by Melendez.

Menageot, François-Guillaume
(1744-1816)

French painter, born in London, died in
Paris. Worked with Deshays and Boucher. In 1765 he took the second, and in
1766 the first, prize in Rome. In 1780 he
was admitted to the Academy, in 1787
appointed director of the French school in
Rome, in 1790 professor at the Ecole des
Beaux-Arts and in 1809 a member of the
Institute. He worked in several Paris
churches, notably Saint-Nicholas du

181

Chardonnet and Saint-Eustache, as well as the church at Neuilly and Saint-Peter's at Douai.

Mengs, Anton Raphael (1728-79)

German painter and writer, born at Aussig, Bohemia, died in Rome. Studied painting in Dresden and Rome, where he became a court painter in 1745. He worked on the decoration of the church of Saint-John in Rome and painted numerous portraits of princes. In 1761 he became principal painter to King Charles III of Spain and worked with Tiepolo on frescoes for the royal palace. He returned to Italy in 1769 and settled in Rome. From 1773 to 1777 he stayed again at the court of the King of Spain. He rose to brilliant glory during his lifetime; likened to Titian, Correge or Raphael, he imposed a veritable dictatorship on his pupils and on painters who occupied less official positions than his own.

Mercier, Philippe (1689-1760)

Genre painter and portraitist, born in Berlin of French parents, died in London. He studied in Berlin, Venice, Florence and Rome. In 1720, after his marriage, he settled in Hanover where he made the acquaintance of the Prince of Wales. He went to London with the Prince and painted several portraits of the British royal family. His rural festival scenes, very much liked in England, were often mistaken for those of Watteau.

Montesquieu (Charles de Secondat, baron de La Brède, et de) (1689-1755)

French writer, born at Chateau de La Brède in the Gironde, died in Paris. Intended to be a magistrate, he succeeded his uncle as adviser to the Bordeaux Parliament, but soon began travelling throughout Europe to gather material for the monumental work on jurisprudence on which he worked all his life. In 1721 Montesquieu wrote his *Discourse on the Transparency of Bodies* and *Observations on Natural History*. His *Persian Letters*, appearing the same year, were a social and even more political satire of his own countrymen and were the forerunner of his *Esprit des Lois*. In 1734 he produced *Causes of the Greatness and Decay of the Romans*, the first work in which the philosophy of history is applied without recourse to theology. But it was his *Esprit des Lois* in 1748, a profound study of the world's legal and political institutions, that first placed jurisprudence into literature and firmly established him in history. Montesquieu put his life's work and meditation into it and it remains a classic today.

Mura (Francesco de) (1696-1782)

Italian painter, born and died in Naples. Studied first under Domenico Piola and later under Solimena. He worked mainly in Naples and Turin. He also painted several portraits of princes and princesses of Savoy and some still-lifes.

Jean-Marc Nattier
The Duke de Boufflers
Rheims, Fine Arts Museum

Natoire, Charles-Joseph (1700-77)

French painter, born at Nîmes, died at Castelgandolfo. Son of the architect and sculptor Florent Natoire, he was a pupil of Lemoine. In 1731 he won the first prize for painting with *Manné offrant un Sacrifice pour obtenir un Fils* (Manné offering a Sacrifice to obtain a Son). He studied in Rome where, at a young age, he acquired a wide reputation. Returning to Paris he exhibited at first in the Place Dauphine. In 1734 he entered the Academy and became professor there three years later. He took part in the decoration of the Hôtel de Soubise and made numerous tapestry cartoons for the royal tapestry works. In 1751 he became director of the French school in Rome. The Stockholm Museum has several of his works.

Nattier, Jean-Marc (1685-1766)

French painter, born and died in Paris, son of Marc Nattier, a portrait painter in

the reign of Louis XIV. Nattier began by making drawings for engravers, including the Rubens of Luxemburg. In 1715 the Tsar summoned him to Amsterdam, where Nattier painted the portraits of the imperial family and other important members of the Russian court, and the *Battle of Poltava*. Returning to Paris, Nattier became a member of the Academy in 1718 and professor in 1752. He worked as a portrait painter, became known in the entourage of the Duke of Orleans and was appointed painter to the royal family in 1745. From 1737 to 1763 he exhibited regularly at the Salon, but died disgraced and generally forgotten.

Nixon, John (*c*. 1760-1818)

English designer and engraver. From 1779 to 1786 he made drawings for the engraver Watts of the stately homes of England and Ireland. From 1784 to 1815 he exhibited at the Royal Academy, in whose catalogues he was listed as the Reverend John Nixon.

Norblin de La Gourdaine, Jean-Pierre (1745-1830)

French historical painter and portraitist, born at Misy-sur-Yonne and died in Paris. He studied in Dresden with Giovanni Casanova. In 1771 he won the grand prize of the Dresden Academy. He founded the Warsaw Academy of Painting and became painter to King Stanislas-August at the Polish court.

183

Octavien, François (1695-1736)

French painter, born in Rome, died in Paris. He was admitted to the Academy in 1725 and was one of the better followers of Watteau with Bar and Pater. His works are in the Louvre and the Nancy Museum.

Opie, John (1761-1807)

English painter and illustrator, died in London. While very young he began portrait painting, but abandoned this rapidly in favour of historical painting. He exhibited at the Royal Academy from 1782 and was made a member in 1787. In 1806 he replaced Fuseli as professor of painting. His works are to be found in London museums.

French painter, born in Paris, died in Beauvais. His father, painter and art dealer, taught him the rudiments of his art, then sent him to the St Luke masters' school. At the age of eighteen he was a pupil of Michel Serre, then painter to the King's galleys in Marseilles. Oudry went there with Serre and did not return to Paris for four years. Then he studied for five years under Largillière. Admitted to the St Luke Academy in 1708, he became professor there in 1717. He tried first religious painting, then portraits, then urban landscapes in 1718. The Academy classified him as historical painter. In 1722 his *Chasse au Sanglier* (Boar Hunt) won him a commission from the King of Sweden; in 1725 he was made painter to the Beauvais factory. In 1743 he succeeded de Troy as professor at the Academy. Oudry was the most sought-after animal painter of the 18th century.

Oudry, Jean-Baptiste (1686-1755)

Panini, Giovanni Paolo (1691-1765)

Italian landscapist, born at Piacenza, died in Rome. He was a pupil of Benedetto Luti and Andrea Locatelli. He carried out large decorative works in Rome. In 1732 he was made a member of the Royal Academy of Painting in Paris, then professor at the French Academy in Rome. He is best known for his landscapes with ruins, which are to be found in many museums throughout Europe.

Paret y Alcazar, Luis (1746-99)

Spanish painter, born and died in Madrid. Worked with Antonio Gonzalez-Velasquez. Several times he won the San Fernando Academy medal and became a member of the Madrid Academy. He illustrated *Don Quixote*. The Prado in Madrid has several of his works.

Parrocel, Charles (1688-1752)

French painter and engraver, born and died in Paris. Was a pupil of Charles de Lafosse. In 1712 he went to Rome. Returning to Paris he was made a member of the Academy in 1721. He followed King Louis XV and painted several portraits of him on horseback during the campaigns of 1744-5. Parrocel exhibited at the Salon from 1737 to 1746. He also made many drawings.

Pater, Jean-Baptiste-Joseph (1695-1736)

French painter, born at Valenciennes, died in Paris. His father was the sculptor Antoine Pater. In 1713 he studied for some time under Watteau in Paris. After a stay at Valenciennes he returned to Paris where he rapidly became the painter of middle-class society. Shortly before he died, Watteau summoned Pater to give him his last advice. In 1725 he was approved by the Academy and admitted in 1728 as a painter of *fêtes galantes*. During the latter part of his life he worked on many commissions and, overworked, died at the age of forty-one.

Pellegrini, Giovanni Antonio (1675-1741)

Italian painter, born and died in Venice. Was a pupil of Sebastiano Ricci and Paolo Pagani. He worked first in Holland where, among other things, he decorated the ceilings of the Mauritshuis in The Hague. Then his travels took him to Italy, England, Germany, Flanders, France and Austria.

Perronneau, Jean-Baptiste (1715-83)

French painter, born in Paris, died in Amsterdam. Studied engraving under Laurent Cars before becoming a pupil of Natoire. From 1743 onwards he painted portraits in pastels rivalling La Tour in this form. In 1746 he was approved by the Academy and admitted in 1753. Then he travelled through France, Italy and Holland. In 1781 he went to Russia and died in Amsterdam on his way back.

Pesne, Antoine (1683-1757)

French painter, born in Paris, died in Berlin. Son of the painter Thomas Pesne and a relative of Charles de Lafosse on his mother's side. First in the competition in Rome in 1703, he left for Venice when the prize was not awarded. Frederick II summoned him to the Prussian court where, in 1711, he was appointed principal painter. He was highly successful there as a portrait painter and then went to Dessau in 1715 and Dresden in 1718. In 1723 and 1724 he went through Paris to London. At the request of Frederick the Great he carried out the decorations for Charlottenburg, Potsdam and Sans-Souci.

Piazzetta, Giambattista (1682-1754)

Italian painter, born and died in Venice. Was a pupil of Antonio Molinari. He worked in Bologna where he came under the influence of Crespi. In 1750 he was named first director of the Venice Academy. He painted frescoes in the church of Saints John and Paul in Venice and the Santo church in Padua.

Pierre, Jean-Baptiste (1713-89)

French painter, born and died in Paris. Studied under Natoire. In 1735 he worked in Rome. Returning to Paris in 1740, he was admitted to the Academy in 1742, became professor in 1748 and director in 1770. In the same year he was appointed principal painter to the King, replacing Boucher. He took part in Academy exhibitions from 1741 to 1769. He decorated public monuments and churches in Paris.

Pillement, Jean (1728-1808)

French painter, born and died in Lyons. He was painter to the Polish court, worked in Vienna and, from 1760 to 1780, exhibited in England. He also showed his works in Paris and became the painter to Marie-Antoinette. His very disperse talents ranged over landscapes, seascapes, genre paintings and flowers. He was also a water-colourist, designer and engraver.

Piranesi, Giovanni Battista (1720-78)

Italian engraver and architect, born at Mozano di Mestre, died in Rome. He

studied archaeology and architecture with the architect-engineer Lucchesi. In 1738 he left for Rome to study architecture, painting and engraving. Later he went to Venice to earn a living as an architect. There he worked on painting with Tiepolo and Polanzani. After a sojourn in Naples, Piranesi made drawings at Herculaneum, Pompeii and Paestum. From 1750 onwards he published numerous engravings in Rome.

Pittoni, Giovanni Battista (1687-1767)

Italian historical painter, born and died in Venice. Was the pupil of his uncle Francesco Pittoni, but later came under the influence of Balestra, then Tiepolo, Sebastiano Ricci and Pompeo Battoni. He became president of the Academy after Tiepolo in 1758. A great part of his work consists of religious and mythological subjects.

Procaccini, Andrea (1671-1734)

Italian painter, engraver and architect, born in Rome, died at San Ildefonso. Studied under Carlo Maratta and worked in the style of his master. A protégé of Pope Clement XI, he carried out several works in Rome churches, particularly in Saint-John Lateran. Summoned to Spain about 1720 by King Philip V, he was appointed painter of the King's chamber. He remained in Spain until he died, and was responsible for the decoration of numerous churches and palaces in that country.

Quillard, Pierre-Antoine (1701-33)

French painter, disciple of Watteau, born in Paris, died in Lisbon. Summoned to Portugal he became painter to the court and member of the Lisbon Academy of Painting. One of his best-known works is the ceiling which he painted for the Queen's bedchamber.

Quinckhardt, Jan Maurits (1688-1772)

Dutch painter, born near Cleves, died in Amsterdam. He was a pupil of Arnold van Boonen and worked in Utrecht and Amsterdam. Quinckhardt painted portraits and mythological and allegorical subjects. The Amsterdam Rijksmuseum has a large number of his paintings.

Ramsay, Allan (1713-84)

English portraitist and essayist, born in Edinburgh, died at Dover. Studied in London and Edinburgh, then in Rome and Naples, where he was a pupil of Solimena. In London, where he settled in 1739, he was court painter to King George III. Ramsay was a portraitist of renown.

Ranc, Jean (1674-1735)

French painter, born in Montpellier, died in Madrid; son of a painter, Antoine Ranc. In 1697, he became a pupil of the Royal Academy in Paris, where he met Hyacinthe Rigaud, whose niece he married. Admitted to the Academy in 1703 he was approved as a history painter the following year. In 1724 Philip V summoned him to Madrid where he painted portraits of the royal family. His works are mainly to be found in the Prado.

Raoux, Jean (1677-1734)

French painter, born in Montpellier, died in Paris. Studied first in Montpellier with Ranc, then became a pupil of Bon Boullongne in Paris. In 1704 he won the Academy first prize, after which he passed three years in Rome and two in Venice. Back in Paris in 1714, he was admitted to the Academy in 1717. He painted *fêtes galantes*, fantasy subjects and allegorical figures.

Restout, Jean (1692-1768)

French painter, born in Rouen, died in Paris, pupil and nephew of Jouvenet. He won first prize in Rome and had a great vogue as historical painter. He was made a member of the Academy in 1720, professor in 1733, rector in 1752, director in 1760 and chancellor in 1761. He exhibited at the Salon from 1737 to 1763.

Reynolds, Sir Joshua (1723-92)

English portrait painter, born at Plympton, Devon, died in London. From 1740 Reynolds worked as apprentice to the portraitist Thomas Hudson. In 1749 he went to Italy and spent two years in Rome to familiarise himself with the techniques of the old masters by copying their works. On his return to London in 1752 he set himself up as portrait painter. Three years later he painted a *Portrait of Commodore Keppel* which won him a claim in high society. From then on he received numerous commissions, and his paintings sold at a high price, enabling him to begin an important collection of art objects, paintings and drawings. In 1760 he founded the Society of Artists, where he exhibited. Eight years later, with a handful of artists of sufficient reputation, he founded the Royal Academy, whose statutes were to be the same as those of the Royal Academy of Paris. He was elected President of the Royal Academy and, between 1769 and 1790, composed and delivered the famous fifteen *Discourses on Art*. His last great portraits were those of *King George III* and *Queen Charlotte*, which he painted in 1779. Towards the end of his life Reynolds painted mythological or allegorical subjects.

Ribera (Juan Vicente de)

Spanish painter who worked in Madrid in the 18th century. In 1725 he was appointed Assessor of Paintings by the Castille Council. He painted religious subjects for the Archbishop's Palace in Madrid.

Ricci, Marco (1676-1729)

Italian painter, born in Belluno, died in Venice, nephew and pupil of Sebastiano Ricci. He worked in Rome where he was noticed as a painter of landscapes and perspectives. Preceding his uncle, he went to England in 1710; his success there was as great as it had been in Rome. In 1730 he published a collection of etchings in Venice.

Ricci, Sebastiano (1659-1734)

Italian painter, born at Cividal di Belluno, died in Venice. In 1674 he was a pupil of Federigo Cervelli in Venice and then, in 1682, he studied in Bologna. He enjoyed the protection of the Duke of Parma. After the latter's death in 1694, Ricci went to Florence, Modena, Parma, Milan and Bergamo, then stayed in Venice for three years. Summoned to the court of Vienna, he decorated the Schönbrunn Palace. Back in Italy he decorated palaces in Florence for the Grand Duke of Tuscany. In 1718 he was admitted to the Royal Academy in Paris and later worked in England until 1728. On his return he settled permanently in Venice, where he painted mainly easel paintings.

Richardson, Samuel (1689-1761)

English writer, born in the county of Derby, whose work greatly influenced that of Diderot and Rousseau. Richardson may be regarded as the creator of the modern English novel. Among his chief works were *The History of Clarissa Harlowe, Pamela, or Virtue Rewarded* and *The History of Sir Charles Grandison.*

Rigaud, Hyacinthe (1659-1743)

French painter, born in Perpignan, died in Paris. At the age of fourteen he went to Montpellier, where he remained for four years, making copies in the workshop of Pézet. After four years in Lyons he arrived in Paris in 1681 and the following year won the first prize for painting at the Paris Royal Academy. He established himself as a portraitist and rapidly became principal painter to Louis XIV, then to the Regent and finally to Louis XV. He was approved by the Academy in 1685, admitted as a member in 1687, made professor in 1710, and rector and director in 1733. Rigaud, who was raised to the peerage in 1709, enjoyed world-wide fame.

Robert, Hubert (1733-1808)

French painter, born and died in Paris. Made his début as a painter in 1753. The following year the Count of Stainville, the future Duke of Choiseul, was named ambassador to the Holy See and took Robert with him to Rome, entering him in the French Academy which was directed by Natoire. There he was influenced by Panini and Piranesi. At a time when the research and theories of Winckelmann were restoring antiquity to fashion, Hubert Robert became a painter of ruins and Natoire encouraged him in this. He met Fragonard, with whom he stayed at

the house of the Abbé St Non in Rome, then in Naples and Paestum. In July 1675 he went back to Paris after spending eleven years in Italy. He painted from the sketches he had made in Italy. In 1766 he was approved by and admitted to the Academy. The King commanded from him an overmantel for the Château de Meudon. At the same time he exhibited at the Salon; criticism was favourable and his canvases from then on were sought after. He was received at the house of the Duke of Choiseul and the salon of Madame Geoffrin. For forty years he moved through Paris making sketches for his canvases. A suspect under the Revolution he was arrested on what the revolutionary new calendar showed as the eighth day of the second month of the year II.

When freed several months later he and Fragonard were named curators of the future Central Museum of Arts.

Rokotov, Fjodor (*c.* 1735-1808)

Russian portraitist, died in St Petersburg. Was a pupil of Pietro Rotari and of L.-J. Le Lorrain. He painted a portrait of Peter III in 1762 and several portraits of Catherine II. He worked for the Russian nobility and the imperial family.

Romney, George (1734-1802)

English painter, born at Dalton-in-Furness, died at Kendal. With Gainsborough and Reynolds, Romney formed the great trio which installed English portrait painting. Son of a cabinet-maker, Romney worked from the age of ten to twenty-one in his father's workshop. In 1755 his father had him apprenticed to the painter Edward Steele, at Kendal. Two years later he set himself up in this town as portrait painter. In 1762 he went to London and from 1763 until 1772 exhibited at the Society of Artists and the Free Society. In 1764 he went to France where he met Vernet. In 1773 he was in Italy. Two years later he returned to London where his rival Reynolds was jealous of his success. He drove himself to work very hard; tired and ill, Romney returned to his family home at Kendal in 1799 and died several years later of a cerebral haemorrhage. The National Gallery in London has a large number of his portraits.

Roslin, Alexander (1718-93)

Swedish painter, born at Malmoe, died in Paris. After spending five years from 1747 to 1752 in Italy, he set himself up in Paris as a portraitist and was highly successful, with a large following among women. He married a young pastel artist, Marie-Suzanne Giroust. He was admitted to the Academy in 1753. His wife was approved in 1770 and exhibited at the Salon the following year. After the death of his wife, Roslin returned to Sweden where he stayed for several years. In 1774 he was elected a member of the Stockholm Academy. A number of portraits he painted are in the Louvre in Paris, the Hermitage in Leningrad and the Stockholm Museum.

Rotari, Pietro (1707-62)

Italian painter, born at Verona, died in St Petersburg. He was a pupil of Antonio Balestra and, from 1727, worked in Rome with Trevisani. After stays in Vienna and Dresden he became principal painter to the Empress of Russia.

Rousseau, Jean-Jacques (1712-78)

French-language writer, born in Geneva, died at Ermenonville. After several years of a vagabond life he went to stay at the home of Madame de Warens from 1732 to 1740, where he read and studied music. In 1741 he went to try his luck in Paris, where he met Voltaire. He frequented the Salons and was associated with the *Encyclopaedia*. In 1750 he wrote *Discourse on the Sciences and Arts* for a Dijon Aca-

demy competition, and won first prize with it. In 1775 he wrote *Discourse on the Origin of Inequality among Men*. It caused a scandal. Rousseau went back to Geneva and was reconverted to Calvinism. In 1756 he stayed at the home of Madame d'Epinay, who discharged him the following year. Rousseau quarrelled with Diderot and replied to an article in the *Encyclopaedia* with his famous *Letter to d'Alembert on Entertainment* (1758). He retired to Montmorency where he wrote *Nouvelle Héloïse* (Julia, or the New Héloïse) (1761), and in 1762 appeared his *Social Contract*, the sequel to an article written in 1753 for the *Encyclopaedia*. Publication of *Emile* (1762) resulted in Rousseau being banned from Paris and

Switzerland. He took refuge in Motiers, stayed there three years and finally was hunted out by the inhabitants. After a stay in London, where he argued with Hume, Rousseau settled permanently in Paris in

191

Thomas Rowlandson
Cheyne Walk
London, London Museum

Gabriel-Jacques de Saint-Aubin
Drawing
Lille Museum

1770. He completed his *Confessions*, published after his death, and from 1772 to 1776 wrote his *Rêveries d'un Promeneur solitaire*. In March 1777 he was invited to stay in a cottage provided by Madame de Girardin at Ermenonville, where he died. He also painted some water-colours to illustrate his *Botanical Dictionary*, published in 1808.

Rowlandson, Thomas (1756-1827)

Painter, engraver and caricaturist, born and died in London. After receiving his first tuition at the Royal Academy, Rowlandson went to Paris where, at the age of sixteen, he entered the Royal Academy school. In 1775 he returned to London and exhibited at the Royal Academy. Inheriting a fortune from an aunt in Paris, he began frequenting London gaming-houses. By about 1782 he had given up practically all artistic work except caricatures, which paid well. It was particularly in this type of art that he excelled.

Saint-Aubin (Gabriel-Jacques de) (1724-80)

French painter and engraver, born and died in Paris. Son of an embroiderer, he was a pupil at the Royal Academy where he drew under the direction of Jeaurat, Colin de Vermont and Boucher, but never won better than a second prize (1750). Saint-Aubin made a number of etchings and oil paintings, but it was particularly his numerous drawings and engravings of Parisian life that made him famous. His works are in the Louvre and Carnavalet Museums.

St Non, Richard (Abbé) (1727-91)

French designer and engraver, born and died in Paris. His family placed him in Holy Orders but, not certain of his vocation, he obtained a post as clerical adviser to the Paris Parliament. Exiled to Poitiers, he devoted himself to engraving between 1752 and 1757. In 1759 he returned to Paris and resigned his post. After a trip to England he went to Rome and became friendly with Fragonard and Hubert Robert. Back in Paris he and a group of artists produced *Picturesque Journey to Naples and Sicily* (1781-6), a publication in five volumes with 542 plates of etchings.

Salon

The French artists' Salon takes its name from the Salon Carré of the Louvre where exhibitions were held. It was held regularly every two years from 1737. At first only artists approved by the Academy were able to exhibit there, but in 1791 participation was freed.

The Salons

In the final years of the reign of Louis XIV the salons were formed out of the ruins of the court. It was through them that writers of the 18th century were able to exert an influence on society. Each salon had its own character and habitués. At the "court" of Sceaux the Duchess du Maine represented the need for amusement which made itself felt towards the end of the reign of Louis XIV. Mademoiselle de Launay, her assistant, paints a picture of this salon in her *Memoirs*. The salon of the Marquise de Lambert in the Mazarin Palace represented the revival of the spirit of 17th-century refinement. The salon of Madame Geoffrin in the rue Saint-Honoré was that of the *Encyclopaedia* and its philosophers; but it was Madame du Deffand's salon in the rue Saint-Dominique which best personified the sceptical mind of the 18th century. There she met Horace Walpole for whom she developed a great but hopeless passion. From their friendship remains correspondence full of curious details. Becoming blind in 1753, Madame du Deffand took Mademoiselle de Lespinasse as a reader; from 1764 the latter opened her own salon in the rue de Bellechasse. This salon, meeting-place for those connected with the *Encyclopaedia*, represented the romantic and ardent element. Atheist meetings were held in the Baron d'Holbach's salon. Necker held a political salon. The widow of Claude-Adrien Helvetius, who retired to Auteuil, in 1771 opened a salon for intellectuals and artists who had shared the philosophical theories of her late husband. Bonaparte, returning from Egypt, visited this salon. Madame d'Epinay, who was the patron of Rousseau, also held a salon and left some interesting *Memoirs*. Bachaumont presided over the salon of Madame Doublet, which was held at the Convent of the Daughters of St. Thomas.

Sani, Domenico Maria (1690-*c*. 1772)

Italian painter, born at Cesena. In 1721 he established himself in Spain where he was painter to King Philip V. Two of his works, *Fou* (Lunatic) and *Mendiant* (Beggar), are in the Prado in Madrid.

Santerre, Jean-Baptiste (1651-1717)

French portraitist and historical painter, born at Magny-en-Vexin and died in Paris. He was a pupil of François Lemaire and of Bon Boullongne. Admitted to the

Academy in 1704, he exhibited at the Salon the same year. He founded an Academy for women at Versailles, and in particular painted portraits and genre.

Schiller (Friedrich von) (1759-1805)

German writer, born at Marbach. In 1773 he entered the Military Academy to study law. He finished his studies in 1780 as a doctor at Stuttgart, but was a poor exponent of the profession. In 1782 he published *The Robbers*. In 1787 he wrote *Don Carlos* and two years later was appointed professor of history at the University of Jena. In this period he wrote *The Thirty Years War* then his *Letters on the Aesthetic Education of Man*, which were printed in 1795. From 1793 to 1794 he was in the Stuttgart district where he met the publisher Gotta, with whom he founded the literary publication *Die Hören*. From this time dates his literary collaboration with Goethe. Goethe's *Wilhelm Meister* appeared in *Die Hören* and in 1796 the two writers published poems in the journal. Schiller eventually gave up the publication in order to complete his *Wallenstein* (1796-9). At Weimar he wrote *Maria Stuart* (1800) and *The Maid of Orleans* (1801). In 1802 he went to Berlin, and a year after completing *William Tell* in 1804 he died at the age of forty-five.

Scott, Samuel (1703-72)

English painter, born in London, died in Bath. He was a close friend of Hogarth. Scott painted marine subjects which were a great success. He was considered one of the leading British water-colourists. He exhibited from 1761 at the Society of Artists, the Free Society and at the Royal Academy in London.

Sedaine, Michel-Jean (1719-97)

French poet, born in Paris. In 1765 he wrote a serious drama, *The Unwitting Philosopher*. He also wrote *The Unexpected Wager* and some pieces for the Opéra-Comique. He was a member of the French Academy.

Servandoni, Jean-Nicolas (1695-1766)

Painter and architect, born in Florence, died in Paris. He studied painting under Jean-Paul Painsic at Piacenza and archi-

Silvestre le Jeune (Louis de) (1675-1760)

French painter, born at Sceaux, died in Paris. First took lessons from his father Israel Silvestre, then from Charles Le Brun and Bon Boullongne. Later he worked in Italy with Carlo Maratti. Returning to Paris he became a member of the Royal Academy in 1702, professor in 1706, rector in 1748 and director in 1752. In 1724 he was appointed first painter to the Court of Dresden and in 1727 became director of the Dresden Academy. He decorated the royal palace in Warsaw and several rooms in the elector's palace at Zwinger. Silvestre exhibited at the Paris Salons of 1704, 1750 and 1757.

tecture under Jean-Joseph Rossi in Rome. After a stay in Portugal he went to Paris, where he was a great success. His masterpiece, which he left incomplete, was the façade of the church of Saint-Sulpice in Paris. In 1731 he became a member of the Royal Academy. In 1749 he went to London where he married. Later he visited Dresden and Vienna. He exhibited at the Salon from 1737 to 1765. His scenographies and decorations for the big public festivals won acclaim for Servandoni throughout Europe.

Silva (Joao Chrisostome Policarpo da) (c. 1734-98)

Portuguese priest, sculptor and painter, born in Merceana, died in Lisbon; was a pupil of Jose de Almeida. Painted religious pictures and sculpted statues for Lisbon churches.

Snyers, Peter (1681-1752)

Flemish painter, born and died in Antwerp. He was a pupil of Alexander van Bredael in 1694. In 1705 he was a master in Brussels and in 1707 in Antwerp. He painted numerous portraits of the peerage in England.

Solimena, Francisco (1657-1747)

Italian painter and architect of the Neapolitan school. Son and pupil of Angelo Solimena. In 1647 he continued his studies in Naples, then worked in Rome copying the works of Pietro da Cortona, Guido Reni and Carlo Maratti. He painted a series of frescoes in Rome (S. Paolo Maggiore). Summoned to Spain by King Philip V in 1702, he painted several works for the Chapel Royal in Madrid. Solimena trained a great number of painters.

Stubbs, George (1724-1806)

English painter, born in Liverpool, died in London. He worked alone, travelled in Italy in 1754, then settled in London in 1760. He exhibited at the Society of Artists from 1761 and became president in 1773. In 1766 he published an important work, *Anatomy of the Horse*. He was admitted to the Academy in 1781. Stubbs painted mainly horses and dogs.

Suvée, Joseph-Benoit (1743-1807)

Flemish painter, born in Bruges, died in Rome. Had as master Mathias de Visch. He went to France, studied under Bachelier and entered the St Luke Academy. In 1771 he won the Rome prize and he stayed in Italy for six years. Returning to Paris in 1778 he became a member of the Academy in 1780. In 1792 he was elected director of the Rome Academy but took up the post only in 1801. He transferred the Academy from the Mancini Palace to the Villa Medici.

Swift, Jonathan (1667-1745)

Irish writer, born and died in Dublin. He passed his life in London, where he was an important figure in literary and political life. His pamphlets on the Irish question made him extremely popular in Ireland. Apart from *Gulliver's Travels* (1726) he wrote the *Drapier's Letters* and *Tale of a Tub*. Swift, a hopeless hypochondriac, spent the last few years of his life insane.

Taraval, Guillaume-Thomas-Raphael (1701-50)

French painter, born in Paris, died in Stockholm. Was a pupil of François Lemoine. At the request of the Swedish ambassador in Paris, he left for Stockholm, where he worked until his death. The Stockholm Museum has several of his genre paintings and animal subjects.

Thornhill, James (1675-1734)

English painter, a pupil of Thomas Highmore. He visited Flanders, France and Holland. Queen Anne commissioned him to decorate the cupola of Saint-Paul's, and he decorated Greenwich hospital and other different monuments in London. He also painted altar-pieces and made some etchings. He was both master and father-in-law of Hogarth.

Tiepolo, Giambattista (1696-1770)

Italian painter, born in Venice, died in Madrid. Tiepolo came from a rich family. His father, a naval captain, died in 1697. A pupil of Gregorio Lazzarini, Tiepolo also was influenced by Piazzetta and Sebastiano Ricci. In 1721 he married the sister of Francesco Guardi: she bore him several children, of whom two were painters, Gian Domenico and Lorenzo. Tiepolo worked in Venice and Venetia for twenty years. In 1733 he was in Bergamo,

in 1737 near Vienna and in 1740 in Milan. From 1750 to 1753 he carried out one of his most important works, the decoration of the archbishop's palace at Wurzburg. After that he returned to Venetia and worked until 1761. King Charles III summoned him to Spain, where he went with his two sons to decorate the royal palace with frescoes. He remained in Madrid until the end of his life, embittered in his old age by rivalry with Mengs. Venetia is rich in frescoes by Tiepolo. For his works he often made sketches in oils, explaining why his canvases are often to be found. He also painted genre and left drawings and etchings.

Tocqué, Louis (1696-1772)

French portraitist, born and died in Paris. Was a pupil of Nicolas Bertin and Hyacinthe Rigaud. He was admitted to the Academy in 1734. From 1737 to 1759 he sent fifty portraits to the Academy exhibitions. In 1740 he painted the portrait of the Dauphin and of Marie Leczinska. He spent two years in Russia (1757) and in 1759 lived in Denmark. With Largillière, Tocqué was one of the favourite painters of the high society of his day. His influence on the painters of foreign countries he visited was considerable: he taught Nordic painters the secret of French elegance.

Traversi, Gaspare (died 1769)

Italian painter, born in Naples. Painted several altar-pieces for churches in Rome and Parma. His works may be found in the museums of Milan, Rome, Aix-en-Provence, Rouen and Strasbourg.

Troost, Cornelis (1697-1750)

Dutch painter, born and died in Amsterdam. Was a pupil of Arnold Van Boonen. He used a special technique for painting, part water-colour, part pastel. He made portraits, genre scenes and paintings of historical subjects. The greater part of his work is in the Amsterdam and The Hague museums.

197

Troy (François de) (1645-1730)

French painter, born in Toulouse, died in Paris. He rapidly gained a reputation as a portrait painter. He was admitted to the Academy in 1675, was appointed professor in 1693 and director in 1708. Louis XIV ordered him to the court of Munich to paint a portrait of Marie-Christine of Bavaria. He painted numerous portraits of celebrated people.

Troy (Jean-François de) (1679-1752)

French painter, born in Paris, died in Rome. Was the son and pupil of François de Troy. He studied at the Royal Academy school then spent six years in Italy (1699-1705). Returning to Paris he was admitted to the Academy in 1708; he rapidly became the fashionable painter and decorated a number of princely mansions. He carried out works for the Paris churches and the royal residences. In 1738 he became director of the French Academy in Rome.

Van Loo, Charles-Amédée (1719-95)

Portraitist and genre-painter, born in Turin, died in Paris. He became a member of the Academy in 1747 and professor in 1770. He was principal painter to the King of Prussia and exhibited at the Salon from 1747 to 1785.

Van Loo, Carle (1705-65)

Brother of Charles-Amédée and the most famous of the Van Loo brothers. He was born in Nice of a line of painters of Dutch descent. Brought up by his father, then in the service of the Prince of Piedmont, he travelled in Italy. In 1724 he won the painter-laureate prize in Rome. He returned to Rome in 1727 with Boucher. Until 1731 he stayed in Turin where he decorated the palace of the King of Sardinia. In 1735 he was admitted to the Academy and in 1748 was placed in charge of the Academy's aided pupils. Painter to the King in 1762 he achieved a considerable success despite his legendary lack of culture and his stupidity. He worked on the Château de Bellevue, the church of Saint-Sulpice and, from 1746 to 1755, painted seven canvases for the church of Notre-Dame-des-Victoires.

Van Loo, Jean-Baptiste (1648-1745)

French painter, born and died at Aix. He was the son of Louis Van Loo and became his pupil. He rapidly made his reputation specialising in historical subjects and portraits. He worked in turn for the families of Savoy and Monaco, in Nice, Turin and Rome. He became a member of the Academy in 1722 and received orders from the Regent. He restored the François I Gallery at Fontainebleau and also painted religiously-inspired pictures. He also painted numerous portraits in London, where he spent four years from 1738 to 1742.

Van Loo, Louis-Michel (1707-71)

Historical painter and portraitist, died in Paris, a brother of Carle and Charles-Amédée. He won first prize at the Academy in 1725. He worked in Rome, then in Spain, where he was first painter to the King. He exhibited at the Salon from 1753 to 1769.

Verbruggen, Gaspar Pieter (1664-1730)

Flemish painter, born and died in Antwerp. Studied with his father. In 1667 he was a master at Antwerp and in 1691 was doyen of the Guild. He worked in The Hague from 1706 to 1723 and was a member of The Hague Academy in 1708. He trained numerous pupils there.

Verhagen, Pierre-Jean-Joseph

Flemish historical painter, born in Aerschot, died in Louvain. Studied at the Antwerp Academy. Was at first a protégé of the Empress Maria Theresa then, in 1771, painter to the Prince of Lorraine. He travelled in France and Italy and was painter to the court of Vienna in 1773. In 1800 he founded a fine arts school in Louvain and was its director. His works are in churches in Louvain, Averbode and Bois-le-Duc.

Vernet, Joseph (1714-89)

French landscapist and marine painter, born in Avignon, where he studied under his father, died in Paris. At Aix he began a career as decorator and painter of seascapes. He went to Italy in 1734 aided by the Marquis de Caumont. In 1743 he was admitted to the St Luke Academy in Rome and in 1746 was approved by the Academy in Paris. From 1745 to 1750 his *Scenes of Roman Life* were highly successful. Between 1750 and 1753 he stayed in Marseilles and painted shipwrecks. At this time he received a commission for fourteen paintings on the ports of France through the Marquis of Marigny, Director-General of Fine Arts and brother of Madame de Pompadour. In 1753 he settled permanently in Paris and in 1766 was named adviser to the Academy.

Vieira de Matos, Francesco
(called Lusitano) (1699-1783)

Portuguese painter, born and died in Lisbon. Studied under Trevisani in Rome. King John V of Portugal commanded numerous pictures from him and he painted a great many pictures for the churches and convents of Lisbon. The year 1755 was disastrous for the artist. An earthquake destroyed many of his works; his wife died in the same year. From then on he renounced painting and spent the rest of his life devoted to religion. The museums of Lisbon and Oporto have some of his works.

Vieira Portuense, Francesco (1765-1806)

Portuguese painter, born in Oporto, died in Madeira. He studied in Italy and lived afterwards in England. He exhibited at the Royal Academy from 1789 to 1799. In Lisbon he was the King's painter. His works may be seen in the Lisbon Museum and the Parma Pinacoteca.

Vien, Joseph-Marie (1716-1809)

French historical painter, born in Montpellier, died in Paris. He went to Paris and became a pupil of Natoire at the Academy school. In 1743 he was a pupil at the Rome School; he spent five years in

Rome, painting pictures for churches. Back in France in 1750 he was admitted to the Academy in 1754 with the support of Boucher. He trained numerous pupils, including Suvée, Vincent and Louis David. In 1755 he was named director of the Rome School where he succeeded Natoire; he held the post until 1782. On his return to France the King granted him a pension. Vien is buried in the Pantheon.

Vigée-Lebrun, Elisabeth (1755-1842)

French painter, born and died in Paris. She was sent to a convent at a very young age, but her father withdrew her and taught her the use of pastels. In 1774 she was approved by the St Luke Academy and rapidly acquired a good reputation as a portraitist. After her marriage to the art dealer Lebrun in 1776, she became painter to Marie-Antoinette, which allowed her to exhibit at the Salon from 1783. The Academy admitted her the same year. When the Revolution began she left for Rome and travelled throughout Europe. She

arrived in St Petersburg, where her reputation had preceded her, and stayed in the Russian court from 1795 to 1802. She returned to Paris and then spent two years in Italy. Banned during the Empire, she left for Switzerland where she met Madame de Staël. Under the Restoration she occupied an important place in the arts; Balzac, Vernet and Gavarni were among those who frequented her salon.

Vincent, François-André (1746-1816)

French historical painter, born and died in Paris. He was a pupil of Vien at the Royal Academy. He won the first prize for painting in 1767 and passed three years at the Rome Academy, where Natoire was then director. Returning to Paris he was admitted to the Academy in 1782 and became a professor ten years later. He was highly successful and was a rival of David. He exhibited at the Salon from 1777 to 1801 and had numerous pupils.

Vivien, Joseph (1657-1734)

French portraitist and pastellist, born in Lyons, died in Bonn. Was a pupil of Charles Le Brun in Paris. He was very successful as a portrait painter and became known as the " French Van Dyck ". His reputation soon spread throughout Europe. In 1701 he was admitted to the Academy. Vivien spent part of his life in Germany where he was painter to the Elector of Bavaria and worked in Cologne and Bonn.

Voltaire (François-Marie Arouet, known as) (1694-1778)

French writer, born in Paris. Because of the great universality of his mind and his longevity, Voltaire was, among the writers of the 18th century, the one who held the most important place in his time. His début into letters came with *Œdipus* in 1719. Following a brush with the Chevalier de Rohan, which landed him in the Bastille, Voltaire was forced to seek refuge in England and spent three years there (1726-9). This stay in England was of decisive importance in the development of Voltaire's literary, philosophical and political ideas. During it he produced his *Philosophical Letters*. On his return to Paris he published *Brutus* and *Zaïre* (1732) and then, influenced by Madame du Châtelet, he turned his attention to the sciences. From the same period date his relations with King Frederick II of Prussia, but it was only in 1750 that he went to the Potsdam court. It was not long, however, before he found this stay unbearable and he left Berlin in 1753 for Délices, an estate near Geneva, and later at Ferney, in the region of Gex. He passed his last years there, exercising a veritable sovereignty over European thought. He returned to Paris to an enthusiastic welcome in February 1778 but died on 30 May of the same year. The model for the narrative story is found in his *Charles XII* (1731), for the political history in *The Age of Louis XIV* (1751) and for the philosophical history in *Essay on the Morals and Spirit of Nations* (1756). His *Correspondance* is a valuable contribution to knowledge of the 18th century.

Watteau, Antoine (1684-1721)

French painter, born at Valenciennes, died at Nogent-sur-Marne. Watteau came from a modest but well-to-do family who did not oppose his vocation. Soon after 1699 Watteau left for Paris, without money, to try his luck there. In 1702, after a course with a painter who had no clients, he went to work as a hack for an art dealer near Notre-Dame. Earning an average £12 monthly, he worked all day at reproducing paintings. About the same time he joined Jean-Jacques Spoede, a young Antwerp artist who was studying at the Academy. At Mariette's he met a number of painters, including Claude Gillot, and lived at the latter's place from 1705 to 1708. But as Watteau soon displayed a talent superior to that of his host, the two parted. He then went to work for Claude Audran, curator of the Luxemburg Palace, and helped him with decoration of the Château de la Muette and Meudon. Audran was instrumental in allowing Watteau to see the great Rubens cycle of the Life of Marie de Medici, an important event in his training. Admitted to the Academy as a pupil, he entered for the Rome prize in 1709 but came only second. Discouraged, he decided to return to Valenciennes for some time. To pay for the journey he sold, through his friend Spoede, a small military painting, *Return from the Campaign*. Sirois gave him 60 francs for it and ordered another which earned 200 francs. In 1710 Watteau went back to Paris with a young artist from Valenciennes, Jean-Baptiste Pater. Sirois invited Watteau to set up with him. About 1710 he painted *Island of Cythera*, a sketch for *Embarkation for the Island of Cythera*. The Academy approved him on 30 July 1712. In 1716 he was with Crozat. Among the works owned by this collector he studied the Flemish and Venetian painters. He quickly left Crozat, returned to Sirois and then set himself up in the rue Cardinal Lemoine until 1719. In August 1717 the Academy had admitted him on presentation of his *Embarkation*. Suffering from tuberculosis, he left for London in 1719 to see a doctor who had been recommended to him. He remained in London for a year. On his return to Paris he stayed for some time with Gersaint, Sirois's son-in-law, and painted for him in a single week the famous *Enseigne de Gersaint*. Before long he went to live at Nogent. Ill, Watteau seemed little by little to become detached from his work. The priest at Nogent even persuaded him to burn his paintings of nudes.

Wilson, Richard (1714-82)

English landscapist, pupil of the portrait painter Thomas Wright in London in 1729. On his arrival in Italy, Francesco Zuccarelli and Joseph Vernet encouraged

him to paint landscapes. He stayed in Rome where he built up a solid reputation for himself. On his return to London in 1755 he received commissions from royalty. He was a founder-member of the Royal Academy.

Winckelmann, Johann Joachim (1717-68)

German writer and archaeologist, born in Stendal (Brandenburg). He studied under a rector whose well-filled library allowed him to learn about antiquity. After his studies he became secretary and librarian to the Count of Bunau, near Dresden. He found treasures in the Dresden Gallery. His love of Italy was said to have prompted his conversion to Catholicism. In 1754 his first important work appeared: *Thoughts on the Imitation of Greek Works in Painting and Sculpture.* The following year he went to Rome where he became librarian to Cardinal Albani. Some time later he was appointed Inspector of Roman Antiquities; it was at this time that he produced his *History of Antique Art.* In 1768 he began a journey into Germany. But hardly had he reached the Tyrol when he began to pine for Italy. He went on as far as Vienna but then went back to Trieste and took a boat for Ancona. On 8 July of the same year he was killed by an Italian traveller.

Witt (Jakob de) (1695-1754)

Dutch painter, born and died in Amsterdam. He was a pupil of Albert Van Spiers. In 1712 he worked in Antwerp with Jakob Van Hal, studied the works of Rubens and Van Dyck. He decorated churches and apartments and painted ceilings.

Zimmermann, Jean-Baptiste (1680-1758)

German fresco painter and stuccoist, born into an artisan family in Wessobrunn, died in Munich. He worked in France as a decorative painter, then with the architect Cuvillies in Munich (salons of the Residence and the Amalienburg and Nymphenburg Palaces). Also collaborated with his brother, the architect Dominic Zimmermann. The Wies church, of which Jean-Baptiste painted the ceiling, is their masterpiece.

Zuccarelli, Francesco (1702-88)

Italian painter, born at Pitigliano, died in Florence. He studied in Florence and Rome. At first he painted historical scenes, then decorative landscapes. He exhibited in London, where he often stayed, from 1765, was a member of the Society of Artists, and in 1768 was one of the founders of the Royal Academy. One room of Windsor Castle is entirely furnished with his works. In 1773 Zuccarelli returned to Florence. His works may be seen in the museums of Budapest, Glasgow, London, Stuttgart and Venice.

Printed in Italy

Bibliography

General Works

E. Faure: *Histoire de l'Art*, vol. IV, Paris 1948.

P.-J. Mariette: *Abecedario*, Paris 1851-60.

A. Michel: *Histoire de l'Art*, vol. VII, Paris 1923.

L. Réau: *L'Europe française au Siècle des Lumières*, Paris 1938.

A. Schoenberger and H. Soehner: *L'Europe du XVIIIe Siècle, l'Art et la Culture*, Paris 1960.

J. Starobinski: *L'Invention de la Liberté* (1700-89), Geneva 1964.

France

H. Borsch-Supan: *Catalogue de l'Exposition " La Peinture française du XVIIIe Siècle à la Cour de Frédéric II"*, Paris 1963.

Diderot: *Salons*.

E. de Goncourt: *Catalogue Raisonné de l'Œuvre de Watteau*, Paris 1875.

E. and J. de Goncourt: *L'Art du XVIIIe Siècle*, Paris 1859-75.

L. Hourticq: *La Peinture française au XVIIIe Siècle*, Paris 1939.

R. Huyghe and H. Adhemar: *Watteau*, Paris 1950.

Lafont de Saint-Yenne: *Réflexions sur quelques causes de l'état de la peinture en France*, Paris 1752.

A. Leroy: *Histoire de la Peinture française*, vol. III, Paris 1937.

A. Leroy: *Quentin de La Tour et la Société française du XVIIIe Siècle*, Paris 1953.

B. Lossky: *Catalogue de l'Exposition " L'Art français et l'Europe aux XVIIe et XVIIIe Siècles"*, Paris 1958.

B. Lossky: *Musée de Tours, Peintures du XVIIIe Siècle*, Tours 1962.

C. Mauclair: *Fragonard*, Paris 1913.

P. de Nolhac: *Boucher*, Paris 1907.

P. Ratouis de Limay: *Le Pastel en France au XVIIIe Siècle*, Paris 1946.

L. Réau: *Histoire de l'Expansion de l'Art français* (4 vols.), Paris 1924-33.

L. Réau: *Histoire de la Peinture française au XVIIIe Siècle* (2 vols.), Paris 1925.

L. Réau: *Fragonard*, Brussels 1956.

G. Schefer: *Chardin*, Paris 1905.

G. Seailles: *Watteau*, Paris 1921.

M. Tourneux: *La Tour*, Paris 1904.

G. Wildenstein: *Chardin*, Zurich 1963.

Italy

G. Beltrami: *Magnasco*, Milan 1913.

H. de Chennevières: *Les Tiepolo*, Paris 1898.

G. Fiocco: *Francesco Guardi*, Florence 1934.

P. Molmenti: *Tiepolo, la Vie et l'Œuvre du Peintre*, Paris 1911.

V. Moschini: *La pittura italiana del Settecento*, Florence 1931.

V. Moschini: *Longhi*, Ed. Martello.

V. Moschini: *Guardi*, Ed. Martello.

R. Palluchini: *La pittura veneziana del Settecento*, Bologna 1952.

O. Uzanne: *Les Deux Canaletto*, Paris 1906.

A. Venturi: *Storia generale dell'Arte italiana*, Milan 1904.

V. Viale: *Catalogue " Mostra del Barocco piemontese"*, Turin 1963.

England

F. Benoit: *Hogarth*, Paris 1904.

Graves and Cronin: *A History of the Works of Sir Joshua Reynolds* (4 vols.), London 1899-1901.

Hogarth: *Analysis of Beauty*, London 1753.

A. Leroy: *Histoire de la Peinture anglaise*, Paris 1939.

G. Mourey: *Gainsborough*, Paris 1914.

G. Mourey: *La Peinture anglaise du XVIIIe Siècle*, Paris 1932.

J. Reynolds: *Discourses on Art*, London 1905.

W. T. Whitley: *Thomas Gainsborough*, 1913.

Other Schools

D. Baud-Bovy: *Peintres genevois* (2 vols.), Geneva 1903.

P. Bautier: *La Peinture belge au XVIIIe Siècle*, Brussels 1945.

P. du Colombier: *L'Art français dans les Cours rhénanes*, Paris 1930.

P. Fierens: *L'Art en Belgique*, Paris 1939.

F. Fosca: *Jean-Etienne Liotard*, Geneva 1928.

F. Fosca: *Histoire de la Peinture suisse*, Geneva 1945.

K. Garas: *Maulbertsch*, Vienna 1960.

Lozoya: *Historia del arte hispanico*, vols. IV and V, Barcelona 1945.

G. Lundberg: *Roslin* (3 vols.), Malmoe 1957.

M. Osborn: *Die Kunst des Rokoko*, Berlin 1929.

L. Réau: *L'Art russe de Pierre le Grand à nos Jours*, Paris 1922.

List of Illustrations

Dictionary

Eighteenth Century Painting

This sixth volume in the series
History of Painting was printed
by the Officine Grafiche
Arnoldo Mondadori in Verona.

The text was composed in Times 10-point type,
and the first and third parts were printed
on machine-coated paper and the second part
on blue cartridge paper.

The cover and lay-out of the inside pages
were designed by Jean-Marie Clerc of
Editions Rencontre.